OUTRAGEOUS FORTUNES

OUTRAGEOUS FORTUNES

The Adventures of
Mary Fortune, Crime-writer,
and Her Criminal Son

Megan Brown and Lucy Sussex

LA TROBE
UNIVERSITY PRESS

IN CONJUNCTION WITH BLACK INC.

Published by La Trobe University Press in conjunction with Black Inc.
Wurundjeri Country
22–24 Northumberland Street
Collingwood VIC 3066, Australia
enquiries@blackincbooks.com
www.blackincbooks.com
www.latrobeuniversitypress.com.au

La Trobe University plays an integral role in Australia's public intellectual life, and is recognised globally for its research excellence and commitment to ideas and debate. La Trobe University Press publishes books of high intellectual quality, aimed at general readers. Titles range across the humanities and sciences, and are written by distinguished and innovative scholars. La Trobe University Press books are produced in conjunction with Black Inc., an independent Australian publishing house. The members of the LTUP Editorial Board are Vice-Chancellor's Fellows Emeritus Professor Robert Manne and Dr Elizabeth Finkel, and Morry Schwartz and Chris Feik of Black Inc.

9781760645052 (paperback)
9781743823880 (ebook)

 A catalogue record for this book is available from the National Library of Australia

Book design and typesetting by Aira Pimping
Cover artwork by Freddie Baer

CONTENTS

THE MYSTERIES OF MARY FORTUNE

ONCE UPON A TIME A WOMAN walked the mean streets of colonial Melbourne. She would carry a basket for market, or a jug for the public house. Sometimes her companion was a cheeky young boy, or a dog; more often she was alone. Her gaze, from underneath a plain black bonnet, saw everything, from the coaches and horses of the wealthy to the ragged children collecting bones and bottles in a hand cart. Her feet, in their elastic-sided boots, went down seedy alleys and along fine thoroughfares. She would chat to a constable on his beat, drop off copy to her editors and printers, exchange nods with detectives and with known criminals. Wherever she went, she took mental notes. She was a pioneering female journalist and detective writer, and her name was Mary Helena Fortune.

Yet she almost vanished from literary history. From 1855 to 1910, Fortune wrote under her initials and various pseudonyms. She was Waif Wander, a self-description, but also W.W., writer of realist police procedurals with a male persona. Her work appeared in Australian magazines and newspapers and was reprinted overseas. She also produced the first book of crime short stories published in Australia, *The Detective's Album*, in 1871. The book was also a world first, being the first detective collection by a woman. Its stories came from the eponymous serial, which was published from 1868 until 1908 and consisted of over 500 stories, the longest early crime series known. Its title came from photography, then a cutting-edge technology. She preceded the police in the use of criminal mugshots, in her case to solve fictional crimes.

And all the while she overstepped the boundaries of her gender. In an era when women had few rights and little status, and middle-class women were expected to be 'angels in the house', valued only for their domestic and childbearing skills, Fortune was a trailblazer. She threw out the rule book and danced on its grave. Her life was lived on her own terms, even if her son George became collateral damage. The story of mother and son ranges across the globe, encompassing colonialism, literature, the newly formed detective force and the criminal class.

In the Victorian era, women writers often used pseudonyms. The Brontë sisters became the Bells, and Mary Ann Evans became George Eliot. Some, such as Eliot and the poet L.E.L. (Letitia Landon), were scandalous by the standards of their time, having sexual lives beyond the bond of wedlock. Pseudonyms could be performative, offering alluring hints of the writer's real identities, like features glimpsed behind a veil. Fortune similarly sprinkled her text with clues, apt for a woman whose métier was mystery.

Although she lived in Melbourne, a centre of literary bohemia, her identity was kept secret. Nobody seemed to know her; or if they did, they kept quiet, even the gossips. To read her is like trying to solve a Victorian-era picture puzzle, in which an image contains a hidden figure. A man laments the loss of his wife while leaning against a tree. 'And there she is. Find her out!' says the caption: the lady is visible in the negative space of leaves and branches. Mary Fortune similarly inhabits negative spaces, hidden in plain sight. She was absent from the many diaries and letters written during her times. When she died, no obituary appeared, and her death record took decades to find.

Had she not left behind some autobiographical journalism and an (unreliable) memoir of her experiences on the Australian goldfields, from 1855 to 1857, research would not have got far. A major reason to persist with this obscured writer was that she was thoroughly engaging. Whether writing as herself or as Detective Mark Sinclair, the narrator of *The Detective's Album*, she addressed the reader directly in a lively and irreverent style. Her prose has an immediacy, a force of personality. In 1869 a newspaper called her 'our old friend' and observed that she was writing 'as freshly and as pleasantly as ever'.[1] Today, her work is like a guided tour into the past.

Amid more typical Victorian verbiage, from writers truly forgettable, her vivid personality stood out. She unapologetically trusted her own taste:

> I have been told by some that I tell horrible stories, and by others that I am not sensational enough; and I have personally come to the conclusion that I shall tell just such stories as I please, and that those who do not like them need not read them.[2]

And she savoured her financial independence:

> my nicely-flavoured tea … tastes unusually good when I remember that I have earned every penny of the money that bought it, myself.[3]

Her writing hinted, moreover, at a very unusual life. She had arrived in the Australian goldfields from Canada with a small son but no husband. She displayed detailed knowledge of crime and the police, including some very dodgy elements, at a time when women were precluded from working in law enforcement or the justice system. How did she know these things?

When the search behind this biography began, little was known beyond her name: Mrs Fortune. To find her meant following her lead as a detective writer, seeking the clues hidden in her vast bibliography. A process of literary detection began. Her game was to drop self-referential fragments – names and events from her life – into her writing.

Reading an author through their work can be a trap: the biographical fallacy – the assumption that writing always derives from life. Such was not true in Mary Fortune's case, for she had a wild imagination. She could write as vividly of a vampire or a vengeful Roma sorceress as of the Victorian goldfields. Yet even at her most sensational her default mode was realist, fed by a tenacious memory. She held grudges interminably and rehashed them in print. Details repeat through the decades of her work, and – thanks to the increasingly digitised world of archives and newspapers – they can be investigated and explained.

Here is someone very unconventional, a bohemian at a time when that term could not be applied to a woman without moral loathing. She innovated as a female *flâneur* (*flâneuse*), a journalist and a significant crime writer. As an itinerant but streetwise reporter writing about violent crime, she confounded notions of Victorian femininity. What she could not write about openly as a woman, she expressed through her male persona – even the unspeakable but all too common crimes of infanticide and gang rape. Her stories are graphic in detail, often with an underlying criticism of the police's failure to protect women. Her range was wide, across genres and modes. She survived as a freelance writer in a hard, bleak market for decades, outliving her male contemporaries and rivals such as Marcus Clarke. Her literary reputation has grown from complete invisibility to translations and reprints. Where once we knew almost nothing, her story can now fill a book.

Her biography is inextricable from that of her second son, George. Mary occupied the artistic upper bohemia, with ventures into the more disreputable lower bohemia. George, in contrast, inhabited the underworld. Mary wrote crime; George committed it. She became one of the most published women of her era yet was almost totally concealed as a person. George's writing appeared in print only once, but his life was public and notorious. What we lack in archival details about Mary's life we have in abundance for George. In prison, what he did and even what he ate every day was recorded. Yet, like Mary, he remains an elusive character. In her 'How I Spent Christmas', a piece of autobiographical journalism, George appears as a small boy with a well-thumbed bible. As an adult he was part of a gang responsible for the most notorious bank robbery in Melbourne in the nineteenth century. How could he be both saint and sinner?

The pair resemble another popular Victorian-era puzzle: the Topsy Turvy. These puzzles took various grotesque forms, expressive of opposites. A Red Riding Hood doll might appear demure until turned upside down, when revealed hiding beneath her long skirt is the wolf. Other puzzles concealed two faces: one a man and the other his wife, or one happy and the other snarling. In a publicity image for Mike Leigh's 1999 film *Topsy-Turvy*, frowning Gilbert inverts to reveal a smiling Sullivan. Female/male, mother/son, crime writer / criminal. Mary and George were two and one, complementary opposites, the outrageous Fortunes.

1
—

ORIGINS OF A CRIME WRITER

THE GRAVE IS UNMARKED, ITS ONLY covering grass. Around it lie the wealthier dead, memorialised in the graveyard of St Nicholas' Church of Ireland, Carrickfergus. The town sits between mountain and the lough of Belfast, with the church built of the same stone as the nearby Norman keep: grey, hard and cold. When new, the grave might have been scattered with forget-me-not seeds – as is another in Mary Fortune's writing. Mary did not recall the site; she was only a baby when the grave was dug. But the castle was her father's workplace, and in the churchyard was buried her mother, one week before Christmas, 18 December 1832.

Little is known of this woman beyond her maiden name: Eleanor Atkinson, as recorded on Mary's second marriage certificate. From her mother Mary inherited the variant middle name of 'Helena'. She also endured regret at what she had never known: 'Motherless! Alas! What a sad term that is to be connected with a girl's name.' Also missing from her life were siblings: daughter and father would comprise a family of two.

He was George Wilson, a civil engineer. The name was common, as was Mary, but it is possible to identify her birthdate and place. Ulster records reveal that on 29 July 1832 a Mary Wilson was born and christened at St Anne's, Church of Ireland, Shankill parish, Belfast. Her mother was recorded as Eleanor, then a relatively unusual name.[1]

In her autobiographical writing, Mary states that her forefathers were lowland Scots.[2] That was typical of colonial Ulster. The church at Carrickfergus symbolised British rule, and the major employer in town at the time of Mary's birth was the Board of Ordnance, operating from the castle. From 1824 until 1842, the board deployed the Royal Engineers in the Survey of Ireland, mapmaking for the purposes of land valuation and ultimately tax. Although the personnel were mostly military, civilians were also employed. A civil engineer had surveying skills and would have been highly employable. Was it from the Royal Engineers that George Wilson acquired the round military travelling tent he took with him when he emigrated to Australia?[3]

The Survey of Ireland began in the north, producing maps but also records of places, people and everything from crops to folklore. The *Ordnance Survey Memoirs* provide a uniquely detailed record of Carrickfergus parish, which was surveyed in 1832. The population was 8000, largely Scots Protestants in origin, with 'little taste for reading or for literature'. In this town, described as 'poor', George Wilson's married life ended.[4]

Although Mary did not know her mother, she did recall Ireland, in stories mostly written for Catholic diaspora publications. Her memories were precise and alert to the natural world. At a Melbourne market, she noted gamebirds (snipe) for sale 'that remind me, though in a different dress [plumage], of the low, marshy banks of the River Shannon. Many thousands of them I have seen brought up in the canvas "coracle" boats of the lower river.'[5]

Elsewhere she recalled Limerick (surveyed in 1841):

If one leaves the 'ancient city of Limerick', in the South of Ireland, by the broad high road known as the Dublin road, after passing the old ruin of *New* Castle, and its noble racecourse, he will find on his right-hand a narrow hawthorn-hedged country-road, which might have almost escaped his notice had he not been on the look-out for it. Following this for a few miles of uninteresting, cultivated, and small holdings, with an occasional 'mud cabin', here and there, he will come all at once upon the pretty rural village of Barrington's Bridge [Droichead Barrington] – so-called from the one-arched iron-railed graceful little bridge that crosses its narrow river, and from the name of the landowner who built it. Passing through the tree-shaded street – if one is justified in calling a street a dozen or two scattered and garden-enclosed houses without any visible sign of business – and on two or three miles more, passing more hawthorn hedges, and more enclosures, and some very disagreeable *bog*, at length we reach the pleasant and beautifully situated Irish village Murroe [Maigh Rua] [...] Behind the village – which was just as unlike a village as Barrington's bridge, by the way – lay the hills and the glens of Glenstal, wild and lovely as any hills and glens in the whole wide world! And oh, the wealth of 'Hurts' (*Anglice* blueberries) that grow upon the hills at Glenstal, up above the new castle built by the Barringtons, and which was for many years called 'Barrington's Folly'; and the wild raspberries and blackberries down in old Cappercullen Glen, and the wealth of half-wild *rhododendrons* that grew down behind the old castle garden.[6]

From 1845 to 1849 Ireland suffered the potato famine, the devastation providing even privileged Protestants with a reason to depart. Mary would later write a story of emigration, 'The Rustling of Wings': 'My father had arranged to leave our pleasant home and to make another for us in a far away land.' It was narrated by teenage Mary, 'a dreamy romantic girl' with a 'growing willfulness'.[7] The title refers to the superstition that hearing angels' wings was a portent of death. During the famine, angelic wings rustled all over Ireland as the staple crop failed. In the story Mary is fourteen, which if autobiographical would date the family's departure to about 1846, when the first starvations began. In another story Fortune would recall 'black, soapy, sticky potatoes, that you would be expatriated [transported] for selling in fair Ireland twenty years ago'.[8]

The Wilsons' destination was the Catholic, Francophone province of Quebec, then called Lower Canada. From the 1830s Canada was widely advertised as an emigrant destination. Crossing the Atlantic by sailing ship took six weeks if the weather was favourable, without fogs, storms or getting becalmed. The New World began with the gulf of St Lawrence, landfall at the quarantine station at Grosse Île and, beyond that, Montreal. Many emigrants would continue onwards, for Ontario or further westward. George Wilson stopped in Quebec, his engineering and surveying skills highly desirable in a developing colony.

With some very well-documented exceptions, such as the Brontës, the early lives of women authors are usually scantly documented. Mary's writings provide some clues to these early years. Consider her Indian-born heroine Emilie Brantome:

a good sensible girl, and without one atom of affectation.

Motherless since her girlhood, and brought up by a soldier-father in the unrestrained freedom of colonial society, it is not to be wondered that Emilie was different from most, nay all, of the young ladies with whom Arthur had come in contact; her manner was more decided, more self-possessed, and more original, and a great fund of shrewd common sense, inherited from Captain Brantome, had been encouraged and fostered by the necessity of self-care in her unprotected situation.

Emilie was not beautiful, but she was decidedly good-looking, and more decidedly good.[9]

Mary Fortune prized such qualities, and the personality revealed in her non-fiction is decided, self-possessed and very original. Being good was another matter, easily prescribed for the Victorian heroine but harder in real life.

A Victorian girlhood meant pinafores, slates, primers and samplers. She mentions making 'peepshows' (collages), using an elaborately carved 'wool wheel' (spinning wheel) and gathering seashells and seaweed on the Irish shore.[10] Girls received far less education than boys and far fewer opportunities, being meant for housekeeping and homemaking. What we know of Mary's cooking is either English, such as gooseberry tart, or from the New World, such as buckwheat cakes:

> To one pound of buckwheat flour, add a little salt, and half a teaspoon of carbonate of soda; mix thoroughly together, and make it into as thick a batter as can be stirred with some milk or buttermilk. Butter a shallow tin (it will not rise so well in a deep one), and bake in a quick oven. The preparation, only made thinner, and poured in spoonfuls on a hot plate – the top of a stove, for instance – forms the well-known 'Flap Jacks' of American cooking. For more delicate ladies prepare it with eggs and cream or milk, and bake it in the same way. Buckwheat is not good baked in any way from a thin dough.[11]

She knew French and snatches of Latin. In another story, a male narrator lamented:

> I often wonder where I got those scraps of 'classic lore', that appear to come so natural to me … Of course it must be a natural ability, that the world – the vicious envious world – has failed to recognize; for I have never been pampered in the school of fashion, and run the wild debasing course entailed by a few years at Oxford.[12]

Her father dabbled in verse, writing a poem for her when she turned eight, a tradition she continued with her own child. She would have read and written with him, and a computer analysis of her writing reveals it has traits of grammar and prosody more usually associated with the masculine (and with better education) than with other women authors of her era. In this aspect Mary Fortune joins a select and exceptional group: Mary Shelley, Emily Brontë and Mary (Perdita) Robinson. Of this quartet, three lost their mothers young, and Mary Robinson's mother was a schoolmistress.[13]

Fortune never described herself as Canadian. Yet when she spent Christmas 1868 at Sandridge (now Port Melbourne), a reminder of Canada had powerful effect:

> I am choking; my face is paler than is its wont, I know, and my knees tremble; there are big tears in my eyes, and my heart has got the pain of long ago in it. Would you know the reason? Read it in golden letters on the stern of that stately vessel, it is but a simple word, but it is the name of 'home'.

'Home', to colonials, usually meant England, but for her it was elsewhere:

> A home lost fifteen weary years ago – a home where Christmas did not find a lonely wanderer, but an envied member of a happy home, where the shadow of death had not yet fallen. A home, where musical sleigh bells danced to the music of friendly wishes, and where Christmas morning awoke to greet a country covered with pure snow, that sparkled like miles of diamonds in the brilliant sun-glow And from that very spot has come this noble vessel, the names of whose owners are almost as familiar to me as my own. I can almost picture, as vivid as a reality, the very spot on the wharf to which she will go back. She will lie at the foot, or rather, opposite to the foot of 'St Francois Xavier-street', where one may see, passing to and fro still, the old French 'habitant', with his coat of 'Etoffe du pays' and his scarlet woollen cap, and eyes will rest on these very timbers – ay, and on that same word in golden letters, that need but pass with a breath to see the glorious shores of the 'L'Isle Jesus', and the broad

> waters of the regal St Lawrence. Oh, let us pass on and forget it all!
> I shall see it again no more![14]

These very specific references are to Montreal. *Habitants* were Francophone smallholders, distinctive in homespun woollens. What she described was Montreal's port, a hemisphere away from where she stood in Australia.

Montreal in the 1840s was a city predominantly French but under English rule. Although colonial, it had centuries of history and much sophistication: a university (McGill); theatres (which attracted Dickens); and a Literary and Historical Society. It was also a major centre for temperance activism. Temperance was a feminist issue, not least because it gave women agency and an excuse to behave badly, smashing up grog saloons. It also enabled women to publish, in fiction and in tracts. Fortune would claim: 'I, myself, did, at one time, write most refreshing temperance tracts, ay, and distribute them too; and I should have no earthly objections to it again, were I as well paid for my labour.'[15]

An old adage was that women were born when they married. The first known record of Mary in Quebec is her marriage certificate from Lady Day (25 March) 1851, when she was eighteen. She wed not in Montreal but in Melbourne village in the Eastern Townships, then a predominantly English-speaking region in southern Quebec, adjoining the American border.

In her poem 'Canada' she mentions birch canoes, used for navigating rivers, which were Canada's main thoroughfares – the alternative being notoriously poor roads. Both roads and rivers were affected by winter conditions, when Canada froze. The solution was the new technology of the railway, which from 1849 was the biggest infrastructure project in Canada. Travel accelerated, enabling unprecedented migration.

George Wilson can be linked to one particular railway, the St Lawrence and Atlantic. This major enterprise began in Montreal and routed through the Eastern Townships to the American border and beyond. Melbourne was situated on the St François River, a tributary of the St Lawrence. The chief engineer in charge of construction was Kazimierz Gzowski, a former Russian Imperial Corps engineer who had come to America as a refugee. Under his direction, a rail trestle bridge was built from Melbourne to Richmond, on the other side of the river, and completed in 1852.

Fifty miles from Montreal, on the Ottawa River, another tributary of the St Lawrence, is a village called Pointe-Fortune. Its modern coat of arms shows a scantily clad and blindfolded woman, walking on water and spilling a cornucopia over a canoe of voyageurs. The motto is *La Fortune aime les audacieux* (Fortune favours the brave). From this place came the Fortunes, including the man who gave a married name to young Mary Wilson.

Mary's new husband, Joseph Fortune, was a 25-year-old surveyor. He lived nearby in Shipton (now Danville), another stop on the St Lawrence and Atlantic railway. The minister at their wedding was the Rev. Daniel Falloon, a missionary with the Anglican Society for the Promotion of the Gospel. The witnesses were George Wilson and Joseph's older sister, Henrietta Fortune. Henrietta was either very distressed at the wedding or ill, for her signature shook like a seismograph.

Unlike the Wilsons, the Fortunes have a name easily traced. It is distinctively Irish, deriving from O'Forkin, from the Gaelic O'Foirtchearn, who occupied the border area of counties Carlow and Wexford. Joseph Fortune's family hailed from Wexford, and before the American revolution they owned a slave plantation in South Carolina. His grandfather William Fortune fought for the English side and after the war fled to Canada as a Loyalist refugee. There he became a colonel in the colonial militia, which was formed to support the resident British army in case of rebellion or US invasion. He acquired land grants that enabled him to settle and name Pointe-Fortune. He named his son Cornwallis Joseph, after the British general Charles Cornwallis.[16]

Both William and his son were surveyors and militiamen. Cornwallis Joseph married Mary Story and they had seven daughters and one son, born in 1826 and christened Joseph John George O'Sullivan Fortune. Although the boy became fatherless at ten, he too followed in his father's and grandfather's surveying footsteps.

In the Canadian census of 1851, which was taken on 12 January 1852, Joseph and Mary Fortune appear, although the only details recorded for Mary are her age at next birthday (twenty), birthplace (Ireland) and religion (Episcopalian, i.e. Anglican). She was then in early pregnancy. The couple had moved to Sherbrooke, the base of operations for the St Lawrence and Atlantic railway project. They kept one servant, Maria Hall, aged twenty-eight, a Methodist from Ireland.

In nearby Windsor, George Wilson, now aged forty-nine, lived in close proximity to gangs of navvies (railroad labourers). He was listed as a contractor, an important role in infrastructure projects at the time. Contractors bridged the gap between the engineers and architects and the navvies who did the hard labour. They brought plans into effect through project management, finance and business nous. They required elan and a certain ruthlessness; the most successful contractors became heroes of speculative capitalism. Gzowski, originally a Polish nobleman, thrived as a contractor, but it was risky work: the job could lead to great riches but more often to bankruptcy, especially since pay could take the form of unreliable railway shares.[17]

In 1851 gold was discovered in Australia, setting off a mass migration. George Wilson saw the opportunity. He likely left by the St Lawrence and Atlantic rail link from Sherbrooke to Montreal. Mary's son Joseph George was born on 12 August 1852, and the railway opened the following month. Did she accompany her father on the first part of his trip, for a quayside farewell? Such a journey might have informed the sense of profound loss in her later recollections of Montreal. Joseph George was christened in December 1852, during the five months when the St Lawrence was impassable because of thick ice. George Wilson was not among the witnesses.

In leaving his daughter, Wilson took a risk. Wives could suddenly become widows, and marriages could fail.[18] Upon marriage, a woman became legally one with her husband: his chattel and his property. Anything she owned also became his: Charlotte Brontë found her new husband automatically owned her literary estate. Marriage was regarded as holy and indissoluble, even if a husband was violent, drunken or debauched. Only the privileged could divorce. When a marriage did founder, the law favoured the husband, whose property included the couple's offspring. When novelists Edward and Rosina Bulwer-Lytton separated in the 1830s, she lost access to her children; their daughter Emily died without Rosina ever seeing her again. A similar case involving English writer Caroline Norton led her to campaign for justice. In 1839, the *Custody of Children Act* was passed by the British parliament. Although it only applied to young children and to mothers of immaculate reputation, it did give custody to women – a major innovation.

Canada, although a British colony, was a patchwork of different jurisdictions and legal codes. Matrimonial law differed from place to place, as it did in the American states. Fortune's contemporary Metta Victor, the first author to write a detective novel in America, married similarly young under the relatively liberal Michigan law, which allowed her to divorce and remarry. Quebec, as a strongly Catholic and former French possession, differed, following the patriarchal Napoleonic Code. Divorce was forbidden, even for Protestants such as the Fortunes.

The law may have been inflexible, but unhappy and determined couples still had options. Canadian legal historians note some Quebec Protestants from this era divorcing by parliamentary decree, a difficult and expensive process. It was easier to cross the American border and divorce there, but the divorce would not be legally recognised in Canada. Such actions were known as 'migratory divorces'.[19]

Typical reasons for marriage breakdowns in Victorian fiction were incompatibility, infidelity, drunkenness and violence. Anne Brontë's bestseller *The Tenant of Wildfell Hall* (1848) depicts a woman deserting her alcoholic husband, taking her son to save him from his father's influence. How many bookish wives with temperance sympathies read it and longed to emulate the heroine?

As a wife, Mary Fortune was legally dependent on her husband – and very much alone. In Quebec, she could have sought a legal separation, *separation de corps*, but if she did so she risked losing her child. The child's welfare would be carefully examined and discretionary judgements made. Maternal custody required a good character and, most importantly, male relatives with repute and means. Mary was very young, and her father was now in Australia – crucial demerits against her. We can never know what went wrong with the Fortunes' marriage, except that there must have been a good reason why Mary took her son to the other side of the world. Possibly the couple parted by mutual agreement or had a trial separation that became permanent. But their child was the only son of an only son, from a family with some standing. Would his father have agreed to his son travelling to the other side of the world? It seems unlikely.

As one Fortune family historian commented, 'Mary must have been very unhappy.' Moreover, she had the willpower to act drastically and some means, at least the gold from her wedding ring and other jewellery. In her fiction, women and their fathers sometimes make property arrangements. In 'Mr Boyce's Daughter', a father opens a bank account for his daughter to use when she comes of age at twenty-one, which for Mary Fortune would have been mid-1853. In 'Delia Loney', a woman begs her father for independence when he withholds her dowry because he disapproves of her choice. By such mechanisms and others, money could have been paid to Mary Fortune: a running-away fund. Such arrangements were invaluable if a marriage broke down; English writer Catherine Crowe, for example, left her husband thanks to provisions in her father's will. Her decision to leave made, how much did Mary secretly plan with George Wilson? The sheer distance meant communication was slow, and the itinerant goldfields life meant Wilson likely had no fixed address. Mary Fortune also had opportunity to flee. Her husband was a surveyor in a province busy with development. His work could have taken him away from home for long periods – and the Eastern Townships where the couple lived were close to the US border.

While this scenario is conjectural, the evidence points to Mary having done a runner with the child. It was an astonishingly brave move for the period. *La Fortune aime les audacieux.* To desert her husband, taking her child, Mary Fortune broke the law, not for the last time in her life.

The easiest escape would have been a ticket to ride on the first border-crossing railway in North America, opened in April 1853 by the St Lawrence and Atlantic, the railroad her menfolk had helped to build. Sherbrooke now linked directly to Portland, Maine, a seaport open throughout winter. She was only seven stations away from the US border at Norton Mills. To use her own description of rail travel, away she 'whirled, with the speed of lightning almost'.[20] Once over the border, she would be beyond Canadian law. While desertion was a criminal offence in many jurisdictions, it was not in the existing extradition treaties between Canada and America, unlike murder, piracy and arson.

From Portland, she could quickly have sailed to England. During the journey her child's name changed from Joseph to George. In her memoir she mentions travelling to Scotland and making useful literary contacts. Then, on 24 June 1855, mother and child embarked from Glasgow to Australia. Once more she crossed 'the beautiful open sea, on which I had spent so many long months of my life'.[21]

Shipping records list a 'Mrs Fortune', aged twenty-five (her age upped by two years) and her son George, aged two (he turned three *en voyage*). They travelled on the *Briseis*, a cargo vessel of 1143 tons with a small complement of passengers, mostly women. On this voyage it transported a very Scots load of oats, salmon and whisky. Mary was an unassisted

Sandridge Pier in 1862.

passenger, paying for her journey, one of the few cabin (first-class) passengers. The ship arrived in Melbourne on 4 October after a voyage of over 100 days. Mother and son made landfall soon afterwards.

There were a good many vessels anchored out in the bay, and from one of them a small sail boat was pushed off, and made for the landing-place. The vessel was a barque of, maybe, a thousand tons. In the boat were several persons, male and female, who passed me toward the station; but the one who was the last to land stood as the others moved on, and looked back toward the ship [...]

'You are a new arrival?' I asked.

'Yes; I've spent one hundred and four days in that old tub out there, and I was just taking a last look at her, and trying not to wish that she might sink at her moorings.'

'I'm glad you tried to discourage so very uncharitable a wish; the poor ship was hardly responsible for your discomfort.'

'She was responsible for a great deal of it. She is leaky, and we had to pump day and night after we passed the Cape.'[22]

Mary Fortune stepped onto the beach, making her first footprints in Australian sand. These were soon effaced – but in the new country she would leave permanent traces, her decades of writing.

2
—

ARRIVAL

M ARY FORTUNE'S UNRELIABLE MEMOIR, 'Twenty-Six Years Ago; or
the Diggings from '55', opens with her arrival in Melbourne. Emigration
meant a new life – but this writer left her previous existence behind so
utterly that she seems a Phoenix, without antecedents. Typically, memoirs
of the Victorian era began with birth and childhood; here a grown woman
simply disembarks from a sailing ship. She provides no self-portrait, and
the reader can only picture her clad in High Victoriana: long, full skirts,
a corseted waist, a shady bonnet tied with ribbon beneath the chin. It
is the dress of a paper doll, from which the face is missing. The writer
was invisible and determined to keep it that way – for excellent reasons.

At the time of the memoir's publication in the 1880s, she had an
established literary reputation. Readers knew her work, her witty, opin-
ionated voice, but not the person behind the pseudonyms. She created
a brand in words but lived privately. As the memoir hints, and research
reveals, here was a highly unconventional woman.

She announces herself first as a wanderer in a mutable world:
'Twenty-six years is a long time to look back upon, and when those
years have been passed in a series of frequent change of place and of
circumstances and of people the time appears longer still.'[1] Next, she
situates herself not in the home, domain of the ideal Victorian woman,
the Angel in the House, but the street.

The past may seem 'a bewildered dream', but she had taken notes: 'I was not old at that distant date, and I had engaged myself to supply some papers [articles] … for a London ladies' magazine called, I think, the *Ladies' Companion*'. Note the active rather than passive phrasing. 'I had engaged myself' suggests she had asked for the job. She had something saleable: an eyewitness account of the Australian goldfields, which in 1855 was of intense interest to prospective emigrants.

The *Ladies' Companion* rates, however, were insufficient for goldfields life, and Fortune never fulfilled the commission: 'Who would write pages at fifteen shillings when one paid nine shillings per day for milk, and for a "woman's" magazine, too! Nay, there was nothing of the namby-pamby elegance of ladies' literature in our stirring, hardy, and eventful life on the early goldfields.' With this forthright declaration she further distances herself from the Angelic Housewives. Life for a middle-class Victorian woman in the Northern Hemisphere was constrained and cosseted. In the Austral colonies, the world turned upside down: servants and masters dug gold side by side, and sheltered misses and matrons did their own housework for the first time. The life might come as a shock, but an adaptable woman could prove tough and resourceful.

She continues with her first impressions, recording:

> the almost impassable condition of Elizabeth-street, and the team of bullocks that hopelessly tried to drag a laden dray out of the clinging mud in the centre of the street (if street it could be called, when only scattered houses, and a here and there visible kerb-stone, outlined a mass of glutinous clay).

Twenty years previously Melbourne had been the bushland of the Wurundjeri; by 1855 it was a very new city. The railway she took to central Melbourne was the first in Victoria and had been operating for only thirteen months.

Mary found somewhere to stay, the Hotel Albion in Bourke Street. The landlord put her '"with the girls", as it would hardly be safe for me to occupy a room alone, if I was the least nervous'. A woman without a man to protect her faced danger, and Mary only had her small son, whom she introduces two paragraphs later as 'my nervous little first-born'. Like Mary herself, he is given no physical description and no name. To the image of a faceless lady in Victorian dress can be added a child with long hair, wearing a short frock. At the time young boys and girls all wore dresses, for reasons of toilet training. The father of this child never appears in Mary's memoir, although Fortune is addressed by those around her as 'Mrs'.

The Fortunes' roommates were the Albion's barmaid and housekeeper, both Irish. Miss Mary Mac, the housekeeper, was 'a decidedly superior and lady-like girl of twenty-three or four'. She was a type that recurs in Fortune's writing: the capable colonial woman. Miss Mac charmed Fortune's little boy and carried him downstairs to the bar for 'lollies and tarts and "tips" of various value, from, no doubt, admirers of kind and pretty Miss Mac'.

While George is downstairs, his mother, who as a decorous matron of the middle class would never enter a bar, sits alone in the 'girls' room' (servants' quarters) and enjoys 'a cup of tea without the ship flavour'. She spends the child-free time taking notes.

I stared to see black satin and black velvet dresses hanging on rusty nails [no hangers yet] against a rough, whitewashed wall, and a handsome cheval glass nearly reaching the low roof, and standing on an uncovered, and not over-cleanly, deal [cheap planking] floor. The bedstead was of ordinary iron, uncurtained and unvalanced; there was a common wash-stand, with common ware [ewer and basin], and an old chest of drawers behind the door, and also behind the door a single stretcher, which was to be mine …

Here she collides with notions of delicacy, for on the chest of drawers is a gentleman's black top hat. Underneath her pillow she finds a common blue-striped man's shirt. They suggested to her two men, of different classes. Why were these clothes there? Did the maids wear drag, or have sweethearts sharing the space? A most indelicate situation is indicated, from the Victorian point of view.

Mary is interrupted when Miss Mac summons her to a scene so typical of goldfields Melbourne it was sketched by the famous artist Samuel Gill: 'Come on; you can see from the drawing-room, and there isn't a soul to see you – hurry, or you'll miss the fun!' Decorum meant a 'lady' should not be seen openly gawking, even if she was a writer. Mary thus becomes an observer who is unobserved, a key mode in her work. She witnesses an open carriage of diggers on the spree, halting outside the Albion. Two women are with them in the carriage, and Mary describes their striking appearance:

The women were both dressed in white of the richest material, and both had apparently vied with each other in donning the showiest and most expensive attire. One dress was of white satin, trimmed with blonde [lace] and clusters of flowers and ribbons; the other was of white watered silk. The coarse, red shoulders of one woman were partially shaded by a handsome lace shawl, which was fastened by a huge colonial gold brooch, and festooned with a ridiculously heavy gold chain; the other had draped around her an expensive China crape scarf, that was embroidered showily in red and blue silk. The head-dresses of these gorgeous dames consisted of white bonnets wreathed with long white ostrich plumes, and each fat, rubicund face was surrounded with a small forest of orange blossoms.

Miss Mac explains:

'Why, that's a wedding party, and those elegant ladies are brides who have just been married.'

'Good gracious!' I exclaimed.

'Yes, and the men are two lucky diggers, just down from Fiery Creek, who never saw the women until yesterday.'

The wedding party guzzles the best champagne, accompanied by spillages, breakages and shrieking laughter. The bill is paid with a handful of notes thrown at the waiter.

'The man is mad, assuredly,' was my comment as they disappeared.

'The sudden possession of gold has that effect very frequently,' said Miss Mac; 'but in this instance I should say his madness is the simple outcome of conceit and drink. I daresay he would be mean and miserable enough if he was poor and sober.'

With this prophecy that the two marriages will be miserable when the money runs out, a favourite theme is introduced: the battle of the sexes. That night it recurs, with a clear sexual threat. Mary tries to sleep, but a band and tramping dancers keep her awake:

Talk of the wild, dark, treacherous seas over which we had so lately crossed! Better the noise of a hundred storms than this of Bourke Street, in Melbourne.

To some such conclusion had I come when the band ceased […] The doors were banged, and there was a scuffling somewhere on the stairs approaching my refuge, while I could hear a woman's laughter stifled, and a pleading voice, which I recognised as that of my friend, Miss Mac. Gradually those noises neared me until they were at the landing outside, and the bumps of struggling bodies were distinctly audible on the door itself. When I discovered, from the incisive assertions of some male voice, that I, myself, was the object of all this to do, I was horrified, and felt so perfectly helpless that, had it not been for the rapid denouement, I believe I should have been new chum enough to faint. As it was, I covered my head up, and drew myself up as well behind the chest of drawers as I could, and listened, shivering.

'Oh, it's no use, Mary; I'm not to be put off. I'm determined on it, so you may as well give in. Let go, for see her I will!'

'Don't I tell you the poor lady is asleep,' Miss Mac cried, 'and the poor child, too. After such a long voyage, and their first night ashore, surely you would never be so cruel as to disturb them. Now, go to bed, Jack, like a good fellow!'

'Good fellow, be blowed!' was uttered in another voice. 'See this new arrival I will. I want to see what a woman looks like that hasn't been kiln-dried in this blessed climate. Stand out of the way, Jack!' and the door was dashed open with a burst. I could not, of course, see the crowd of faces that I knew were within a few feet of me, nor do I to this day know what occasioned the sudden lull and quiet departure of the boarders, unless it was the sight of my sleeping child's face.

The next day Fortune found more permanent lodgings and went to the office of *The Argus* newspaper to place a notice informing George Wilson of her arrival. The paper's 'Missing, Friends, Messages, &c.' column was a vital communication tool for a population frequently on the move from rush to rush. It comprises a rich social history: lost legatees and lost lovers, people seeking 'first-rate rat-dogs', and dressmakers with uncollected, unpaid-for frocks. Mary's notice appeared on 5 October 1855. Like many of the mysterious notices of assignation found in the column, what she wrote could be decoded by one person only.

Mr George Wilson. Mary and Georgie have arrived. Inquire at W. Finlay's, Tranent Cottage, Collingwood.

William Finlay was an emigrant Scot and builder, 'a man of considerable practical ability and public usefulness'. He had a pregnant wife, was president of the Collingwood Philanthropic Society, and would later become a local councillor. His views on the 'sensual indulgence of eating and drinking, which tend to debase youth' suggests that his dinner table tended to the dismal. Lodging with Finlay meant spending Sundays at the brand-new Chalmer's Church, which belonged to the Free Church of Scotland (Evangelical Presbyterians), of which Finlay was a committee member.[2] People like the Finlays – busy, public-spirited and pious – would become a moneyed elite in Marvellous Melbourne, as wealth from the goldfields made it one of the richest cities on the planet.

More akin to Fortune was John W. Semple, subeditor at *The Argus* and correspondent to the *Sydney Morning Herald*. She had a letter of introduction to him from 'a Scotch literary gentleman'. She presented herself as a woman of letters, unusual in colonial Australia but not unique. *The Argus'* Adelaide correspondent, ostensibly John Brodie Spence, was actually his sister Catherine Helen Spence, the first woman journalist in Australia. The previous year she had published anonymously in England the novel *Clara Morison*. The two women may never have met, but they were linked by locality: Melrose, in Scotland, was Spence's birthplace and an ancestral site for Mary Fortune.

The Spences had emigrated due to money troubles, but Semple had left Scotland under a spectacular cloud, if Fortune's memoir can be believed. In Scotland she had heard gossip about this 'clever but erratic' man:

He was [...] ordained minister of a Scotch church in the ancient town of Peebles, but the pulpit was the last place a handsome young man who valued his position only as it afforded him facilities for pleasure, more especially in the shape of young ladies' society, should have occupied. Poor Semple was accused of other, and more unbecoming vices too, and he lost his gown in consequence of them, leaving Scotland engaged to *two* women, with both of whom I was personally acquainted.

The colonies enabled transformation. On the goldfields men lost identities and class, wearing rough workingmen's clothes, growing beards, assuming nicknames. Mary never gives her name in the memoirs, and in its early pages she disguises George Wilson as James Grieve, describing him as her uncle rather than her father. By the second instalment, published four months later, she forgets and calls him Uncle Barry, while her child addresses him as 'dear old Daddy'.

George Wilson was a common name, and Mary's advertisement went unnoticed by its intended recipient. Nobody enquired for her at the Finlays. What might have happened to Wilson during their long voyage to Australia?

Of course, some people did not want to be found. The following notice appeared on the front page of *The Argus* on 9 October:

ELIZA CHARLTON, wife of Peter Charlton, having left her husband on the 6th August, in company with another man, taking with her a male child, twelve months old, for the safety of which the father is most anxious; he will thankfully reward any person who can give such information as may lead to the recovery of the same. PETER CHARLTON. Address Post Office, Maldon, Tarrengower.

A father had absolute patriarchal rights over his child. Peter Charlton might not want his faithless wife back, but he did want his son. Fortune may have made use of this advertisement; she had the habit of tweaking fact into fiction. In the memoir she encounters a lucky miner, Jack Dawson, who is deserted in similar circumstances. They first meet as fellow passages on an omnibus, before Dawson has discovered his wife's betrayal:

'I've just come down from Fiery Creek with a belt full of gold. Thank God, there'll be no sad faces in our home any more! I've plenty, and to spare. See here!' and he drew a handful of sovereigns from his pocket, shoving one each into the children's hands … 'I've been six months away, and my lass doesn't expect me home to-day. How surprised and glad she will be! my kind Nell! Look, that's my cottage; but the door is shut – she must be out.'

Fortune meets all three Dawsons later in the memoir. The encounter may be fictional, but with it she set up a plot line. She also expressed a hidden anxiety: she too had left her husband, taking their child.

During the wait for news of Wilson, Semple initiated contact with Mary via his own advertisement in *The Argus*. 'Mr Semple was very genial and attentive to me,' she recalled. He was an enthusiast for Scotland and its poetry, fond of amateur dramatics and giving public lectures. If the two managed a discreet flirtation under the eyes of Melbourne's unco guid, the rigidly religious Scots, then it could go no further.[3]

On 20 October Mary advertised for the third time, this time giving her name and two possible locations for the man she sought. Finally George Wilson responded, from the Castlemaine district, where he had a goldfields store – easier and more lucrative work than mining. She packed up her child and waved Melbourne goodbye for the moment. Semple would also later head for Castlemaine, to work for *The Mount Alexander Mail*, but she never saw him again. Or so she said.

Tracing George Wilson through colonial Victoria is difficult: in 1856 over twenty George Wilsons appeared on the electoral roll for the first Legislative Assembly. This significant reform extended voting rights to men over twenty-one who owned property. Property included holdings as small as a miner's right, the cost of which had been significantly reduced following the Eureka unrest in 1854, when miners at Ballarat had clashed with government forces in a dispute over licence fees. Mary's father was likely the George Wilson recorded at Kangaroo [Flat],

Loddon, in the Fryerstown district near Castlemaine. He had a miner's right and had been resident for at least three months, no mean feat on the rushes.

Mary and young Georgie took a Cobb & Co. coach to join George Wilson on the diggings. There was one other female passenger, 'to keep me in countenance' (composed, another suggestion of nervousness); the rest were male. Of this woman, a Mrs Blackett, Fortune commented that she 'impressed me unfavourably in every way', and foreshadowed that they would meet again – another plot line in the memoir.

The coach traversed the 80 miles to Castlemaine:

Flocks of sheep there were, with strangely dirty and dingy fleeces, and ranges of blue hazy hills in the distance, and, as for the rest, it is to me a blank, save one scene of plunging horses and broken traces on a bush track, where our Jehu seemed to thread the mazes of dead and living timber like a phantom driver with a team of phantom horses under his spirit power. One other memory I have of that journey to the diggings, and it is the memory of a pretty scene, though I had nearly forgotten it. Along the edge of a wooded slope, and among the beautiful green undergrowth, where one of the many tracks ran, we saw a conveyance, of strange and strong build, being driven with a velocity that seemed dangerous to us new chums, and behind and before it rode a mounted escort of red-coated soldiers. The rattle of its wheels as it passed us, the sharp crack of the driver's whip, the cheery salute as the clatter of hoofs and the cloud of dust they raised overtook us and disappeared, was like a vision or a dream. We had met the famous gold escort from Castlemaine.

At day's end, waiting in a hotel for the next stage of the journey, Fortune recorded a woman's lament:

'What ever came over me at all to come to such an outlandish place!' she sobbed. 'I didn't know when I was well off, or I'd have stopped among my own people.'

Ah! Many of us have come to the same conclusion many a hundred times since our voluntary expatriation … as the twilight deepened and my sleeping boy lay snugly and quiet in my arms, I began to realise that I was on the borders of a new life. All the perils of the sea were over, and it lay an impassable barrier between me and the old happy Canadian life.

Finally she alighted at George Wilson's store in Kangaroo Flat. He peered 'into her face to read the record of years' and wept to see his daughter again.

3

—

ON THE GOLDFIELDS

THE AUSTRALIAN GOLDFIELDS OF THE 1850S were exciting, dangerous, a lottery of backbreaking work. Thousands converged on auriferous areas, creating a moonscape of dirt, tents and mineshafts. When the claims were exhausted, miners simply moved to the next rush. The process created a national identity of prosperity through mining which persists even today.

Kangaroo Flat, Mary's first goldrush, is now Tarilta, desolate farmland. In late 1855 it was a thriving alluvial goldfield, with hotels, bowling alleys, boarding houses, libraries, private schools, concerts and balls. 'Sticking-up and horse stealing', however, were 'said to be rather more rife than desirable'.[1]

This alien environment would intensely inform Mary's work, making her as a writer. She mined a rich subject:

> To fall asleep and dream dreams that change as quickly as the forms in an unsteady kaleidoscope, and to awaken with a bewildered feeling that you are not yourself but have changed places with some other identity, must be a sensation akin to that I experienced when I opened my eyes in the morning after my first sleep on the diggings. I had been too tired the night before than to thankfully follow my child to bed without finding enough energy to even

31

wonder at my strange, not to say uncouth surroundings, and in the morning the extraordinary and unaccustomed objects that presented themselves to me suggested the dregs of a nightmare.[2]

The Mount Alexander diggings in 1852, in an engraving by S.T. Gill.

Her home was a tent that also housed a general store. S.T. Gill's goldfields illustrations provide a visual complement: a miner's gold being weighed by the storekeeper behind his counter, the stock on display ranging from cheese to candles. At the back were private quarters, with primitive furniture: crates for seats, a bed cut from saplings, the posts sunk into the ground, a chimney of bullock hide, no windows but slits in the canvas for ventilation. On the floor were tailings, by-products of mining: smooth pebbles, a solution to the fleas when sluiced with water daily. Mary's light kid boots sank into this novel flooring – to walk in the goldfields, she would need less ladylike footwear.

I saw the piles of uprooted soil, where the diggers were burrowing like moles, and heard the monotonous rock of a hundred cradles [sieves for washing gold-bearing dirt] that went 'swish, swish' down by the creek that wound through the Flat. It was from thence also that I saw the long double lines of business tents that formed the street, and the waving of gay flags of all nationalities, from the rough flag poles in front of store, or restaurant, or billiard-room, or what-not.[3]

Flags were used as identifiers for a population not always literate. Wilson was doing well, able to afford licences for mining and business. Every meal was home-delivered from a nearby restaurant:

chops, that were burnt into cinders and swimming in fat, several thick slices of dirty-looking bread, and about a pound of *awful* butter rolled up in a bit of green paper that I afterwards discovered to be a part of an ancient play bill. Two enamelled dinner plates that had seen rough usage and fire, black-handled and stained knives and forks, two enamelled cups without saucers, and a *billy* full of tea completed the preparations for breakfast. There was no milk or eggs procurable ...[4]

Although her writing is vivid, Kangaroo Flat is where Fortune's narrative becomes unreliable. This text was a hybrid: first travelogue, then completed years later as memoir. It also partakes of fiction, which was not considered a fault in Victorian life-writing – however annoying to the historian. The modes of detective writing and melodrama infest the memoir: even when describing verified events, Fortune adds sensation. Her habitual concealment is another factor, and there were issues she simply could not describe with complete honesty, such as true crime.

Here the past was indeed a different country. Guns were unrestricted and miners discharged them at dusk to warn thieves. In Fortune's story 'The Star-Spangled Banner', even a woman shoots. Capital punishment applied to a range of offences, including rape. At a time when there was no social welfare, most crime was petty, committed by people simply trying to survive. Vagrancy was a catch-all charge, with those unable to prove some kind of employment fined or incarcerated.

Drug abuse was rampant: opium was legal and available from pharmacies, mixed with alcohol to make laudanum. Other combinations were more alarming, such as the cocktail 'Blowhisskulloff': opium, spirits, cayenne pepper and *Cocculus indicus*, a berry otherwise used to stun fish. Alcohol posed the greatest danger. Historian F.B. Smith noted the laxness of colonial law regarding levels of proof alcohol (higher than in France) and adulteration. In her journalism, Fortune reported a comment: 'But it was always the way; if a man happened to get a drop of bad stuff (and that F. did keep some shocking beer on tap) the women were sure to say he was drunk.'[5] Imported spirits would be watered down and cut with anything for potency: opiates, tobacco, kerosene or methanol. Drug-related violence consequently went off the charts: historian Janet McCalman compares the effects to those of methamphetamines today. Newspapers frequently noted 'the blue devils': people drinking themselves into delirium tremens, with delusions and hallucinations. Often those affected were committed to an asylum to dry out, and on release many offenders would relapse. They would be readmitted, if their preferred tipple did not kill them first.[6]

On the goldfields, an attempt was made to limit trade to licensed hotels, where some degree of regulation applied. The failure of this prohibition is shown in Fortune's description of a flooded creek as a sea of bobbing corks. Here an uneasy undercurrent of her memoir surfaces. Without drink, she reflects, 'How much less accommodation would have been required in asylum, gaol, and churchyard!'[7]

Mary Fortune's relationship with alcohol was, like much in her life, complicated. In the memoir she disapproves of drink, but in her fiction she shows goldfields stores such as Wilson's to be dependent on sly grog. Her 1899 story 'A Trooper's Tale', set on Kangaroo Flat, notes that the few women present mostly 'had their time fully occupied in some or other kind of business connected with the sale of drink'.

Others concurred. Gill depicted a tent with the sign 'Coffee and Meals', but a woman is shown pouring grog into a miner's pannikin. Future police commissioner Frederick Standish recalled an Irishwoman at Bendigo carrying milk cans of grog with the cheery cry, 'Milk ho!' He had partaken of the trade as an unsuccessful miner and storekeeper. When two thirsty policemen visited his store, he sold them lemonade but gave them 'the illicit' gratis, a common ruse. Subsequently warned of imminent raids, he hurriedly sold off his alcohol. Being caught meant a £50 fine, which few could afford, or four months in gaol for a first offence.[8]

Worse crimes than sly grog occurred. William Jones, a miner, cohabited with Sarah Williams, and during a drunken row struck her with a pick, hitting her jugular vein. Jones fled and was eventually arrested at Creswick while shaving off his beard.[9] Kangaroo Flat united in the manhunt:

> Every place of business, every claim and shaft, every bend and nook of creek and hill was tramped over by willing men, eager to see justice done on the wretch who had shed blood at their very doors, as it were; and that it was a woman's blood did not render them any the less rancorous or anxious to succeed ...[10]

In Fortune's memoir the killing is fictionalised but recognisable, the woman attacked as she tries to flee: 'Poor soul, she has been on the bolt, and he found it out.' In December 1855 Jones was convicted of manslaughter and sentenced to seven years' hard labour on the roads.

That same month, Fortune sent *The Mount Alexander Mail* a poem, which was accepted. 'Song of the Gold Diggers' appeared with her initials and location. It was revolutionary, reflecting her milieu. Fortune recalled the 'noisy political argument' of goldminers, with that December being the first anniversary of the Eureka Stockade.[11] Three years earlier, a monster meeting of miners had occurred on the Mount Alexander diggings, with some 15,000 men peacefully gathering to protest a hike in licence fees – and the government had backed down.

Hurrah for the free new land!
And hurrah for the diggers bold!
And hurrah for the strong unfettered right
To search in the hills for gold!
Turn up the sods my strong free mates,
And dig with a fearless hand:
For there's not a castled lordling here,
In all this glorious land!

Women poets could be politically radical during this period, as with the English Chartists and Ellen Young, the 'Ballarat Poetess' of Eureka. Fortune's 'genial' John Semple at *The Argus* also had radical sympathies; with Ebenezer Syme of *The Age*, he provided bail for Henry Seekamp, editor of the Ballarat *Star*. That showed courage, for the charge was sedition, Seekamp being the only person jailed over Eureka. Semple called Seekamp a 'brother of the quill'.[12]

In the memoirs, Fortune downplays her politics:

Coming almost directly from America, and being young you know, perhaps it was natural that, in a new land and among scenes in which law was of but little account, I should bloom in the Poet's Corner as a thorough Democrat.[13]

Was a copy of *The Mount Alexander Mail* left on the counter of Wilson's store, with the oh-so-casual enquiry to customers: 'Anything in the paper today?' And the response: 'Who is this M.H.F. fellow?' 'No idea!' – with a sly smile.

The poem was reprinted in other colonial newspapers. Fortune herself revisited it, notably in her second novel, *Dora Carleton* (1866), in which a miner sings the ditty. A listener comments: 'Wasn't the fellow that wrote that a ninny. Unfettered right – eh? I wonder if that chap ever paid a pound for a "miner's right," when he hadn't the price of a loaf left.'

The singer agrees: 'Hanging is too good for the author of such trash.'[14] Such in-jokes often featured in Fortune's work.

Others rated the poem more highly. When rediscovered by Castlemaine historians, it would be recited during goldfields tours and in 2000 was even recorded for an album of songs from the diggings.[15]

A week after the poem was printed, another more accomplished, if less political, verse by 'M.H.F.' appeared: 'To xxxx'.

Thou art away, away
I see thee not
Mid thy new circling ones
Am I forgot?
Oh! In the red faint light
Of a dying sun,
Think thou of me, thine own –
Thy distant one

Christmas came, with gold running low. Miners prepared to leave and so did the storekeepers. On 28 December, *The Mount Alexander Mail* printed another of Fortune's poems, 'Climb Up the Hill', with revolutionary themes similar to those seen in 'Song of the Gold Diggers'. In the same issue, the paper's editor requested: 'M.H.F will oblige by calling at this office at his earliest convenience.'

That day Wilson packed his business onto a bullock dray, with Fortune riding atop the load. They stopped at the *Mail*'s office in Castlemaine, Fortune being 'very much tickled at the personal pronoun, and curious too'. When she presented herself:

I was interviewed by a man who stared in open-eyed wonder at me and my youngster, who I led by the hand.

'Are *you* "M.H.F."?' he questioned with evident disbelief.

'Yes.'

'I can hardly credit it. You had better see Mr Saint; but as for the request that M.H.F. would call, we want a reporter and sub-editor, and thought he might suit.'[16]

Charles Saint (1824–1886) was born to a printing family in England and worked as a journalist prior to emigration. In Castlemaine he became a crusading editor, and his career would take him from the Melbourne *Herald* to Hong Kong. The 'strong radical sense, energy, and literary talent' he brought to *The Mount Alexander Mail* made it influential, only surpassed on the goldfields by Seekamp's *Ballarat Star*. Saint might have been approachable, amiable and just, a supporter of the Chinese, but he was no feminist. Although skilled writers were scarce on the goldfields, he did not employ this talent he had spotted. In any case, Fortune had the care of a small child, and Wilson's trade was peripatetic.[17]

That evening Fortune visited Saint and his wife Sarah at home, and the next day he showed her the police court. The star attraction was lawyer Butler Cole Aspinall, famed as the Eureka defence lawyer. He was an ex-journalist, handsome and witty. In 1856 he would be elected to the colonial parliament.

Fortune's memoir here obscures her personal narrative by leaping ahead in time. Aspinall did defend two cases of sly grogging on 29 December 1855, yet what she described in the memoir was a major police operation, which occupied the police court for days. In fact it occurred the following year, in March 1856, with up to forty defendants charged with sly grogging. Nearly all were from the vicinity of Taradale, near Castlemaine, a rush Fortune claimed to have visited for only half a day. Fortune quoted Saint: 'There is a great deal of talk and not a little indignation about it, for it is reported that the people were arrested before they were out of bed, and actually marched to the Sawpit Gully.'[18] They were walked 4 kilometres, in handcuffs, to what is now Elphinstone, where a police magistrate was situated.

In her memoir, Fortune does not reveal any personal involvement in the arrests. In 1893, however, in an authorial aside to a goldfields crime story, she wrote:

> There may be persons inclined to carp at a statement that a mounted policeman went to Curlew's to *arrest* Joe on a charge of sly-grog selling. In 1856, I, the writer of this, saw several men arrested at Yankee Point, Taradale, and marched on foot to Castlemaine lockup, *handcuffed,* on the charge of selling spirits without a licence.[19]

Fortune knew the mechanisms behind such raids. Says the police narrator of her first crime story:

> I received orders to 'stick up' all stores and shanties that sold grog without a license, and although I much disliked the work of a 'dirty informer' [...] my instructions were strict, and so my first step was to find a man willing, for a bonus of ten pounds, five on engagement and five on conviction [...]
>
> I settled on my man – a low sneaking looking wretch – and after engaging him to do some fencing at the camp, I sounded him out on the point; and he agreed to be my fellow informer – two witnesses in these affairs being required by law [...] we succeeded in drinking nobblers [shots of spirits] and not paying for them at seven or eight different stores and shanties. Of course I summoned them all, and plenty of black looks I got in consequence.[20]

In the March 1856 cases, two hired informers met a hostile reception when the cases came to trial. Only minor operators had been arrested, including women and children. Newspapers commented that some notorious offenders had not been raided, imputing they had paid police bribes. Standish himself recalled 'the general impression' that certain Castlemaine businesses were 'winked at' by police.[21]

Aspinall appeared for the defence and was 'an excellent pleader and examiner', wrote Fortune. He accused the police of deliberately targeting women, whose husbands would pay the fine to ensure their wives avoided jail. In the *Mail*, Saint editorialised that the whole affair was an exercise in 'sly revenue', designed to fill governmental coffers. On the final afternoon of the trials, the remaining cases were all dismissed.[22]

Was Fortune simply a curious observer, or did she have a closer interest in the March 1856 cases? Did she know, say, defendant Robert Blair of Taradale, who kept a small circulating library? She would later depict such a reading room in 'The Little Widow'. Combining books and alcohol was an unusual but calculated risk.[23]

Was George Wilson arrested? The possibility exists, since records are incomplete and aliases common. Or was Mary arrested? A number of women were charged. Her memoir describes the Castlemaine lock-up, built so roughly that tobacco could be passed through the cracks between the logs that made up the walls. In a later novel, she describes the lock-up from within: her narrator watches the moon through the cracks and, being rather a 'dainty fellow', can slip off his handcuffs 'as easily as you would a piece of greased eel skin'. If Mary was locked up after the Taradale raids, it was not for the last time.[24]

The *Mail* wrote that the arrested were 'almost without exception persons of good character and position, men respected by their neighbours and women of superior education and breeding'. That fitted Wilson and Fortune. Yet a sly-grog charge was unsuitable for a Victorian lady's memoir, even if the prosecutions largely collapsed due to inconsistent evidence and perjury.[25]

Behind such raids could be murky motives. Fanny Finch, a Castlemaine businesswoman of African descent, is now famous for being one of the first women to vote in Australia. But in 1855 she was fined for selling sly grog. A 'Constant Reader' of *The Mount Alexander Mail* alleged the real reason was sexual harassment:

I believe I state correctly when I say that war is declared against her for not acceding to the infamous wishes and proposals made by one of the camp officials, and which has been followed up without success by the subordinates as a matter of course, for these gentry make a point of imitating those above them in rank in all their vices and folly. It is high time such proceedings were stopped, and individuals allowed to live unmolested by them.[26]

Some raids were commercially motivated. In the memoir, Fortune's fellow coach passenger, Mrs Blackett, is described as living and working at a local landmark, the Taradale Hotel. In real life, Geraldine Nicholson, a widow aged thirty-nine, was its owner, and in 1856 would become its licensee, the first woman to run a public house in the Castlemaine region. A historic plaque today describes her as Taradale's 'best known publican'. In Fortune's depiction, Mrs Blackett takes charge of the business, not letting her menfolk interfere.

Again, however, Fortune adds melodrama, making Mrs Blackett a villainess who drops dead from apoplexy in her own bar. What had Geraldine Nicholson done to deserve such a lurid fictionalisation? It reads like a personal grudge – Fortune settling a score. A female publican on the goldfields needed to be hard to succeed. Just as a licence to dig gold was a lottery, so too was a licence to dispense alcohol. The investment was expensive, with thin profit margins and the risk of insolvency.[27] The unlicensed sly-grog shanties represented serious rivalry; Fortune herself noted that they could be 'more frequented than the hotels'. Here the interests of publicans and the police could coincide. 'Information was laid', in the contemporary phrase: a licensed publican might make a complaint, naming and locating the sly groggers. In these circumstances, dobbing in the competition would have been sound business practice. That Nicholson was a successful publican for twelve years suggests a force of character and commercial skills, but not necessarily scruples.

Did Fortune believe Nicholson was behind the raids? Most of those arrested were from Taradale. If Fortune was taking literary revenge, she fudged the details: in the memoir, Mrs Blackett is arrested in the sly-grog raids. Notices of Nicholson's death, in Taradale, appeared in the Melbourne papers in early 1882, months before Fortune's memoir began serialisation. If the news stirred up memories, then Fortune killed Nicholson again in print, damning Mrs Blackett as 'vicious'.[28]

Victorian moralisers might have applied the same word to Fortune herself. Angels in the house did not live in sly-grog shanties, nor did they have sex outside of marriage. The raids coincided with Fortune getting pregnant; she gave birth on 3 November 1856, nine months later. The evasions and distortions of time in the memoir conceal her illegitimate baby.

A liaison could never have been mentioned in her memoir. The ideal was female purity, but in real life women were more complicated. Consider Ellen Clacy, who wrote the bestselling 1853 travelogue *A Lady's Visit to the Gold Diggings of Australia*. In the narrative, Clacy travels to Australia with an elder brother, goes gold-digging for several months and marries before returning to Britain. Family research has revealed a different tale. Clacy was pregnant out of wedlock, having conceived before arriving in Australia. Two months after her departure her daughter was born at sea. The immense distances travelled by Clacy hid her impropriety. Moreover, the contemporary female fashions – corsets, wide skirts supported by stiff horsehair petticoats, topped with a shawl or a loose pelisse – concealed pregnancy even when advanced.

Back in England with the baby, she published as Mrs Charles Clacy, although she did not marry this man until the following year. If he was the father, his tardiness in tying the knot may be reflected in a melodramatic subplot of Clacy's book, in which a pregnant young woman is twice left at the altar. Clacy presents this story with the conventional trappings of sin, ruin and penitent death: the mother, her seducer and their baby all die. But in life Clacy, like Fortune, was not a conventional Victorian women. For both writers, melodrama expressed what was otherwise too indelicate to mention, and both survived and became published authors. Clacy's daughter, also called Ellen, became a noted artist.

Fortune did not marry her baby's father. Colonial Australia had a significant gender imbalance, with the goldfields noted for having 'very little of crinoline about them'. An anonymous goldfields memoirist, travelling with a mother and daughter, recalled that the two women received enthusiastic male attention, 'a species of persecution not readily punished, nor easy to get rid of'. Both left quickly for peaceful employment at a bush station.[29]

Fortune does not describe such pestering in her memoirs, but in fiction with a male narrator she was able to depict sexual violence. The settings tend to be on the goldfields. One storekeeper's daughter is 'besieged with suitors' and is warned to watch her company and 'where she goes', lest a man take 'jealous revenge'. Another sneaks out after dark to meet an admirer and is murdered, her clothing 'disordered and torn'.[30]

Fortune's second crime story featured a serial rapist and murderer, something unprecedented in fiction by woman writers of her era:

> One dark night, in a tent in the very centre of a crowded thoroughfare, a female had been preparing to retire to rest, her husband being in the habit of remaining at the public-house until a late hour, when a man with a crape mask – who must have gained an earlier entrance – seized her, and in the prosecution of a criminal offence, had injured and abused the unfortunate woman so much that her life was despaired of.[31]

An old adage held that rape was a fate worse than death. In Victorian fiction, victims of sexual assault conventionally die. That trope avoided the real-life consequences: pregnancy, venereal disease and, if the assault was made public, the label of fallen woman.

The closest Fortune gets in the memoirs to sexual peril is at the Albion Hotel soon after she arrives in Melbourne. What she did not write of directly, however, other women did. Martha Clendinning, a Ballarat storekeeper, published her goldfields recollections in 1906. Her doctor husband 'was occasionally absent at night, a fact easily known to anyone who watched his movements, and thought of visiting at night a dwelling in which no man was in charge [...] with an evil design in view.' Although not a nervous lady, she took precautions, undressing in the dark and always being within 'screeching distance' of a neighbour. One night she closed the business at dusk and after putting her daughter to bed, read by candlelight. The premises comprised tent and wooden lean-to, and she sat with her chair against the locked door:

> After a while I heard the step of a man passing by. He stopped for a moment, then crept noiselessly nearer. The fine twigs of the firewood crackled under his foot, and I became unpleasantly aware that he was standing against the door outside, peering through a chink close to where my head was leaning on the inside.

Nearby her child slept, breathing heavily. Clendinning cleverly improvised, addressing the little snorer as her husband, and eventually the prowler stole away. She spent a sleepless night, but did not encounter further danger.[32]

Court reports in Victorian newspapers show that relatively few rape cases were prosecuted. Only ten men hanged for the offence between 1842 and 1900, compared to nearly 150 murderers. In court, misogyny ruled. Consider the 1856 experience of Mrs Ann Gray of Richmond in Melbourne, described in reportage as forty and 'stout'. She was alone, walking along the road one evening after waiting unsuccessfully at a Kew public house for a dray to take her home. Two men 'violated' her, crushing her bonnet but not her fighting spirit. She went immediately to police.

Butler Cole Aspinall argued for the defence that Gray had been drunk at the time and had an 'indifferent' character. Whether or not she had been drinking, Gray had been in a pub. Justice Redmond Barry told the jury: 'although a woman may not make any statement, yet by her conduct she may make a man believe her to be a woman of bad character'. The all-male jury agreed.[33]

That the case even got to court was unusual for assaults involving adult women. More commonly tried were offences against girls, where purity could not be questioned. Of the ten hanged rapists, six of their victims were prepubescent girls, including two cases of fatherly incest. Yet examination of the newspapers shows that in many cases juries did not convict.

Mary Fortune wrote about many things with unwomanly authority, and one of them was rape. Other Victorian women writers, such as her French goldfields contemporary Céleste de Chabrillan, have their heroines faint and awake to find themselves pregnant. De Chabrillan, despite having been a Parisian courtesan, published her novel *Les Voleurs d'Or* (1857) under her own name and conformed to the prevailing standards of modesty. Fortune, writing under a male pseudonym, was not so constrained. She writes sexual attack unflinchingly. Whatever happened in Taradale in March 1856, sexual violence remained a constant threat, even beyond the goldfields.

4

—

A FATHERLESS CHILD

Subsequent to the autumn 1856 raids Wilson's store packed up again for a longer trip, to a new rush at the White Hills, Buninyong, near Ballarat. On the road Mary met a colourful character she had first encountered at Kangaroo Flat, Fritz the Bellman (actually Fitz, his full name being William Fitzgerald), a town crier: a walking, shouting advertisement for local businesses described as an 'eccentric little manikin'. In January 1856 he had been charged with theft while drunk at Castlemaine and sentenced to two months' hard labour. His release is further proof that Fortune spent longer in the Castlemaine region than she would admit.[1]

She also re-encountered Jack Dawson, who was seeking his lost family, 'with what dread intentions I could but guess shudderingly'. At Buninyong she met his wife, Nell, and their son; both mother and child were miserable. Nell functions as a contrast to Fortune, and is part of a longer discourse about goldfields motherhood. Melodrama strikes again when Dawson confronts Nell: 'Faithless and vile that you are, give me my child!' The mother has no legal redress, 'everyone dropping from her as from one visibly infected with sin'. Even her son abandons her happily. Much later, Fortune sees Nell working as a barmaid, 'with a haggard painted face and much jewelry', among a 'crowd of flattering diggers'.[2] Behind the melodrama, was there a personal anxiety that could not be openly expressed? Peter Charlton from *The Argus* advertisement might never have found his child. Certainly Joseph Fortune, far distant in Canada, did not claim his patriarchal rights.

Buninyong rush had a population of 12,000 in early 1856. Mary drew it vividly:

> Let us try if we can to distinguish among the miles of heaped-up pipe-clay, from which the rush took its name, the hundreds of gay flags fluttering or drooping from their poles, the thousands of windlasses and moving diggers' forms, the strange hum of a busy multitude, and the astonished and bewildered faces of newcomers who, like myself, had not hitherto seen a 'great rush' – let us get there and find ourself camped for the night almost among the very holes where miners were working, while already the men of our party were driving in posts and raising rafters for Grieve's Store.
>
> It was a pleasant experience to sit or stand at the open side of our temporary shelter, and idly watch the scores of busy workers within view. There were some odd scenes exposed to the public in those days, and even refined women got accustomed to perform wholly domestic duties without even a screen between them and the moving, talking, laughing, eating, or working population around them. On the occasion I write of one party at a short distance were busily getting up the wooden frame of a tent, while a young woman was coolly washing a baby near an American cooking stove that was set up on the unsheltered ground and on which several pots were bubbling and steaming in the process of cooking.
>
> The noise was shocking, and toward evening deafening. Hammering, chopping, bellringing, band-playing, shouting, laughing, fighting, and singing were all represented horridly in the babel of a new rush, and one heard and saw as in a dream in which the dreamer's identity is lost.[3]

Buninyong was a 'deep sinking', with the gold far underground in a 'lead' or gutter. Alluvial deposits followed ancient watercourses that trapped and concentrated the gold. Following the lead was guesswork; miners dug shafts, creating tunnels shored with timber and lit with candles. In Fortune's writing the shafts frequently collapse.

Again she observed without being seen:

I and my boy amused ourselves by watching what was going on through the interstices of a sapling erection at the back of the storeroom, which served as a sort of kitchen or scullery, and abutted so close on the lead that every word of the men at the nearest windlasses could be distinctly heard by us.'[4]

In a tent encampment, little was private from watching eyes, whether they belonged to a budding writer or to the police. Fortune's detective Sinclair observes: 'I used to think [...] that people who lived so entirely in public could have no fear of police supervision, but I am a suspicious fellow, and I soon changed my opinion on that subject.'[5]

The White Hills proved unprofitable, and the family moved to the nearby Green Hills. Here they lingered some months, 'simply waiting for a more attractive goldfield to turn up'. This dig was smaller, and 'in this quiet season was more like a very quiet and friendly suburb than anything else'.[6]

Fortune's pregnancy would now have been nearing its third trimester, but this was unmentionable in the memoir. Instead she relates a story, concerning not her but a neighbour, Mrs Mack, a restaurant-keeper with children and no husband. She was 'in an interesting way, and dependent on the doctor for attendance during an interesting event'.[7]

On the goldfields, medical attention was expensive. The poor avoided it unless vitally necessary. Fortune depicts the rush's doctor as incompetent and alcoholic, the object of a cruel and dangerous prank played by the miners. They conspired with Mrs Mack's ten-year-old son to get the doctor dead drunk, thus unable to attend the birth. Some termed the ruse shameful; others suggested it had averted medical manslaughter. Mrs Mack gave birth unassisted and survived. The doctor woke chained in the Macks' dog kennel, the dog wearing his nightcap.

Other pregnant women on the goldfields, as newspapers and diarists attest, died for lack of medical attention. Or from a drunken doctor: in December 1855, Dr William Henry Haddon drank his way through a confinement at which both mother and baby died. Found guilty of neglect, he was sentenced to three years on the roads.[8]

When Fortune gave birth on 3 November to a baby boy, a Dr Curtayne of Ballarat, respectable medical practitioner, attended. Fortune would use his name later in her fictions, apparently in gratitude. The birth may have had complications; Fortune would continue to be sexually active, but she bore no other children.

Although none of her writing from this period survives, she tells us in the memoir that her 'occasional squibs in the shape of "Sketches"' appeared in the *Buninyong Advertiser*. Started by printer Samuel Goode as a sheet of advertisements, by January 1857 the *Advertiser* 'had advanced to the dignity of a trim little weekly'.[9]

Two small children limited her time, however, and this second acquaintance with the press proved short-lived. The family now moved to Chinaman's Flat, about 80 kilometres north, near Maryborough. The *Maryborough and Dunolly Advertiser* was as new as her baby, but its editor, Julius Vogel, was not simpatico. A correspondent for *The Argus*, he was not without feminist and literary interests – he later wrote the utopian *Anno Domini 2000; or, Women's Destiny* (1889) – but his paper did not give space to sketches or poems.

Travelling to Chinaman's Flat was arduous. In the fourth installment of the memoir, Fortune wrote:

It was in the hottest days of a hot summer, and was a series of misfortunes of one kind or another. Fortunately none of them were very serious, decidedly the worst being an enforced encampment of four days on the then Ballarat racecourse, in consequence of all the bullocks of the party being lost.

I shall never forget that wretched camping ground, or the frightful hot winds we had to endure there. Persons who had no experience of out-door life in our Victorian interior some twenty-six years ago can get but a faint idea of the hot winds of that time in the hot winds of to-day, and never had I a better opportunity of feeling them than during those days in a shelterless camp.

There was not a tree or a shrub on the burnt up level course, and not a roof save that of a sort of roadside store or inn, which we could just discern on a bleak track that had no charms for the wearied eye. Bullock drivers had a way of keeping their loads together in those days when it not unfrequently happened that a loaded dray got 'bogged', and rendered it necessary for the bullocks of one dray to be yoked to help those of another out of the mire; so there were five or six drays together, making a total of some fifty bullocks, who took it into their wise heads to leave on a private pleasure excursion, while we awaited their leisure in the delightful enjoyment of camping out on a shadowless plain.[10]

Again Fortune depicts a neighbour's experience of motherhood, as if projecting her own anxieties. She describes a baby three months old – the same age as Fortune's child at the time – 'an unhappy, puny looking little creature', lying in a basket in the shade. His mother, Ann Rashbone, had post-natal mental illness and eventually killed the child. At the time it was known that post-partum mental disturbance had a 50 per cent recovery rate, and in most cases the prognosis was simply to wait. Fortune does not blame Ann, who goes on to die in an asylum, but attributes her illness to mistreatment by her husband and mother-in-law.

At Chinaman's Flat the family experienced greater prosperity: she now had a real table, with a rough boarded floor instead of tailings.

In her story 'In the Cellar', set at Chinaman's Flat, such a floor conceals illicit liquor. She had also 'a convenient little American cooking stove that was afterwards put to illegal use'. The criminal uses of such a stove were limited: it must surely have been used as a still.[11]

As the text progresses, it becomes less of a memoir, for she could not write with complete honesty, for fear of censure. A series of seemingly fictional sketches appear: a murder mystery, another comic prank and more melodrama. Something changes. The narrator is no longer the vital and assertive young woman of letters, the centre of the tale. Fortune retreats from her own experience, becoming a bit-player in what is no longer her story.

At Inkerman goldfields, she encounters another depressed young mother (called first Mrs Clark and later Mrs Deasey, Fortune again forgetting names between instalments): 'The woman was pale and delicate looking, though not ill; but that she was a helpless sort of creature was evident.' The woman neglects her three-year-old daughter, nicknamed Little Possy, and does little but weep. She feels out of place on the goldfields and hates the camping life.

Fortune admonishes her:

'You are as young as I am and, I hope, healthy; you have your husband and the dearest little girl, *how* can you feel anything unpleasant in your surroundings? As for myself, I do think I was never happier in my life!'

The woman responds: 'Ah, *you* can't understand; you wasn't brought up as I was.' (A cunning class indicator here is the poor grammar. Here is cash, but not education.)

'I don't know what you call being brought up,' I returned, with a red heat glowing in my face, 'but if *you* had been well brought up you would have been trying to do your duty in whatever state of life it met you in, instead of crying for nothing and making both your husband and child unhappy.'[12]

When the unhappy young woman takes to drink, the narrative mixes melodrama with the conventions of the Victorian temperance novel. The neglected Possy wanders off and drowns in a nearby creek. The husband berates his wife as a murderess, a term Fortune also uses. The memoir ends with this tragedy, most abruptly: 'It was a sad story, but, after the usual inquiry, poor little Possy was buried, and the wretched mother went home to her friends in town.' No inquest fitting the story can be traced. However, it was typical: in April 1857 the *Bendigo Advertiser* wrote that child drownings comprised three quarters of all inquests.[13]

In the memoir, Fortune anticipated one final destination: Kingower, ten miles away, with a population of 1000 in early 1857. The field was rich but nuggety, and Wilson noted the potential financial risks: 'A digger must be able to risk not seeing the colour [gold] for weeks or months, when a grand find might make him a wealthy man in one hour; and the storekeeper would find it impossible to do a business if he was not in a position to give credit when it was asked for.'[14]

Their arrival was at latest mid-year, for she registered the birth of her second son at Kingower in June 1857. The baby was by now eight months old but had been neither named nor christened. Mary stated that the father was Joseph Fortune – a geographic impossibility – but the alternative was to declare the child illegitimate. Much later the baby's full name would be officially recorded as Eastbourne Vaudrey Fortune, which sounds inexplicably like a stage villain.

In August, Kingower became famous, an event Fortune describes in her first surviving story, the 1865 'Recollections of a Digger'. The narrator claims to have been only 'a few feet away' when in August 1857 the Blanche Barkly nugget was discovered.[15] It was the largest nugget then found, roughly the size and shape of a leg of mutton and named for the Victorian governor's daughter.

The nugget was unearthed on Kingower Flat by two sets of brothers, the Napiers (from Canada) and the Ambroses. They kept the discovery secret, buried under the table in their tent. After three months they packed up and drove a one-horse cart 240 kilometres to Melbourne, with the nugget hidden in a box and covered with old clothes. The brothers had only a pistol and shotgun for self-defence but met no bushrangers on the trip. Only when safe in Melbourne did they reveal the find – sparking a major rush to Kingower.[16]

The fact that Fortune does not mention the discovery in the memoir, although it would have been a fitting climax to her tale, suggests that she too was concerned with secrecy. Did her life resemble this fictional scene from her story 'Delia Loney'?:

There was a woman kept a shanty on Kingower – she was young and handsome, too, and she was a widow, they said; but there were a couple of little children. Well, she just sat and nursed the youngest, and let the boys [miners] help themselves. When a man shouted, or that, he just put his money on the top of an old clock, that stood on the sort of counter, or table, and took his change out of what was there before. The woman made money like winking ...[17]

If this passage is self-referential, it is the only time she depicts both her children. In the memoir, Kingower is, like Taradale, a place where Fortune creates a temporal and spatial twist in the narrative. She elides an incident too painful to be recalled in words, and which might identify her.

The omission is confirmed by an examination of the dates. Fortune's first summer in Australia was that of 1855–56, which she spent in the Castlemaine region. Her second, 1856–57, included the family's relocation to Chinaman's Flat. Her third summer in Australia, 1857–58, was spent in Kingower.

The last glimpse of her eldest son in the memoirs is 'in the latter end of February' 1858. The details are specific: on a drowsy, pleasant afternoon, she sits sewing under a blue gum tree at Inkerman, to the sound of rippling water and rustling leaves, watching her boy 'delightedly engaged with hammer and nails, monstrously proud of helping to put up uncle's store'.[18]

The memory is vivid – but in terms of place and date it is false. By February 1858 the family were at Kingower, and Mary's firstborn was dead.

5

—

BIGAMY

SHE WAS UNABLE TO WRITE THE child's death, even after twenty-six years. Only in 1903 could Fortune physically describe her eldest son. In 'Little Georgie's Grandpa', he is pale, with large blue eyes: 'He was far from being a robust boy but looked like some delicate flower that had shot up tall and slender among frail and tender leaves.' She gives most detail to his clothes:

> It was long before there were such things as knickerbockers for little children's wear, and this little boy was dressed in short petticoats, that showed frilled drawers and short, openwork [summerwear] white socks, with strap shoes of patent leather. The shoes were sadly dusty and a little worn, and the white Holland jumper [a linen dress] strapped around the waist by a soft, leather belt, with an ornamental metal buckle, was dusty and crumpled too. A little straw hat, with a blue ribband was on the child's head …[1]

Georgie Fortune's death certificate, dated 25 January 1858, was signed by the attending doctor, Charles Archibald Campbell, also the district registrar. He had met Mary Fortune when she registered her baby. In the formality and grief, something went unnoticed: her signature varied, written with a backwards slant in 1857, while in 1858 it slanted forwards.

The cause of death was 'convulsions', the illness lasting one day. The sudden onset suggests meningitis, likely caused by tainted water. Before antibiotics it was invariably fatal, a quick but horrible way to die. In the 1904 story 'Her Death Warrant', set in Kingower, Fortune wrote of 'the five years old son of Bell, and when the little fellow died of convulsions one hot summer day … Mrs Bell's heart was almost broken'.

Georgie Fortune was buried the day after he died, prudent in summer conditions. The funeral service was performed by the only Protestant clergyman for miles, William Hall, also the local squatter. 'Her Death Warrant' includes a description of the child's grave:

> The shade of them big trees made the sun look kindly on the few graves, and fell right on the big white boulder we put at little Harry's head. I got over the fence, and pulled out the weeds where we planted that flower-seed I brought from Bendigo, and there's a lot of forget-me-nots in full blossom.[2]

She never forgot.

~

Kingower was then the northernmost goldfield in the colony. Around it grew mallee bush, from which granite ranges or outcroppings rose. Its gold, discovered in 1854, took the form of nuggets found in the deep sinkings or veins in quartz rock, which were extracted by crushing and processing. In the early rushes the gold was alluvial, found by washing dirt – a process cheap and democratic, involving little beyond spades and a cradle. Quartz-crushing, by contrast, was complex and polluting: arsenic, mercury and acids were used and discarded freely, a lasting, lethal residue. The expense meant that companies with shareholders formed to extract the precious metal.

In the late 1850s, Kingower had no road as such, no magistrate and no gold escort. In 'Her Death Warrant', a carter hides little bags of nuggets in loose straw, driving with them underfoot. The geology of the goldfields made it into the newspapers, but other stories noted the arrival of Chinese miners who were 'immediately supplied with their passports and quitted in great haste' and the rush's first cricket pitch. Others were the matter of Fortune's fiction: murder, suicide and delirium tremens.[3]

What made her a pioneering writer of what would be termed police procedurals was a young man in uniform: Percy Rollo Brett. Their association was brief, but Mary mined it for the rest of her life. Brett in 1857 became the mounted constable in charge of the small police camp at Kingower. He was born in Ireland, Rathmacknee in Wexford, on 21 July 1838, the eldest son in a family of twelve children. His parents were Sarah, née Bredin, and Edward E. Brett, an Anglican rector who had previously been an army chaplain. The Bretts prized association with wealth or titles, such as the Annesleys, Earls of Anglesea, landowners in Wexford. Usually one Brett per generation was given the name Annesley.[4]

Mary Fortune listened intently to Percy Brett. He would later appear in her fiction:

> I was the son of a poor country clergyman who was not able to give his family more than the most ordinary of educations, and until I was twenty I had the run of my father's parsonage without one idea that I was sadly encroaching on the income I ought rather to have been increasing by my own exertions [...] An occupation of any kind to provide for my future at all was never hinted at, and as my father's position gave me an air of respectability, and an admittance to the restricted society alone open in the neighbourhood, I passed my time in a very jolly, selfish fashion, while poor dad was poring over his sermons or making 'poetry', to which unremunerative occupation he was much addicted.
>
> Ours was a hunting neighbourhood, and I was at least a fearless rider. It was my only accomplishment, but it sufficed to gain

me the attention of our richest magnate, Squire Baytown. I have no doubt I was some use to him in a certain way among the dogs, of whom I was a judge, and with the horses, whose society I preferred, I think, to that of the most engaging girls. At all events, the Squire never let me want a mount. I had only to choose from his stables, and my time was passed very pleasantly indeed until the Crimean war broke out, and all the regulars were sent out to help against Russia.

Then my father seemed to suddenly remember that I was unprovided for entirely [...] so, without consulting me in the matter, he requested the squire's influence to get me into the militia that was being called out to do duty at home in place of those that had been sent out to fight for the honour of old England.

I hardly know how it came about, but I soon found myself an ensign of militia, and for a time was very proud of my new uniform. That did not last long, however – it was a foot regiment, and I missed my horse and the delightful runs with the C— hounds across country; so that it was found necessary for me to be moved in some way or other, and they moved me with my full consent to Victoria, with very little money in my pocket and a brilliant letter of introduction from my true friend, the squire, to Captain Southfield, an old college friend of his, and a then squatter [...]

'What can you do, Ned?' [Southfield] asked, plainly, and I answered as plainly, 'Nothing earthly but ride, and that I can do with any living man.'

'Hum – um. I might put you on the station as super, but you say you cannot keep accounts.'

'Can hardly do a sum in simple division and write an execrable scrawl.'

'Upon my word, Ned, I'm afraid there's nothing for you but the mounted police.'[5]

Mounted police would have been familiar to Brett, as the colonial model drew on the Royal Irish Constabulary, essentially a force of occupation. The town police, meanwhile, derived from Sir Robert Peel's Bobbies.

Brett emigrated as an unassisted passenger; in shipping records he is described as a clerk. He disembarked in Melbourne in December 1856 and nine days later joined the police. His Defaulters' Sheet (personnel file) stated that he had been an ensign in the Dorsetshire militia for a year, he was single, and his religion was Church of England. His complexion was fresh, hair light, eyes blue and height five foot nine. His age was given as nineteen, although he was a year younger.

Fortune made repeated use of Brett's backstory, variations of his name and his physical description. His youthful beauty she drew as near-feminine, something she admired in other 'downy-faced' and lissom male characters. She may even have cherished his photograph. In her one crime novel, *The Bushranger's Autobiography* (1871–72), the hero is Eber Pierce, a clergyman's son, from Wexford and fond of hunting.

Well, I was getting on for nineteen years of age when this daguerreotype [photograph] was taken, and it pictures the face of what ladies would term a 'sweetly' handsome boy. The nose is aristocratically aquiline, and the nostrils as fine as a thoroughbred's. The eyes are almost as blue as the turquoise (Mary used to say they reminded her of forget-me-nots!) and the mouth should have been a woman's [...] that face, with the white teeth showing between the soft silky moustache, and the sun-bright hair resting wavily on a white forehead, almost as guileless as a child's! They were such dainty hands, too: the one resting on the sword that lay harmlessly across the knee, with its gay ring displayed, as well as its delicate outline, telling of the 'blue blood' of which my mother was so proud. The likeness was taken in the uniform of an ensign [...] of foot.[6]

Recruits to the mounted police were considered to be of a high calibre. They were permitted moustaches and spurs, along with other perks, as described in *The Bushranger's Autobiography*:

> The uniform was a becoming one, and calculated to set off a slight, good figure, such as mine was in those days. It was blue, laced with silver [...] when in full uniform and on duty, we carried sword and carbine, and pistols in the holster pipes at our saddle bows [...] the youngest and vainest among us need not have wished for a handsomer dress.[7]

Their duties included road patrol, special pursuit of offenders, delivering despatches and summonses, acting at court proceedings, and escorting prisoners and gold. It was hard work with long hours, and new recruits had to learn on the job.

After depot training, Brett was sent to Maryborough, arriving in 1857 after Fortune had quit the town. That September he made the local paper when a local carter broke into a tent while drunk. The carter fought with the married couple inside, punching the wife. She complained to the police, and Constable Brett arrested the offender.

In arresting the man, Brett had made a major procedural error, as revealed in the police court next day. For a common assault that Brett had not actually witnessed, he should have delivered a summons, not arrested the accused without a warrant. He had exceeded his duty. In the *Maryborough and Dunolly Advertiser*, the editor and court reporter, Julius Vogel, fulminated:

> Now we contend that the arrest was not only an infringement on the liberty of the subject, which the law does not sanction, but that the apprehending constable, Brett, displayed gross ignorance of his duty as a police officer, and committed a breach of the rules of the force, which ought not to be allowed to pass unnoticed.

Vogel warned that Constable Brett's error, 'if allowed to go unnoticed might at some future time lead him to the commission of errors of a much more serious kind'. In context, the case appears more an instance of an inexperienced, overzealous, even chivalrous young man. Vogel considered the incident to have been 'hushed up', and certainly it is not noted on Brett's file.

The day after Vogel's editorial appeared, Brett accompanied Inspector Hare to a bloodstained tent at Chinaman's Flat. There they found the body of Jane Fyfe, who had fallen into financial hardship while her husband was away at a distant rush. Her seven-year-old daughter testified: 'I saw mother go and take a little knife out of a case and cut her neck; she then laid down to sleep; I spoke to her and she did not answer.' Brett also testified at the inquest. Recruits were expected to become inured to such horrors, as Fortune would later have a character observe: 'I had not been a year mounted when I could lie down by the side of a corpse and sleep as soundly and comfortably as though alone.'[8]

The controversial arrest aside, Brett showed enough competence to be put in charge of Kingower's two-man station. *The Age*'s correspondent described him and Constable Gilmore as very intelligent. The pair occupied a single building with wooden walls, iron roof and a lock-up constructed of logs.[9] Details of police life appear in Mary Fortune's stories, gleaned from close observation and alert listening:

> Sometimes a brother trap would spend a night with us on his way with despatches to some further up station perhaps, and then we managed to get up a little excitement over a game at all-fours [gambling with cards], or a gossip about old times, or a round of abuse at the Inspector maybe; and such chances, with an occasional ride into the surrounding bush country, or a stroll down the dead-and-alive street [of the rush], were all that circumstances afforded us to keep life from fairly stagnating …[10]

Police reports from Brett's time in Kingower contain such excitements as an interminable dispute over hay, which Brett dealt with in a handwriting not execrable. In such conditions, a young man's thoughts might wander. In 'The Double Cross on the Rock', Fortune's fictional detective expresses his yearning for feminine company: 'I felt the want of female influence very sadly, for there was scarcely half a dozen girls within as many miles of the station.'[11]

In 'The Stolen Specimens', the unnamed narrator is a mounted constable in a place much like Kingower in the late 1850s:

> Eight years ago, then, I was stationed within two miles of diggings, where so many large nuggets had been turned up, but where the fine gold was so scarce that a poor man had no chance. The consequence was, that it never was a large rush, the diggers being limited to those who could afford to wait for weeks or months on the chance of finding a 'big one'. The camp had been originally in what had appeared the most convenient locality [in Kingower, at the Springs], but the richness of distant gullies had led the population away from its neighborhood and at the time I write of, it stood [...] at the inconvenient distance of two miles from the nearest tent.[12]

In this story two women appear. Both live in grog shanties, and one is the narrator's washerwoman, a recurring theme. Washerwomen could provide police with a means to meet and pass money to their female informants. Perhaps Fortune took in washing for Brett? Certainly she knew something about police washing. In 'Grey's Gold', a policeman explains the logistics of washing his cap cover (a white cloth cover placed over the policeman's cap):

> When I first joined the force I used to send my cap covers to the washerwoman to be starched and ironed, not knowing that neither

process was the thing, and that the cover had to be put on and fitted while it was wet, and allowed to dry on the cap.[13]

It is also possible that Fortune met Brett via grog-selling. Consider this 'most entirely colonial' establishment from *Dora Carleton*:

Belette was a 'general storekeeper', and his shop was crowded with articles of every variety, from a screw nail to a lady's crinoline. The counter was untidily littered with a quantity of drapery, tobacco, glasses, pewter pots, and bottles; and the floor with gin cases, flour bags, bars of iron, and coils of rope, not to mention many other things indispensable to the well furnishing of a country store.[14]

In this scene Belette serves a mixed group of men, including a mounted trooper in uniform – nominally a sackable offence for the constable. Other stories feature barmaids:

I thought her perfection in every way; and to make a long story short, fell over head and heels in love with her, making of myself the veriest spooney that ever disgraced the silver striped arm of Her Majesty's blue police jacket.[15]

In the memoirs, women selling illicit alcohol are depicted as dishonest if not actually depraved, but the fiction shows more nuance. Fortune's most interesting and powerful female character is Kate Juniper in 'The Star-Spangled Banner' (1895). The narrator policeman, Percy Butt, is, like Brett, a former ensign of militia. Kate is described as 'no creature of the imagination. There are many diggers yet living who will recognise the favourite of more than one "rush" in the early days.'[16] The motif of attraction between a young constable and a woman selling grog recurs. Kate runs her own business and has an innocent fondness for pretty young men, serving them 'soft drinks': claret with lumps of sugar in it. She is also a dashing horsewoman and handy with a pistol. '[S]he's as masterful and independent – ay, and powerful – as any ordinary man, though she has a heart soft as honey for sickness or trouble, for all that.'

Kate wears simple, elegant black. She will not be bought with gold, preferring grass flowers tied into a knot. Although only in her twenties, she is a bereaved mother: 'Then the little boy died and Kate was nearly broken-hearted; that was how she took up the grog-selling business.' A tough woman on the frontier could not let grief destroy her.[17]

Mary Fortune fragmented her experience into fiction. The shards recombine in patterns like a kaleidoscope, the original components just visible. In life, she was unconventional; in her fiction, she allowed convention and morality to determine the ends of the stories. In 'The Star-Spangled Banner', Kate dies from male violence – but Fortune survived.

Other stories hint at Brett and Fortune's courtship. In 'The Double Cross on the Rock', the policeman recalls:

In a hundred ways I managed to make myself useful and welcome to old Mr Davis, the father of my new laundress [...] supplying him with books, he being a quietly disposed old man, and an inveterate reader. Many a long ride I took to some distant township for paper or book, to insure my welcome at the little cottage behind the camp.[18]

On 29 October 1858, Fortune and Brett travelled twenty-four miles to Dunolly, where, in an Anglican service, Brett took Mary Fortune to be his lawful wedded wife. The legality of their marriage was uncertain. As one of Fortune's autobiographical characters would declare: 'I am already the wife of one man, and I do not know that I am his widow!'[19]

On the marriage certificate, Brett declared that he was single, and Mary Fortune that she was a widow. Did she wear the conventional black, like Kate Juniper, or the dulcet shades of half-mourning, grey and lavender? She gave no further detail, although the form required a previous spouse's date of death. A conscientious clergyman would have insisted on it: in the colonies, with their highly mobile population, marriages could dissolve with distance. Another significant omission was Fortune's two children, living and dead. She did not bring her nearly two-year-old son to the ceremony – somebody looked after him in Kingower. He would have dated her 'widowhood' and prompted questions.

Brett again gave his age incorrectly. The groom and bride were recorded as being twenty-four and twenty-five respectively, Brett adding four years to his age. Another curious thing was Fortune's signature. In her Canadian wedding, her signature slanted forwards, as it did on Georgie's death certificate in 1858. She used a backwards slant to register her second son in June 1857 and again when she married Brett the following year. A person's signature might change – if there is a hand injury, say, and the other hand is used. But Fortune alternated, as if deliberately disguising her handwriting. It also suggests a possible dissociation between the respectable young wife in Canada, the grieving mother and a woman who was something quite different.

Why did Mary and Percy marry at Dunolly, when there was a Protestant minister in Kingower (William Hall, who had performed Georgie's funeral)? The Reverend made other people's morals his business, especially a woman with young children and no visible husband. While he had buried Georgie with all due ceremony, a marriage was another matter. Hall was dutiful or suspicious enough to have asked the awkward questions that Richard Stephens of Dunolly, a lay missionary acting as curate, did not.

Did George Wilson approve of his daughter's second marriage, and had Brett asked his permission to marry his daughter, as was conventional? Wilson was not a witness at the wedding, as he had been at Mary's marriage to Joseph Fortune. What was behind his absence? As a member of the colonial police, Brett was also obliged to ask permission to marry. Such requests were hardly ever refused, but it would have prompted scrutiny to establish whether or not the bride and her family were likely to 'bring discredit upon the force'. The bride, moreover, could not work once she was married without special permission. Colonial police records usually note when a marriage occurred, but they do not record Brett's marriage to Mary Fortune. Was this an omission, an elopement or a secret marriage?[20]

Dunolly school house, circa 1861.

The pair wed on a Friday. The Anglican church at Dunolly was also used for schooling; if they were married during teaching hours, they would have had an audience. Fortune did not describe such a scene, but an anonymous writer described a marriage of another couple in similar circumstances:

the parson was fished up somewhere and the ceremony was gone through in the school house, the only place available for the purpose [...] It was truly the pursuit of marriage under difficulties, as the whole of the pupils of the school were supposed to be going on with their exercises at the same time as the ceremony was proceeding, which to say the least of it was a thing impossible with the little girls whose eyes could not for a moment leave the bride.[21]

The wedding over, the couple perhaps spent the weekend celebrating in Dunolly. When they returned to Kingower, it was to a police station without married quarters. The single iron bed was not built for two. Three weeks later, the police inspector called unexpectedly. Usually, the troopers' bush telegraph gave warnings of such visits, giving time for officers or their wives to ensure that cap covers had been washed and the camp made immaculate.

Samuel Stackpole Furnell, inspector first class, was Irish, from Limerick, and had taken part in storming the Eureka Stockade. Former policeman George Buckmaster recalled Furnell was a target for Julius Vogel, whose 'caustic pen exposed the poor stupid Inspector's constant blunderings'. Yet Buckmaster also described Furnell as 'a fine soldierly looking fellow [...] what is called a "swell"', and considered him 'a good police officer and a strict disciplinarian'. That strictness got Brett into trouble, for he mislaid 'several of his appointments' – items issued to police, including signal rattle, rifle, bayonet, baton, handcuffs and belt. For losing items and not reporting the losses, Furnell fined Brett five shillings.[22]

The incident must have rankled, for references to Furnell recur in Fortune's writing:

Inspector 'S.S.F.' cheated Government out of his very handsome pay, by driving round in his buggy – he would have made it a carriage if the roads had permitted – and seeing that our carbines and swords were properly polished, and that there was not a single button off our jumpers.[23]

Fortune accuses Furnell of corruption – not uncommon in the force – and of rorting his travel expenses. She may also hint at what the missing appointments were. A laundress, even a policeman's wife, could be held responsible for the buttons, and for the fine.

The narrator of 'The Stolen Specimens', aware that he could not marry a shanty-house woman and remain in the police, recalled:

> I saw the foolery of the course I was pursuing, but at last we settled it all comfortably thus. After a little time I was to resign, marry my inamorata, and keep a shanty myself for all I knew; nothing of that sort troubled me; only let me become the happy possessor of my angel, and everything else might go to old Nick, Her Majesty's police in the bargain![24]

Brett resigned from the police force on New Year's Eve, 1858.

6

—

THE LADY VANISHES

THE FIRST THREE YEARS MARY FORTUNE spent in Australia are a goldmine: her memoirs can be cross-referenced via newspapers, her later fictions and archives. The next seven are a near blank. She did not refer to them in her writing, at least not as obviously, and she completely vanishes from sight. Of course she wrote – that was her vocation – and reared her surviving son. Whatever else she did during this time, it was not childbearing, remarrying or getting arrested – as far as we know.

Percy Brett similarly is a blank in the records. Certainly the marriage did not last long. At some point Brett must have realised that Mary may not have been widowed, and that her son was of dubious legitimacy. Brett was very young, and he was proud of his family and status.

Mary Fortune's obsessive recycling of Brett suggests the parting was not by mutual consent.

Love in the breast of some burns like hot iron, in others it explodes like [gun]powder; in the one it sears and hardens like the branding metal, in the other it destroys the very spot which has sheltered it, so that it can shelter again no more. In the heart of one, it is a more than mortal strength to live, and to work, and to feel; in that of another, a crushing of the very power of existence, until there remains only the strength to suffer.[1]

69

Couples in the Austral colonies could not divorce until 1873. Even then it was easier for men, who could cite adultery, while women had to prove multiple misdemeanours. Once divorce was available, it was restricted, slow and expensive. Small wonder bigamy was known as 'poor man's divorce'. A notable example was journalist Daisy Bates, who wed Breaker Morant in Queensland in 1885. After their separation she travelled to New South Wales and contracted two bigamous marriages within fifteen months.

Although Fortune committed bigamy, there is no record that she used the name Brett. Injured pride could have figured, as with another woman in her fiction with a failed marriage: 'my husband deserted me, and I will not bear *his* name again. I am Mrs Nemo.'[2] Or perhaps she could see the situation from Brett's point of view. In 'Mary Hester Armour', she wrote of a deserting husband: 'He had done what many a young man has had to regret – married a woman older than himself, whose cold, hard, and exacting nature never assimilated with his own, and after some months of misery he had deserted her.'[3]

In her autobiographical 'Yatalonga', Fortune wrote:

I had a husband who proved false to me; he left me [...] with the avowed intention of going to England to take possession of some hereditary property, and I have never seen nor heard of him since, nor have I ever grieved until this moment that I never attempted to trace him.[4]

Brett family history records that Percy was in the public service in Victoria – an ambiguous statement which could refer to the police – and that he then became a goldminer in Bendigo, thirty miles from Kingower. A newspaper report from October 1862 places a Mrs Fortune in Bendigo too. A theft occurred at Kearney's store at the quartz mine of Specimen Hill, the heist including a gold watch and chain. The thief was arrested and jailed, but the watch was not recovered:

> Of course, all hope of its restoration was given up, when, to the surprise of the owner, it was brought in to the store on Monday afternoon by a Mrs Fortune. She stated that as she was proceeding up Wattle Gully, by the bush road, she happened to glance into the hollow of an old stump as she passed, and that her attention was attracted by a glittering substance, which on further examination, proved to be the watch and chain in question […]

She was 'liberally rewarded' for this lucky discovery. By this time, there were other Mrs Fortunes, and even Mary Fortunes, in Victoria. But this incident reads remarkably like one of our Mary's fictions.[5]

Subsequently, Brett family history holds that Brett worked on rural properties in the western district of Victoria, where his expertise with horses would have been handy. His death certificate from 1900 states that he lived seven years in Victoria and thirty-eight in New South Wales, suggesting he left Victoria in about 1862. A man could easily vanish in nineteenth-century Australia, growing a beard, moving to another rush, using an alias or nickname. An errant husband could not easily be traced, particularly if he crossed a colonial border. Brett only reappears in June 1865, at Jerilderie in New South Wales, working as a pound-keeper. This post, which had responsibility for stray stock, was important. It settled him in the southern Riverina, a man gaining increasing respect and influence.

Some clues to Mary Fortune's missing years can be found in her writing. The evidence suggests she remained mostly in the central north of Victoria. She does draw other locales with authority, among them the Murray River borderland, but not with the same affinity.

She drew on personal experience in describing people, too. The names of mounted troopers who worked with Brett appear in her stories, among them Harry Downing, depicted as a brave but pretty and foppish youth. In real life Henry Downing was the police sergeant (first-class) at Dunolly and was promoted in April 1860. In 'Dead and

Alive', Fortune recalled that he 'was so proud of his stripes (he was sub-Inspector)'.[6]

What else did she know about? Selling sly-grog – and making it, with the cooking stove. Distilling spirits was a useful skill in Ireland, in rural Quebec or in the bush, wherever there was a demand for moonshine. In 'The Murderer's Claim', an Irishman cites his experience making the Irish version of moonshine.

'Many a dozen gallons of poteen I've made,' he enthuses. He and his friend kindle 'the fire and made all preparations for breaking the law with quite enjoyable feelings.'[7]

In remote districts, supplying spirits meant expensive transportation. It was easier to make your own. Mary's fiction includes examples of sly-groggers using the Granites, rocky outcrops with clefts and caves near Kingower, as ideal hiding places for stills. These caves were also hide-outs for bushrangers, such as the real-life Captain Melville.

The raw ingredients for distilling were a secluded hut or a cave; water, preferably a creek; malt for the whisky, Scots-style; fire, with a chimney to diffuse the smoke; and someone to oversee the operation, even if they imbibed and slept during the stages which did not require close watch. The equipment was largely improvised or repurposed: a boiler, barrels and tubs, and the distinctive 'worm', used to create condensation. In 'Jim Dickson', Fortune describes its operation in detail:

> The still, although of rough formation, was in complete working order. The boiler stood over the hot ashes, among which still remained red embers, and the head and worm were attached; and the worm carried its convolutions down through a large hogshead of cold water, discharging the 'mountain dew' by a pipe near the bottom ...[8]

She knew the terminology, and also the rate of police fines. These created an incentive for the police to raid the hidden distilleries, as officers kept a percentage of the fines collected. They also inspired grim determination among the distillers to avoid discovery. 'Dead or Alive' begins with a mounted constable, Dunn (another name borrowed from real life), returning from carousing at Dunolly. He stops for the night, in a bush scene richly evoked:

> Or, if perhaps, you were sleepless for a while, you watched the stealthy 'possums crawl along the boughs in the moonlight, their lithe little bodies outlined darkly against the clear sky. Or you listened to the mopoke's solemn monotone in the swamp, the weird scream of the curlew down by the creek, the tinkle of the bullock bell, or the crisp break of the dewy grass as your horse grazed peacefully within call of you.
>
> And then, as your eyes closed, you felt, almost unconsciously, the delicious night breeze on your face and stealing softly among your hair.[9]

Dunn is joined by a man with a loaded cart, who leaves early next morning so stealthily the constable fails to wake. Suspicious, Dunn examines the only traces left of the man – the tracks – and discovers grains of kilned barley and malt, intended for a still.

Another means by which Fortune can be located during her lost years is via allusions in her stories to real crimes. Her 'The Dead Man in the Scrub' may have drawn on a case from Kingower in late 1859, when the rush was clearing out for Inglewood. As *The Mount Alexander Mail* reported, a tent was found in a lonely part of the bush; 'perceiving a very strong smell issuing therefrom, they looked in, when they discovered the body of a man in an advanced state of decomposition.'[10]

Compare Fortune's account in 'The Dead Man in the Scrub' (1867):

> Inside the tent, which was quite closed up, a continuous buzz, suggestive of innumerable myriads of flies met the ears of the horrified

mates, who were now quite certain that death, in some shape, inhabited this little white calico home in the mallee [...] What to do was the question; the tent, as I have already said, was fastened, the door being apparently secured closely inside, while the slight movement one of the men made in ascertaining this fact, seemed to disturb the feasters upon the dead; they rose in such terrible clouds through the thin calico one could see them, as they came buzzing in millions against its sides.[11]

There is nothing else like this uniquely Australian scene in Australian letters until the *Bulletin* writers of the 1890s, and even Henry Lawson and Barbara Baynton would have hesitated at being so gruesome. In real life, as in fiction, the tent had been closed from the outside, a locked tent mystery. The case was never solved, except in Fortune's story.

Fortune had written of a serial sex murderer in 'Traces of Crime', and she knew a man accused of being a real-life serial killer. Joseph Sullivan was a transportee, and during his time in Victoria was associated with the bushrangers Black Douglas and Gipsy Smith. He informed to police when the law got too close. From 1857 he lived in Korong, and from the early 1860s ran a shanty on the road to Inglewood. Fortune describes it in her story 'Gustav Kupper': 'a collection of slab huts adhering to each other like a cluster of mussels [with] a glitter of bottles showing through the open door'. She describes Sullivan in detail: his age, build and the 'shrewd, hard face, the blue eyes deeply set'. She fictionalises a murder of which he was suspected, describing his modus operandi:

'Bill's Trap – is it a shanty?'

'Yes; a roadside house of accommodation [...] most calls it 'Bill's Trap' [...] when Bill once gets a man into his place he don't very easily get out again.'

'Hocusses?' [doping]

'Oh mun; least's said soonest mended.'[12]

One of Sullivan's victims told the police that Sullivan had choked him senseless and stole £40 pounds and a gold watch. The man was instructed to get a warrant from Dunolly, but instead was found dead on the Kingower road, his corpse set on fire for good measure. At least four other murders of travellers, hawkers such as Kupper in Fortune's story, were ascribed to Sullivan, but he was never charged. Even when he struck a policeman he was only fined £10.[13]

On Christmas Day 1868, Fortune saw Sullivan featured in the Chamber of Horrors, Madame Sohier's waxworks in Melbourne. The figure had been modelled by Ellen Williams, Sohier's common-law wife, and was a poor likeness, said Fortune. Sullivan had impressed himself upon the wax of her memory, and in 1866 he gained international notoriety from New Zealand's 1866 Maungatapu murders, in which Sullivan and a gang of three other men robbed and murdered five travellers. Sullivan escaped hanging by informing against his associates, all of whom were executed.

Sullivan is an extreme example of how true crime informed Mary Fortune's fiction. The milieu in which she lived, the remote goldfields, was a dangerous place, even for women with male protectors – and she had none. Brett had gone, and George Wilson also disappears from the records. None of the George Wilsons whose deaths were recorded in Australia during this period seems to fit. People who died in remote areas were often buried without official notification.

Did Mary and her father part on bad terms after Fortune's marriage to Brett? In the 1883 story 'Coals of Fire', an old man's daughter deserts him for a 'wild young scamp'. The elopement in the story occurred in about 1858, the same year Mary married Brett. Another possibility is that, for whatever reason, George Wilson assumed a goldfields alias and died under that false name – just like in a Fortune story.

Did Fortune mine gold herself? She writes with authority, particularly of the deep sinkings.

[…] a good many ladies were digging in the old days, miss, and there will be a couple here soon, I guess. My missus will be helping me, and in my private opinion she's the first and best lady in the land. Oh, you needn't shake your head, old woman – every word's true. On old Chinaman's Flat there was a reef called Petticoat Reef, because a woman took shift and shift about with her husband at the windlass [which carried miners and their buckets up and down the shafts]. She was a German, she was, but, all the same, she was a decent, honest, hard-working woman, and a good wife. Then at Jericho, on the Granite Reef, a woman ran the claim, so to speak, and worked with her husband and his mates as well as any man could. But […] I'm afraid poor Mrs Maloney was no lady. She drank and swore most awful.[14]

Here again occurs a slight folding of the map, a fictionalisation of geography. Some reefs and mining claims were given picturesque names (Psalm Singers Gully, Poverty Gully). Petticoat Reef existed and was indeed worked by a woman. It was not at Chinaman's Flat, but Jericho (later Wehla), near Kingower.[15]

'Our Golden Girl' depicts a young woman mining her claim, with little more than work gear of a short skirt and rough jacket, pick, shovel and bucket. She loosens the 'stuff' with the pick and shovels it into the bucket, to be carried to the creek for washing. In a detail recurring in other Fortune stories, one shovel-load is too heavy to lift. The reason: a 'brown, stone-like thing': a gold nugget.

Fortune also knew about quartz-crushing, not only from living in its noisy vicinity: 'the monotonous never-ending sound of quartz stampers dinning our ears through the live-long day and night'.[16] It figures in her fiction, as in 'Simple Sam':

If you have never seen a crushing machine in the dark (that's very Irish, isn't it?) I can hardly give you an idea of its weirdness. Of course I mean a machine which is not working during the day, and which stands, silent and desolate-looking, by its deep dam, in the partially starlit darkness of midnight.

Carter's dam was a broad sheet of water, fringed with young trees; and as I crept around it, I could see the lights of the far up reef reflected in its still bosom. Between me and the sky rose the huge timbers and towering chimney of the machine; and even the belts and wheels of the engine-room could be traced darkly against the less dark western sky.

As I passed the dam I thought it looked wondrous cold and deathly. Little did I think – well, never mind. I remembered dams and Simple Sam in connection for many long days after.

There was not a sound in the place as I went cautiously inside. I was well acquainted with the premises, and intended to make for the 'tables,' as they are called – viz., the place where the pulverised quartz flows over quicksilvered ripples, and leaves the gold, in the form of amalgam, behind. I wondered at the quietness as I went on, knowing as I did that strict guard was kept on the premises at night; but I had not much time to wonder, as I shall tell you.

This suspenseful passage sets up Mark, the narrator-detective, for a stealth attack. Not many crime writers would set their story beside the battery of quartz stampers, with Mark 'pounded unmercifully [...] Like stampers themselves', and then thrown into the dam. Fortune used whatever she could of her varied experience.[17]

Her words are complemented by images: the new technology of photography. Fortune even namedrops Emily O'Shannessy, co-partner in a Melbourne photographic studio, in 'The Wattle-Farm Tragedy'. This interest in photography might reflect some amateur experience, or even a professional association, like her character Miss Marks, who works for a Melbourne photographer in 'The Lady's Hair-Net'.

During the 1860s the Batchelder brothers formed an intercolonial photography firm, with offices in Melbourne, Sydney and Bendigo. Benjamin, the Bendigo Batchelder, was described by a miner, Laurence Chubb, as having 'the reputation of being the best in that line out of Melbourne'. Benjamin twice got official commissions for intercolonial and even international exhibitions. His work forms a contemporary album of places Fortune either mentioned or that can be associated with her.[18]

Gus Peirce, an enterprising young Yankee, worked for Benjamin. He recalled in his memoir, *Knocking About*, that 'We were furnished with a little black push-cart holding the camera and other necessaries, and we were to get pictures of all objects of interest [...] the work was most disagreeable, owing to the heat and dust'. The 'objects of interest' included landscapes; industry, including gold operations; and notable buildings, like the homes of the squattocracy.[19] These albumen silver photographs have extraordinary detail, depicting a land scarred from mining.

As the alluvial gold ran out, the rushes became more settled and large mining operations created some permanence. A miner might plant a garden or vines, build a slab hut. Now that gold had cleared the land, pastoralists exploited it. In the process, the democratic spirit of the Eureka rebellion gave way to capitalism.

Fortune reminisced:

The many valuable finds of those days – when one went to work, perhaps, sixpenceless, and returned at dinner-time worth hundreds – have disappeared; and one hears but very occasionally indeed of a nugget of much worth having been 'dropped upon'. The very term 'lucky digger,' has given rise to the more recent and much more respected term of 'rich reefer'; and we now see men, instead of sinking energetically to reach the 'bottom', looking about the surface in some promising district, in hopes of perceiving the 'cropping out' of a new reef, the very working of which will require machinery and appliances so complicated and expensive, as to throw completely into the shade the old tub and cradle [...][20]

Two views survive of Kingower, the first from the east. It shows dirt hummocks, few trees or houses, and carts, their drivers and passengers disembarked for the photographer. The nearest man holds his horse's head lest it move and blur the photograph. The largest building in sight is the Bridge Hotel. An anonymous traveller in May 1864 noted its fine hospitality and the pleasant homes and gardens of Kingower.[21]

The photograph of Melville's cave, an enduring local landmark, shows granite boulders piled high on the hill. The image was praised, and is striking even by modern standards. The 1864 traveller found the place 'a scene of romantic beauty rarely surpassed'. Fortune, who knew the site well, saw it differently. Her police narrator comments: 'I have, at times, been romantic enough to scan its nooks pretty closely in search for the bushranger's plant.'[22]

Particularly significant is a photograph of the nearby settlement of Jericho. It was eight miles from Kingower, a trip Fortune wryly described as 'as picturesque as need be', the road being steep, winding and narrow.[23] Here are yet more mining operations, bare earth, trunks and saplings, with again a notable hotel. The township comprised an accretion of small businesses and households around the dirt main drag, with associated gardens and domestic animals.

Jericho existed for the gold reefs, and for quartz-mining. In 1863 an entire hill collapsed into the mine. The incident does not appear in Fortune's writing, suggesting her absence at the time. Three years later came another collapse, with a miner dying soon after being brought to the surface. This seems the source for a similar death in 'The Dead Man in the Scrub'.[24]

The 1864 traveller found Jericho quiet, with stores, including shanties, and 'some twenty-five or thirty tents and huts'. The Prince of Wales mining company had just begun operations, causing the town to boom again. That was why the traveller visited; both he and the photographer found the mine the only notable feature.[25]

Off-camera, was Mary watching the photographer at work and enquiring about his craft? She might have been living in Jericho as a de facto 'Reefer's Wife', the title of a story of hers set there; perhaps she kept a store or shanty. Hints and shadows of what Fortune did appear in her fictions, but the first sure sign of her after seven missing years is in Jericho, September 1865.

FORTUNE WRITES

'Well, she had a weekly copy of the *Australian Journal* spread
carefully on her aproned knee, and she was reading it – so intently
that my foot was unheard.' —'Looking for Lodgings'

IMAGINE MARY FORTUNE IN 1865: A woman in her early thirties
reading in what spare time she had as the single mother of an eight-
year-old boy. If she was not in a de facto relationship, then she had
their living to earn. As a woman in the bush, her dress was simple and
serviceable. Her long hair was neatly coiled and pinned, less for fashion than for practicality, and she wore little jewellery other than her
wedding ring.

Fortune called herself a widow, and that was now true. In October 1861 her first husband, Joseph Fortune, had died, aged thirty-five,
at Knowlton Falls (now Warden) in Quebec's Eastern Townships. Did
she know that? In the Canadian census, taken at the beginning of that
year, Joseph was living with his sisters near Montreal, and all the siblings stated that they were unmarried. In law, a spouse who deserted
or disappeared could be declared dead after seven years, permitting
remarriage. If Mary had left in about 1854, Joseph was legally single.

Her second husband, Percy Brett, was still living, although she
probably did not know where. He too could remarry, for her bigamy

invalidated their marriage – but he may not have known that. Mary did not wed again, although she was free to do so. Such complications were not uncommon in the colonies.

Her surviving child bore the Fortune surname and she called him George. With high infant mortality, families would reuse a dead child's name; it was not considered bad luck.

Fortune now sought to become a professional author. As well as it being her vocation, it would enable her to work from home and secure economic independence. For that she needed regular and reliable literary employment. Before her now was an opportunity golden as a nugget: the first issue of a weekly magazine, the *Australian Journal* (*AJ*), published 2 September 1865. It had come from Melbourne, a day's journey of steam trains and horsepower.[1]

Although Fortune lived in the bush, she could access the small colonial literary world. She submitted to the *AJ* prior to its publication, being in the loop of possible contributors. Likely a journalist or editor she knew – kindly Charles Saint? – tipped her off. She sent off poems on spec, under her initials. Only when the debut issue arrived in Jericho could she really see what the *AJ* was.

The magazine cost threepence for sixteen pages dense with type: over a thousand words per page. Its subtitle was 'a weekly record of Amusing and Instructive Literature, Science, and the Arts'. The masthead depicted a classical nymph with a pen, to her left the symbols of agricultural Australia. To her right were the arts, given equal importance.

Most of the content was fiction. In the Victorian era reading was a major activity: virtuous, with the Bible; educational, with schooling increasingly compulsory; and for entertainment, with Dickens attracting a huge audience. Significantly, the *AJ* stated its fiction would be by 'colonial pens'. The journal opened with 'Force and Fraud: A Tale of the Bush' by Mrs Arthur Davitt. Next came 'The Shepherd's Hut [...] Being Memoirs of an Australian Police Officer', published anonymously but identified later as written by James Skipp Borlase. The third contribution was a medieval romance, à la *Ivanhoe,* by Borlase, followed by the non-fiction 'Street Life in the Colonies' by 'Robin Goodfellow'.

All were written to be continued. In an era when most books were expensive but magazines cheap, serialisations brought novels to the public in instalments. The reader became hooked: what happens next? They sold magazines, issue after issue. Serials had particular importance in the colonies, where book production costs were high.

The magazine was produced by Clarson, Shallard & Co., printers in both Melbourne and Sydney. Their work ranged from auction catalogues and wedding invitations to pamphlets and booklets such as that by Louis L. Smith, a doctor and member of the Victorian parliament, proposing that since three-quarters of the body was fluid, weight reduction would occur on a dehydrating diet of one pint of water a day, biscuits or toast, meat and dried vegetables. Such books were produced via commission – in modern parlance, it was a vanity press, meaning the author paid.

Producing a journal in Australia was financially risky: the audience was small and the distances vast. Postage was high – tuppence a copy, almost doubling the price of the *AJ.* Cunningly, by printing the magazine in two cities, intercolonial postal charges were avoided.[2]

The *AJ* aimed at a wide audience. 'What could readers of the "servant gal" species deserve more than this?' sniffed one newspaper, while another noted its 'considerable literary merit'. The design ripped off the popular imported fiction magazines the *London Journal* and the *Family Herald.* The business plan and package would prove astute: the *AJ* survived for nearly a century.[3]

Those responsible were a small and motley band. Editor George Arthur Walstab (1834–1909), had sought colonial adventure but turned to writing and journalism after being wounded during the First War of Indian Independence. He was a dandy who gave exhibitions of fencing. 'Robin Goodfellow' was Thomas Harrison (1827–1897), the pseudonym necessary because he was a moonlighting public servant. Harrison was hearing and sight impaired but a keen amateur geologist.[4]

Of the other two writers, the widowed Ellen Davitt (1812–1879) had been a prominent educationalist and was approaching public intellectual status. She exhibited her artwork and did lecture tours, daring for a woman at the time. James Skipp Borlase (1839–1902) was a lawyer with experience of English fiction magazines. He emigrated to Australia in 1864, only to desert his wife, Rosanna, and flee to Tasmania. Unlike in America and Canada, intercolonial desertion in Australia was subject to extradition, and Borlase was returned to Melbourne. Fast talking resolved the marriage, with no offence recorded, but he had damaged his legal career.[5]

Over half the content of the *AJ* had Australian settings, a key departure from the English models. Fortune would record the vox populi reaction of an *AJ* reader and shopkeeper:

' ... I can't say as ever it comes natural to me like the old *Family Herald* Mr Garton used to take in for the kitchen. There's some very fine stories in it, I daresay, but they're all about the colonies, and I would rather read about home [England] any day [...] I don't see what pleasure nobody can take in reading about possums, and bushrangers, and such like. However, I daresay they knows best themselves what brings in the money.'[6]

They did know. The shopkeeper voiced the cultural cringe, but other settlers differed. Theatre audiences applauded 'localisations': imported plays with colonial content added, such as pantomimes with kangaroos and topical political jokes. Although nobody then knew the term, they sought self-validation. The *AJ*, decades before the bush nationalism of *The Bulletin*, provided it via popular fiction.

The rural Victoria in which Fortune lived was no cultural desert. Mechanics' Institutes, providing adult education for the masses, flourished with their associated 'Literary Institutes' (free libraries). Amateur concerts were held for fundraising and fun. Inglewood had a theatre, which drew touring international dramatic troupes. Yet it lacked a literary outlet, the *Inglewood Advertiser* tending to piracy from overseas writers, including Dickens' *Great Expectations*. In contrast the *AJ* invited contributions 'from the whole of the Colonies'.

In the second issue, a week later, appeared Fortune's poem 'To My Little Son on His Birthday'. The poem began as a private gift. With its publication, George became not only her subject but also subjected to his mother's view of him, set in print like concrete. Affection met affect, not happily. To write – and have the subject know – is a means of exerting control, an unhealthy habit, particularly within the family. Consider Christopher Robin Milne, who suffered from his father's writing his childhood into a bestseller. George Fortune was a vulnerable subject, to use the terms of modern life writing.[7]

Fortune signed the poem with her initials and location, as she had for *The Mount Alexander Mail*. In a large goldfield she had anonymity, but Jericho was small: how many women with those initials had a fatherless son of eight? It could identify her, something unwanted. For subsequent publications she assumed the pseudonym 'Waif Wander' and used it for the rest of her writing life. It protected her privacy and reputation, permitting a long literary career.

What's in a name? Waif Wander was an odd choice for a woman in an era when femininity meant domesticity. Both words connoted homelessness. Furthermore, waif is a legal term, signifying among other things lack of ownership – and a woman without a legal owner in the Victorian era was beyond the control of husband or father. It also connotes being outcast, which for a woman meant the loss of virtue.

Within five issues she published three poems and 'Recollections of a Digger', a short, fictionalised goldfields memoir from a male viewpoint. These works were good but not startlingly original. What genuinely broke new ground was the short story 'The Stolen Specimens'. She wrote it in response to the magazine's first issue, pioneering in a new genre: detective fiction.

The *AJ*'s English models favoured romances and melodrama, but the *AJ* chose crime, not only 'The Shepherd's Hut', but also Davitt's *Force and Fraud*, the first Australian murder-mystery novel.[8] Someone on the staff knew their audience. Both sexes in the nineteenth century were fascinated by crime. Gory cases were perused in newspapers, and trials and public executions keenly attended. In Australia the interest was acute due to the national origins as a penal colony. Crime begat European Australia, with much of the population from prisons such as Newgate; some were famously featured in *The Newgate Calendar*, a bestselling compilation of villains.

This interest found expression, first in convict ballads, then in crime fiction, a form slowly developing over the nineteenth century, worldwide. Australia's first novelist, John Lang, was a lawyer and the grandson of a First Fleet convict. He wrote of convict Sydney, where crime intertwined with the setting.

During the 1800s, the detective gained prominence, but the translation from fact to fiction proved problematic. Today police procedurals are award-winning entertainment but then, class was a factor: the police were working class, hardly heroic for middle-class readers. Lang put a 'thief-taker' (a proto-detective) in his 1856 novel *The Forger's Wife*, based on the real-life Israel Chapman. Most novelists put police in minor or secondary roles, as with Dickens' Inspector Bucket in *Bleak House*. Preferable was Poe's Chevalier Dupin, a talented amateur, or Sherlock Holmes, an upper-class diletante, cleverer than Inspector Lestrade.

Nonetheless police were heroes in what were termed casebooks, popular short stories with professionals – initially mostly lawyers and later police – as narrators. The first was William Russell's 'Recollections of a Police Officer' (1849), narrated by Waters, a gentleman reduced to joining the force. Casebooks presented readers with a series of self-contained stories, each featuring the same detective. Initially the narratives were simple adventures, but they gradually became ratiocinative, with the detective using logic and intelligence to solve cases.

Modern readers know the form from Sherlock Holmes, and Arthur Conan Doyle claimed to have invented it, but it preceded him by decades. In 1864 this sub-genre even featured two female sleuths – a fiction, for women would not have an official role in the police force, let alone detection, until the next century.

Australian newspapers reprinted casebooks, and the form inevitably became as naturalised as the fox. 'William Burrows' wrote *Adventures of a Mounted Trooper in the Australian Constabulary*, a book of travelogue and fictionalised memoir published in London in 1859. That was followed in 1863 by the anonymous short story series 'Recollections of an Australian Detective' in *The Leader* and *The Age*, starting in 1863, which mixed true crime and fiction. 'An Australian Detective's Story; or "Murder Will Out"', attributed to 'B' and published in 1864, was pure fiction; it appeared in Australian newspapers as well as in English and American magazines. Marcus Clarke, writing as 'M.C.' while still a teenager, published the spoof 'Wonderful! When You Come to Think of It' in the *Hamilton Spectator* in January 1865. In September 1865, Borlase's 'The Shepherd's Hut' appeared in the first issue of the *AJ*, as we have seen.[9]

September 1865 also marked an auspicious French debut. Émile Gaboriau began the serialised *L'Affaire Lerouge*, which included Monsieur Lecoq as detective. It was the first *roman policier* (police novel).

The early Australian casebooks were generally set and published in Victoria, and this was no accident. During the 1850s, Victoria recruited middle-class young men as mounted cadets to create an elite police force. Some had military experience, others were simply adventurous. They included Percy Brett and George Walstab, editor of the *AJ*. In South Australia, a similar young policeman was Adam Lindsay Gordon. This notion of a 'gentlemanly' police did not last long, although one cadet, Hussey Malone Chomley, became police commissioner. Yet it represented a goldmine for crime writers. The problem of class could be avoided, for the hero was a gentleman.

Walstab drew upon his cadet experience for his 1864 novel *Looking Back*. However, his editorial workload meant delegating casebooks to Borlase, a lawyer. Borlase's 'The Shepherd's Hut' was published anonymously, because the casebooks claimed the authenticity of being written by actual police.

In 1867 Borlase collected his casebook stories as a book, *The Night Fossickers* (referring to thieving among miners), published in England under his own name. A reviewer commented: 'Whether Mr. Borlase ever held in reality as well as in imagination a prominent place in the Melbourne police force, or whether [...] he merely makes bold use of one of the licenses permitted to writers of fiction, we do not care to enquire.'[10]

A reader who knew casebooks and the police would have seen the 'license' taken by Borlase, and Mary Fortune used it to her own advantage. Other women of her era, such as the novelists Mary Braddon and Ellen Wood, wrote crime and investigation. Fortune went further with a casebook, breaking new ground. Fortune was the first woman known to write a male detective in the first person, impersonating the police in print.

She began with 'The Stolen Specimens', responding to 'The Shepherd's Hut'. The voice was direct, colloquial and realist, performative mimicry:

> We, members of the police force of Victoria, are, I think, a little –
> a very little – less despised in this year of grace, eighteen hundred
> and sixty-five, than we were when I first donned the uniform twelve
> years ago.
>
> I was a 'Cadet' then, and now I'm a — ; but I dare say you don't
> care what I am, so I may go on with my adventures.[11]

The piece is beginner's work, the author writing herself into the narrative with increasing confidence. Featured is matter typically Fortune: sly grogging, a sweetheart shanty-keeper, alcoholism. It is also ratiocinative, with a gold theft solved via a sprig of ti-tree. As a story it mixes crime with romance and horror, and its greatest success is its narrative voice. Ex-cadet Walstab would have seen its authority.

The *AJ*'s records have not survived. Fortune's relationship with the journal is conjectural, apart from the *AJ*'s 'Answers to Correspondents' column, in which the editors replied to readers' letters and submissions. Answering contributors via this column saved postage and meant would-be contributors had to buy the magazine. From the column Fortune's submissions can be traced, both as Waif Wander and as her new alter ego, 'An Australian Police Officer' – a cheeky borrowing of Borlase's pseudonym. Her first story submitted under this pen name was accepted with 'much thanks' at the end of September, and appeared a fortnight later under the pseudonym 'An Australian Mounted Trooper'.

Fortune liked literary games, such as punning on her (hidden) name. Sending the *AJ* contributions under different pseudonyms, however, required other ploys to keep her identity concealed. At Jericho, mail had to be enquired for at the local store, which doubled as the post office. A century later, the science-fiction writer James Tiptree Jr. (Alice Sheldon) set up a separate PO Box for her alter-ego, a car drive away. Fortune could similarly have ridden or walked to Kingower, where she had her firstborn's grave to tend, and the nearest library, a room in the Bridge Hotel with 300 donated books.[12]

Tiptree's ruse was facilitated by typewriter, invented in 1867. In an age of pen and paper, how did Fortune avoid her handwriting being recognised? She had already disguised it when registering her illegitimate son and bigamously marrying Brett. It would not be easy to do at length, but contemporary court cases and crime fiction contain many instances of forged handwriting. Tiptree had three signatures, one as herself and two for her different personas; Fortune had at least two.

When did the *AJ* discover this policeman wore petticoats? Walstab saw an opportunity in 'The Stolen Specimens'. Borlase had paused his casebooks, but an extra writer meant the *AJ* could commission a series.

It needed reliable supply, and the firm knew nothing about the new author. A meeting can be posited, an editorial negotiation. Fortune's 'The Murderer's Doom' (1894) described travelling between Melbourne and Jericho in the 1860s:

> ... at the time I write of, the place was difficult of access. You took the 7pm train to Sandhurst [Bendigo], which latter place you reached sometime before midnight if you were lucky; and then you sat by the fire in the bar in the old Shamrock Hotel, if you were wise, so as not by any chance to miss the Inglewood coach, starting at 4am. At Inglewood you caught the express wagon that carried mail and passengers, and, after passing through poor old 'Golden Kingower', you got into Jericho by 2 pm.[13]

The long journey meant staying in the city, a chance to walk the streets, observing and seeking material. Two fictions Fortune published in 1866 describe a dead woman pulled from the Yarra, an apparent suicide. The devil is in her details: easy enough to envisage a dripping corpse, but not the police 'conversing unconcernedly' while the body lay on the grass. In Spring 1865, Henriette Nieman drowned herself in the Yarra. If Fortune did witness the body's recovery, her trip to Melbourne can be dated to early October, shortly after the acceptance of 'The Stolen Specimens'. Such timing would indicate that the story had an immediate effect on Fortune's career.[14]

Gruesome witnessing aside, from the evidence of Fortune's fictions, in Melbourne she attended the theatre and a labour hire office, a private job agency. Were Walstab and Borlase confounded by her arrival at the *AJ*? Borlase was only twenty-six, dark and intense in looks. Walstab, observed diarist Annie Baxter Dawbin in 1863, was fair and 'extremely good looking [...] tho' very yellow [jaundiced] from the effects of Indian climate'. He wore mourning – in June his two youngest children had died within six days of each other.[15]

Fortune had surprised editors in person before, at the *Mount Alexander Mail*. Her gender had precluded a newspaper job in 1855, but now she was a freelancer with a desirable commodity. They could overlook that she was a woman, if nobody else knew.

Another person in the know would have been Alfred Massina, a young and entrepreneurial printer at the firm who would become the dominant partner, and then proprietor, of the *AJ*. He would have noted her goldfields writing, having nearly starved on the rushes. Erroneously or not, he was recalled as stating that Fortune was the widow of a police detective, writing up her husband's cases – which explained both her authority and her need for work.[16]

Whatever she told the men of the *AJ*, they bought it. In early November the magazine announced a series, written alternately by 'the respective authors of "*The Shepherd's Hut*" and "*The Golden* [sic] *Specimens*"'.[17]

IMPERSONATING THE POLICE

IN THE HISTORY OF CRIME FICTION, the nineteenth century belonged to men. Poe was the originator, followed by Wilkie Collins, followed by Doyle: a patriarchal succession. In fact, women wrote crime fiction from its beginnings. For every early major male crime writer existed a female counterpart. Consider Catherine Crowe's 1842 *Susan Hopley; or Circumstantial Evidence*. This murder mystery achieved success both as a novel and play – the title character was a maidservant and amateur detective. It appeared months before Poe's 'The Murders in the Rue Morgue'. Wilkie Collins' 'sensation' novels were similarly rivalled by Mary Braddon's.

Fortune was not the only female crime writer in the *AJ*, which also published Davitt's serial *Force and Fraud*. Crime fiction historian Stephen Knight comments that 'nobody before Davitt, whether in England, Australia or America, of either gender', had structured crime and its solution into 'such a well-controlled over-arching narrative, especially one richly embodying her theme that crime comes from both' high and low society.[1]

That two women crime authors debuted in the magazine within a few weeks of each other is coincidental but not unusual in the genre. Any meeting between the pair is conjectural. Both women were fiercely independent from living by their wits in colonial Australia. They also shared personal knowledge of crime. The fraud in Davitt's novel derived from her father, a Yorkshire bank manager who speculated with his customers' money.

Davitt had excellent literary connections: her sister Rose was married to the famous novelist Anthony Trollope. Yet she was forgotten, despite the many biographers of the Trollope family, and so was *Force and Fraud*. Since its rediscovery in the 1990s, it has been reprinted three times, and the annual Sisters in Crime awards for crime fiction, the Davitt Awards, are named for her.

Davitt wrote only one crime novel, but also some fine crime stories. The most interesting is 'The Highlander's Revenge' (1867), an extraordinary examination of atrocities against Indigenous Australians. It drew on actual events in Gippsland, being clearly informed by an eyewitness. Like sex offences and infanticide, this crime occurred in real life more often than it appeared in contemporary fiction.[2]

While Ellen Davitt only touched briefly on crime writing, police procedurals became Mary Fortune's vocation. The knowledge she had absorbed from Brett powered her fiction. Another major source was colonial newspapers, full of gory inspiration and readily accessible even in the bush: 'tho' it was only a bit of a Mechanics Institute as John subscribed to, there was hardly a colonial paper you couldn't a got a read of there.'[3]

Yet her first crime series met difficulties. Two writers alternating weekly was ambitious, especially as they lived a day's journey apart with no communication but the post. While the series ran without break for six weeks, it was largely Borlase's work. Fortune's 'Traces of Crime' failed to appear as scheduled. Unreliable mail or unreliable writer? Or perhaps editorial delay prompted by its unusual subject, a serial sex killer? Whatever the reason, an extract from John Lang's novel *The Forger's Wife* appeared instead. Lang could hardly protest this piracy, for he had died in India the previous year.

The series broke for Christmas and resumed in late January with five more stories, showing Fortune's growing confidence with writing crime fiction. 'Traces' had been an improvement on 'The Stolen Specimens', and now she provided an even better story: 'The Dead Witness; Or, The Bush Waterhole', the first in the anonymous series to be attributed to Waif Wander. 'The Dead Witness' would have a long afterlife, being the title story for two anthologies over a century after its first publication.

The story has been described as the first police procedural by a woman – incorrectly, for 'Traces' and 'The Stolen Specimens' preceded it, as did a story by American writer Harriet Prescott Spofford (1835–1921), which appeared nine months earlier. Spofford's story may have contributed literary DNA to 'The Dead Witness'.

Spofford was Bostonian, well educated, but obliged from the age of twenty-one to support her family by writing. In 1859 she sent the prestigious *Atlantic Magazine* 'In a Cellar', a detective story so stylish that the editor suspected it was a translation from the French. Although her sleuth was amateur rather than a police officer, the story made Prescott the first American woman known to write detective fiction. In April 1865, *Harper's New Monthly* published her 'Mr Furbush', a third-person police casebook set in New York.

Not only people travelled great distances in the Victorian era; so did texts. The colonial book trade relied on imports from England and North America. The latter reached the Austral colonies by cross-Pacific steamships within weeks. It is not impossible that Borlase and Fortune read and drew inspiration from 'Mr Furbush'. In 'The Dead Witness', the protagonist is James Brooke – the name of Borlase's detective. Stephen Knight has argued that 'The Dead Witness' was intended as a Borlase story, but with time constraints, he gave the task (and his detective) to Fortune.

'Mr Furbush' contained a brilliant idea, from the new technology of photography. The story begins with a murder in a hotel. Coincidentally a parade is passing in the street outside, recorded by the photographic studio directly opposite. Later, Detective Furbush, visiting the studio for a portrait, sees the photographs of the parade and examines them:

procuring, though channels always open to him, the strongest glasses and most accurate instruments, [he] had the one chosen window in that picture [the window opening onto the murder scene] magnified and photographed, remagnified and rephotographed, till under their powerful, careful, prolonged and patient labour, a speck came into sight that would perhaps well reward them.[4]

His prize is an image that identifies the killer. Crime revealed via magnified photographs has appeared in films from Michelangelo Antonioni's *Blow-Up* (1966) to Ridley Scott's *Blade Runner* (1982), but it began far earlier. Prescott used the motif, and so did Fortune.

'The Dead Witness' begins with Brooke riding through the bush, showcasing Fortune's nature writing:

I can scarcely fancy anything more enjoyable to a mind at ease with itself than a spring ride through the Australian bush [...] for to a man accustomed to the sights and sounds of nature around him there is nothing distracting in the warble of the magpie or tinkle of the 'bell bird'. The little lizards that sit here and there upon logs and stumps, and look at the passer-by with their heads on one side, and such a funny air of knowing stupidity in their small eyes, are such everyday affairs to an old colonist that they scarcely attract any notice from him, and even should a monstrous iguana [goanna] dart across his path and trail his four feet length up a neighbouring tree, it is not a matter of much curiosity to him.[5]

Brooke investigates the disappearance of an itinerant photographer. He examines the missing man's photographic plates and discovers a suspicious image, which when enlarged shows a local shepherd. The suspect avoids a particular waterhole, and in an exquisitely melodramatic denouement, Brooke discovers why: 'A fearful, dripping *thing* rose to the surface – a white ghastly face followed – and then, up – up – waist high out of the water, rose the corpse of the murdered artist!' Gases from decomposition can bring a submerged body abruptly to the surface, a phenomenon that recurs in Fortune's writing.

In this story Fortune strikingly married setting, investigation and photography. If she had watched Gus Pierce or Benjamin Batchelder at work, then she wrote her observations into a murder mystery. Did she ask too many pesky questions, get short shrift, and in return gruesomely imagine clobbering a photographer while his head was under 'the black rag'?[6] The result was an outstanding early detective story.

The Literary Detective

All the stories in the *AJ*'s casebook series, bar 'The Dead Witness', were published anonymously. So how can it be proved who wrote what – who dunnit? The major evidence came from Borlase's *The Night Fossickers*. It reprinted seven stories from the series with additional new material. The remaining five *AJ* stories contained themes and motifs found in Fortune's work. The settings were part of her personal geography: both 'Traces of Crime' and 'A Struggle for Life' are set in Chinaman's Flat. They read like Fortune, and modern technology has supplied proof.

To make absolutely sure of the authorship, the stories were submitted to forensic linguistic testing. Language is like a fingerprint, a unique marker of identity, with literary style quantifiable at the level of grammar. In the nineteenth century, it was particularly marked in writers with different levels of education: men who had attended grammar schools, for example, wrote differently from women and from working-class men. With the aid of Professor John Burrows of the University of Newcastle, the *AJ*'s casebook stories were put into machine-readable form and compared with *The Night Fossickers* and with subsequent crime stories definitely by Fortune. We expected this testing to prove that all the *AJ*'s crime series stories not written by either Borlase or Lang were Fortune's work. But the computer had some surprises in store.

While the five *AJ* stories not in *The Night Fossickers* did strongly resemble Fortune's later work, they also had slight similarities to Borlase's texts. The obvious explanation was that Borlase edited Fortune. The relationship between the two can be seen as intimate and complex. They were both writing as police, and they swapped detectives. Borlase can be seen to have learnt from the relationship. The *AJ* stories he wrote were adventure thrillers, heavily coincidental, but in *The Night Fossickers* his new fictions were ratiocinative, making use of clues – a lost, distinctive button, mimicking 'The Stolen Specimens' and some of Fortune's other stories.

Furthermore, Borlase was a literary thief, freely helping himself to others' texts. His 'Pursuing and Pursued' contained an uncredited extract from William Burrows' *Adventures of a Mounted Trooper*. *The Night Fossickers* contained at least three other plagiarisms, with the title story borrowing from Ellen Clacy and another story from an anonymous author who contributed a travelogue to the *AJ*. The third plagiarism was of Mary Fortune.

Plagiarism encourages paranoia: one proven instance in the work of an author has the tendency to make all their other writing suspect. Borlase tended to borrow when in need, something which would in 1866 get him sacked from the *AJ*. The magazine would claim his contributions had 'more than a mere "family likeness" to "Ivanhoe", and other obscure productions of an *unknown* Scottish baronet'.[7] He would embark on a slow tour of the colonies, trying his literary luck alongside legal work, but he kept in contact with Mary Fortune.

Borlase's appropriations of Clacy et cetera were too small – a paragraph here, a paragraph there – to be statistically significant. In contrast, 'Mystery and Murder' was an entire story. When put through the computer, testing for features such as grammatical patterns and word frequency, it proved to be aligned not with Borlase's other texts but with Fortune's stories. It was very definitely hers, although it appeared under his name.

'Mystery and Murder' is set in Hobart, where the wealthy Mr Longmore is plagued by an apparent hoax ghost. The apparition resembles Longmore's wife, who eloped with a sea captain years before. When the ghost manifests, the detective follows it to the shores of the Derwent, where it vanishes on a patch of disturbed soil. Underneath is a box containing the corpse of Mrs Longmore, recently murdered.

'Mystery and Murder' was unique among the *AJ* casebooks for its Tasmanian setting. Borlase fled there after deserting his wife, Rosanna. As the story featured a runaway wife, it could be read as authorial reversal, inverting real-life into fiction. But, when cast adrift from its putative author, the story's elements – gore, supernature vs rationality, female sexuality – are far more Fortune's preoccupations.

The final story in the serial, 'The Deserted Hut', proved a true collaboration. It comprised a frame story of a detective encountering a madman, and the latter's confession. Computer analysis showed it was by both Fortune and Borlase, he writing the frame, she the confession. Was it a story Borlase began and Fortune finished? That mystery is unsolved.

While forensics solved the whodunnit of 'Mystery and Murder', other evidence concerning the snatching of this body of words is not forthcoming. It is possible that some transaction occurred between Fortune and Borlase – that he paid her for the (unacknowledged) reprint. Stephen Knight has suggested that as Fortune had written stories for Borlase, using his characters, he may have regarded her as his ghostwriter. John Burrows wondered if she never knew; or could see no means of redress; or that she regarded it as 'recompense for his editorial labours on her apprentice work'. After Borlase left the *AJ* he acted as a packager and agent for other writers, including Fortune, suggesting the pair remained on good business terms. Recent research by Christopher Philippo has shown that after Borlase's return to England he would freely reprint *AJ* stories, including Fortune's, under his own name.[8]

There is one further irony. In 1986, scholar Cecil Hadgraft published an anthology, *The Australian Short Story Before Lawson*. During his research he read both *The Night Fossickers* and W.W.'s one book, the 1871 *The Detective's Album*. He was unimpressed by the latter while appreciating Borlase's 'sheer readability'. Yet the story he chose to reprint was 'Mystery and Murder'.[9]

9

—

THE YEAR OF NOVELS

IN THE *AJ*'S FIRST MONTHS, FORTUNE printed three poems and five short stories. In the new year, 1866, she appeared nearly every week. Between March 1866 and March 1867, she published four serialised novels.

This astounding output resulted from personnel changes. Nearly all those involved in the first issues departed, some permanently. They found other outlets, newspapers and rivals such as *The Australian Monthly Magazine*, which debuted the same month as the *AJ*. Walstab left to found his own magazine, the *Australasian Monthly Review*, a venture ponderous, literary and more expensive, with a cover price of two shillings and sixpence. It largely featured Walstab and lasted two issues.

Pay would have spurred Fortune, although colonial rates were poor. Borlase found Australia unsuitable for 'the man of letters': even the compositors got better wages. He complained the *AJ* paid a quarter of the *Family Herald*'s rates (the *AJ* bitterly disputed this claim). Borlase struggled financially until he returned to England and a minor career in popular fiction.[1]

Four novels, however, would earn a useful sum for Fortune, a running-away fund, even if she only received a fraction of the male salary. As journalist Alice Henry noted in 1901: 'Women writers of more than ordinary ability receive less than half the remuneration given to men whose writing is of far inferior merit ...'[2]

The *AJ* advertised Fortune's first novel, *Bertha's Legacy*, with high praise: 'by far the best and most cleverly written tale of Australian origin'.[3] At the time the national literature was new – the first Australian novels date from the 1830s – so the claim had some justification. Here *Bertha* was rated above the work of the other *AJ* authors, as well as the likes of Catherine Helen Spence, whose books had been published overseas. Nobody seems to have disagreed, although reviews only mention the novel in passing.

The *AJ* also said the novel had been written for the magazine, a dubious claim. Both it and Davitt's *Force and Fraud* are polished, without signs of haste. Likely they were written before the *AJ* and rejected by other outlets, possibly even English publishers.

Bertha's Legacy has an English setting, with only the final chapters concerning Australia. Its theme is illegitimacy and the legal and social biases to which it was subject. The heroine begins the narrative as a 'child of shame' who is both beautiful and good. Though nature vs nurture was not then argued in those terms, Fortune protests against 'the fate marked out for [Bertha] by the wickedness of others'. Chance or poor upbringing ruins a life, rather than inherited sin.[4]

The same theme applies to three young women in the novel. Bertha proves to be legitimate, an aristocratic heiress. The situation is reversed for the other two. Her cousin Jane, an apparent moral guardian, turns out to be dishonest, with an unknown father. The other, Lady Georgiana Bassingholt, is Bertha's younger half-sister, the product of an unintended bigamy. The arrival of Bertha effectively disinherits her, and Georgiana progresses downwards, from spoilt and wilful darling to adulterer.

Such plot twists were common in the 1860s sensation novels, which were decried by moralists but loved by the public. They could reflect the lives of the writers themselves. Mary Braddon, for instance, cohabited with her publisher and had six children. Wilkie Collins had two concurrent mistresses and three illegitimate children. Their readership was blissfully unaware of these complexities, as was the *AJ's* audience when it came to the life of Waif Wander.

If there was a real-life parallel to the novel, it concerned another illegitimate child: young George Fortune. Bertha's middle-class uncle reared her and paid for a ladylike education, which ended when she was sixteen. In contrast Fortune was a single mother with an uncertain income. Schooling in the colony of Victoria was free, but only at primary school level. George Fortune's formal education would cease before he was a teenager, and he faced an uncertain future.

The novel contains an interesting authorial interjection:

I stick up for Bertha Beverly, and I say that it is hateful to owe bread, and butter, and clothes to your back, or any thing that money will purchase, to those on whose kindness or support you have no legitimate claim; and it is worse than hateful, when you feel it *may* be grudged, and when you are willing to work for your own bread and butter and cannot get the work to do![5]

Fortune here eschewed charity: she wanted economic independence. Writing was the means to achieve it. *Bertha's Legacy* concluded at the end of May 1866. In June four short stories appeared, and in July began *Dora Carleton: A Tale of Australia.* This novel was less polished but more vital. It contained a murder, recognisable and recent, from Daylesford, in December 1864. Margaret Graham, a teenage newlywed, had been attacked while she lay in bed in a humble miner's cottage. Although she struggled fiercely, her throat was cut. Fortune termed the case 'fearful' and said it would ' long remain a terror to Australian women'.[6]

Clearly Fortune had read the newspaper coverage, and her use of verbatim details suggests she compiled crime scrapbooks. Although changing names and referring to the town of D—, she does allude to the killer entering via the chimney, low and easily accessed from the single-storey roof. In the Graham case, David Young, an ex-convict from

Tasmania, was tried and hanged in August 1865, although he protested his innocence. Fortune makes the killer a man named Gart, drawing on descriptions of Young. Gart flees with blood on his face and incriminates himself further by reacting to a crime-scene photograph of the victim.

Although forensic photography was then not standard police practice in Australia, Daylesford had a photographer, Thomas Foster Chuck. Margaret Graham's body was photographed, but only Chuck's image of the cottage survives. In *Dora Carleton*, Fortune describes the image of the victim freely circulating via *cartes de visite* (small photographic prints on cardboard).[7]

The novel does not involve a detective – amateurs and a mounted trooper solve the case together. Its form is the 'howcatchem' or inverted detective story, predominant in early crime fiction until the whodunnit gained primacy. The reader knows from the outset that Gart is the killer.

The other part of the narrative concerns the heroine Dora Carleton, who has emigrated to Melbourne and married a wealthy squatter. There she employs Mabel, a young working-class woman from D—, as a companion. What Mabel finds is a household at odds. Husband and wife are near-estranged, and Dora seems bent on compromising herself with an Irishman, Annesly de Vesey.

The novel is most self-referential. In the opening chapter, Fortune quotes 'Song of the Gold Diggers' ironically, and Samuel Stackpole Turnhill is named, a light disguise for Samuel Stackpole Furnell, the inspector who had fined Percy Brett and was still prominent in the colonial police. The name of Annesly de Vesey draws on Brett family names: Percy would name two of his sons Annesley and de Renzie. Brett himself is clearly drawn in caustic terms – suggesting that Fortune hoped he read the serial:

> a slight, young, military-looking man, with a soft, glossy head of
> fair hair, and a delicate moustache and beard, inclining to be sandy.
> The face of this young man was very handsome; his nose was small

and aquiline, his teeth white and regular, his lips full and rosy, and
his forehead broad and full; but there was a look of weakness and
inanity in the light blue eyes – a want of firmness in the formation
of his chin, and a self-satisfied simper on his lip, that left upon the
close observer an impression of weakness of character.[8]

This passage appeared in July 1866. Three weeks earlier, Brett had
married seventeen-year-old Mary Ann Leek. They met in Jerilderie and
wed in Corowa, near the Murray border between New South Wales and
Victoria. The couple had eloped, riding 70 miles. Mary Ann Leek is
remembered as a superb rider, but her horse was so restive that it had to
be blindfolded before she could mount.

A family story is that Mary Ann's father had doubts about the marriage and had travelled to Ireland to discover more about Brett. Eloping
forestalled any adverse findings – although if Brett and his first Mary
parted soon after their 1858 marriage, then the seven-year rule applied
and he was free to remarry. Brett now became again what he had been
in Ireland: a horsy countryman but who also worked as Justice of the
Peace and coroner. The marriage produced eleven children.

In *Dora Carleton*, Annesley has faked his death to avoid gambling
debts, then followed Dora to Australia. Believing him dead, she unwit-
tingly committed bigamy. Although Annesley is presented as a ne'er do
well, Dora respects her marriage vow. The couple eventually reconcile,
but only after Annesley has redeemed himself by helping in the pursuit
and killing of Gart, now a bushranger.

Dora Carleton has vivid descriptions of 1860s Melbourne, including an employment agency. Mrs Overdon's Labour Office advertises 'in
the catchpenny advertisements paraded in every daily paper'. It sati-
rises a Melbourne institution, 'Mrs Brown's Offices', that lasted into the
1900s. Brown and Overdon(e) – a cheeky cookery allusion.[9]

In November 1866 the *AJ* ran an article titled 'The Labour Mart',
noting the 'peculiarly Australian' nature of the institution. In England,

a servant's references could be checked; in the colonies, people reinvented themselves. The Labour marts vetted their applicants, acting as intermediaries for immigrants seeking work. Employers in remote areas needed a reliable source of labour, and the marts obliged. As both Fortune and the article noted, female servants could bargain their pay and conditions with a boldness quite unknown in old England. The article was illustrated by a fine engraving by Nicholas Chevalier.[10]

Dora Carleton's Mabel travels to Melbourne to find work that is 'respectable' and 'not menial', precisely what Fortune would have sought. Mabel applies unsuccessfully for governessing, schoolteaching and a housekeeper's position but is warned against Mrs Overdon: 'The old creature makes a perfect mint out of the advertisements she puts in for highly-educated governesses which are never required.' The advertisements are fake, always just beyond the abilities of the applicants, who pay fees to remain interminably on the agency's books.[11] At the theatre, Mabel and Dora observe Mrs Overdon, overdressed. 'It takes two tired and faded-looking governesses, Mabel, to furnish the price of that dress seat.' Did Fortune again settle a score in print? The pseudonym of Waif Wander protected the author.[12]

As the *AJ* had now survived a year, it celebrated with a redesign. The lead serial for each week gained a half-page engraving, echoing the *Family Herald*. The production costs were offset by the increased visual appeal, intended to boost the circulation. Fortune's next serial, *The Secrets of Balbrooke,* was illustrated, if crudely.

Bertha's Legacy and *Dora Carleton* had been realist in style, but *The Secrets of Balbrooke* was melodrama in a purely English setting. The title refers to a stately home whose heir is the splendidly named villain Massy Barthwayt. Secret passages, a madwoman and incriminating documents all figure, as well as the machinations of no less than ten lovers. Half have names beginning with A, including two blondes confusingly both named Alice. Ultimately the plot is too complicated for its own good but enjoyable in parts.

The fourth novel, *Clyzia the Dwarf*, was undisputedly Gothic, a genre whose advent and major popularity roughly coincided with the early settlement of Australia. The depiction of the new land by Europeans drew upon the Gothic uncanny – but *Clyzia* displayed a very dark imagination. It may be the first genuinely Gothic novel written in Australia, although set entirely in early modern England. The novel is historical and fantastical; the title character is a deformed Roma woman skilled in magic and murder.

Clyzia the Dwarf.

The novel begins quietly, even elegantly:

We were not so very wise in those days; we could not with such facility seize the lightning of heaven, and make it whisper our wishes, in a few moments, to the most distant kingdoms on the face of the earth [the telegraph] … There are few dealers in the occult sciences to-day. We speculate in railway debentures, or in bubble companies, but we trouble ourselves little concerning the movements of the stars in connection with our speculations. We forge iron and steel into machinery which shall produce gold for us by labour stronger and swifter than that of our own arms; but we never dream of attempting, by a combination of chemicals, to produce the philosopher's stone.[13]

It is also a temperance novel, with its villain, Rupert Adderfield, an alcoholic. Clyzia is an anti-heroine who knows both chemistry and the occult and taking revenge on the Adderfields for her mother's seduction. Her weapon is a magical snake necklace, which on command comes alive and bites her victims. The result is a glorious female revenge fantasy, as shown in the illustration for Chapter XIV, depicting Rupert hexed by Clyzia. While the novel is excessive, it is also very well written. The *AJ* wrote that 'no previous story has equalled in interest and power'.[14] There was nothing like it in the small world of Australian literature.

Mary Fortune's four novels were a burst of wordage, as if she had published all of *The Lord of the Rings* in one year. *Dora Carleton* seems written contemporaneously. The others could easily have been produced during Fortune's seven lost years. She was a compulsive writer, and that time could have been spent learning the novel-writing craft.

Possibly *Clyzia the Dwarf* was first submitted under a different title. In the *AJ* for 2 December 1865, Waif Wander's 'The Old House in the Forest' was rejected: 'We cannot let any material creep into our journal of a *bigoted* and sectarian nature. MS is returned for revision.'[15] The material in question was likely anti-Catholic, a familiar trope in English novels, such as Wilkie Collins' 1881 *The Black Robe*. The title 'The Old House in the Forest' could describe the ancestral mansion in *Clyzia*, situated near Sherwood Forest. The need to revise *Clyzia* could explain why it appears last in the sequence.

With Fortune's year of novels over, Ellen Davitt returned with her last known serial, *The Wreck of the Atlanta*. A court case connected with this work reveals the precarity of the colonial literary freelancer. In August 1867, Davitt, described as an authoress, was sued for a debt of £18 for 'board &c'. She explained that she had only earned £12 since March but had 'a very large amount of money due to her'. That money seems to have been for the serial, which ran in the *AJ* between April and July 1867.[16]

Fortune now returned to the short story, her preferred mode. In the same issue as *Clyzia* finished, 30 March, the *AJ* announced that its 'Police Stories' would return 'as the leisure of the writer permits'[17]. This time she was not working with Borlase. If her association with him had been an apprenticeship from which both learnt, now she was masterful in her crime writing.

10
——

THE DETECTIVE'S ALBUM

IN 1867, FORTUNE LIVED ON THE 'Farm of Five' in what would become Kelly country: Oxley in Victoria's King River District, a grain-growing area. She would depict it ruefully:

> How we scanned the weather for weeks previously, and how we calculated the increasing gold of the waving crops. Should we, or should we not be, harvested before Christmas Day, or should we lose the pleasant day we had promised at Reedy Station?
>
> Sadly, the threshing machine arrived on Christmas Eve.
>
> If you have never been a farmer, or a farmer's wife, or a farmer's servant, or a farmer's something or other, in Victoria, I need not explain our feelings to you. What do you know about baking bread for thirty men, or cooking five meals a day for ditto? That's what we did on Christmas Day, however, and only in thought did we sadly visit the holiday pleasures of Reedy Station.[1]

The 'Farm of Five' can be identified as the 'Farmers Five', a group of young miners who found the gold in grain-farming. One of them, George Brown, was progenitor of Brown Brothers' Winery at nearby Milawa.[2]

On that Christmas Day, Fortune had no leisure to write. When she did, it was short stories, necessitating a new nom de plume. Waif

Wander had become gendered after her year of novels, three of which had female protagonists. Her police stories, with their masculine true-crime pretence, needed a new byline. It appeared in early 1867 with 'The Lost Shepherd', by W.W. Her modes of writing were thus differentiated. Most of her work would appear under this new name.

She wrote crime because she liked it, but also because the case-book form had a keen audience. Here Borlase provided an exemplar. He aggressively sought markets, with 'The Shepherd's Hut' reprinted under his name in the English *Reynolds's Miscellany* in early 1866. The following year, *The Night Fossickers* appeared and was well received; it was compared to Poe and was reprinted into the 1890s. It proved that a book of Australian crime stories was publishable. As crime writing became more sophisticated, Borlase found a niche in the boys' own adventure market.

Some of Fortune's early crime stories were among her best. In 'The Midnight Watch' she introduced the police horse Vino: 'she was almost as good a detective as I was myself'. At a rural inn, Vino reacts to a teamster suspiciously, as does the barmaid. When the detective shadows the teamster into the midnight bush, this woman also follows.[3]

Fortune works on two levels here: the woman writing the male detective, who in turn observes a woman. At the inn, the detective waylays the barmaid, grabbing her wrist and dragging her into his room, locking the door. For a woman the scenario is sexually threatening, even from a man identified as police: he feels her tremble violently, and when a candle is lit, she proves white with fear. 'She was not a timid woman,' he observes, oblivious to why she might be so afraid. The barmaid is also a detective, if amateur; two years ago, her husband went missing, presumed murdered, and she has followed his trail for justice. Now she has recognised her husband's ox-team, being driven by a stranger. The detective takes over the chase, but when he releases the barmaid, she threatens: 'if you play me false in this I will find this man out [...] until I die myself, or he is hanged!'[4]

In this story, crime arises organically from the milieu – the details unusual but credible and compelling. The detective follows the ox-team, riding parallel to them but invisible in the bush, guided by the sounds of wheels and whip. When the villain confesses, he says that he struck his victim with an axe as the man was putting his billy on the fire. The dead man fell into the flames, a convenient cremation.

Other strong stories also pit a woman against male authority. 'Circumstantial Evidence' begins with a mounted constable on a 'bleak and dreary night', in the New South Wales–Victoria border country. He discovers a girl.

'Good heavens! What brought you here? You are at least five miles from the nearest hearth!'

'I have lost my way.'

'Lost your way! I should think so! Where on earth are you going?'

'I don't know. With you, I think, if you will permit, as I am afraid of being in the bush at night.'

[…] And the strange traveller approached, and placing her foot on mine, with the assistance of my hand, vaulted lightly behind me.[5]

She rides, holding on with an arm around his waist. The proximity has erotic frisson, although the constable is more irate at the girl's self-possession, her polite deflection of his questions. He consults the *Police Gazette* and discovers she is a teenage runaway, possibly guilty of infanticide. But he is biased; the girl is innocent.

The most striking story was not colonial at all. Waif Wander's 'The White Maniac: A Doctor's Story' is set in England, another Gothic horror. A young woman is imprisoned by her family in an entirely white environment, for seeing colour makes her homicidal. The tale reads like a vampiric version of 'The Yellow Wallpaper' by Charlotte Perkins Gilman, rewritten by Angela Carter during her fascination with red/white menstrual imagery. Such a topic was indelicate; here it remains unexpressed but nonetheless present, particularly for the woman reader. Again, the story is written on two gender levels. Of all Fortune's fictions, 'The White Maniac' has been the most reprinted. In 2020 it was included in *Visions of the Vampire*, the British Library's anthology of vampire fiction, alongside the best in the field, including Polidori, Stoker and indeed Carter. A French translation has been published, and the story has also drawn film interest.[6]

Another powerful story was 'The Family Secret, a True Tale of the Colonies'. Like *Clyzia*, it had a temperance message, but this time depicted a middle-class female alcoholic. Such women were then considered especially reprehensible. Her police magistrate husband has to transfer to a new town and her son loses his fiancée. In their new home, the woman, otherwise a gentle soul, discovers her husband's stash of spirits: 'husband, son and self were engulphed in the oblivion of a desperate craving.'

Addiction is presented with some sympathy, and as something uncontrollable. Unmentioned is why this good wife started drinking. Although both her menfolk are supportive, she suicides:

> She slept, while the pale moon rose up and cast shadows of waving branches upon the window – slept, until it crept above them, and lay, cold and pale, upon her dead face – slept, till it went frightened away and left the dark shadows of the verandah on the calm, still form of the escaped intoxicant.[7]

'Escaped' is the key word, indicating what modern studies of alcoholism have found: abuse is not only social but palliative, and liquor a readily available anaesthetic. Fortune herself had problems with alcohol. No treatment then existed, nor counselling apart from the Bible or taking the pledge. Nor had she the option of suicide, as in the story. She had a young son, with nobody else to care for him.

Otherwise, Fortune worked towards a second casebook series. If it succeeded, she would have continued literary employment without the stress of maintaining a novel's narrative. It took several attempts. In May 1867, 'Stories of My Chignon', by Waif Wander, drew upon the current fashion craze for hairpieces, second-hand crowning glories. The next year, W.W. produced 'The Trooper's Bivouac', with police, camped in the bush for the night, reminiscing. Neither series lasted for more than a few stories.

Consciously or not, she took another approach. Rather than settling on a series theme first, she wrote crime stories in which a compelling series narrator gradually emerged. It took over a year of writing in the evenings after a full day's work on the farm. A 'Mark P.' appeared in the June 1867 crime story 'The Medal Case', complaining about (Samuel Stackpole) Furnell. Next month, in 'The Wedding Bonnet', Mark gained the surname Sinclair. He developed into a sardonic but effective series detective, cantankerous and not overscrupulous in his pursuit of crime. Sinclair had a distinctive voice, very like Fortune's in her non-fiction, but the detective was not simply the authoress in male drag, for he voiced the prevailing misogyny. His persona enabled Fortune to write the male-dominated world of justice for the rest of her literary career.

Fortune had her character, and the form of the casebook. Now she added another of her interests: photography. She realised, even before the real-life colonial police did, that photography would change the justice system. This new technology fixed identity, so that it became harder to do as she had and disappear for a new life. Pentridge Prison would photograph villains; so would the Victorian Detective Office. But Fortune's fiction got there first.[8]

In September 1868, three years after her first crime writing, she published 'Mr Medlet's Wedding', in which she gave Detective Mark Sinclair a photograph album.

I turned to my album to have a look at the pictured face of Koëler, the 'wanted'. Yes, young ladies, we detectives patronise albums, too; and I can assure you that they are far more interesting than any of your collections of forms and faces on pasteboard. I have not in my album a single *carte* with the original of which I have not had professional dealings, and about whom I could not tell some terrible stories. You may read a few of these stories of my album some of these days.[9]

The readers did. *The Detective's Album* debuted in early November 1868 and drew upon her experience. It ranged widely, from the goldfields, the bush and bushrangers to Melbourne's criminal underworld. Although the stories started short, in time they stretched to 10,000 words and more, near novelette length.

The Detective's Album would become the longest running crime serial of early crime fiction, lasting forty years and over 500 stories. Here Fortune's inside knowledge provided an edge, creating the most realist police procedural of her era.

Journalism

The month before the first instalment of *The Detective's Album* appeared, Fortune removed to Melbourne from Oxley. She wrote the trip up as a travelogue. Her model was the bestselling Fanny Fern, aka Sara Willis Parton (1811–1872), who, like Fortune, was witty, outspoken and lively. Fern was a novelist who became the first paid female newspaper columnist in the USA and also the highest paid. She was reprinted widely in colonial periodicals; Fern's 'Joyless Homes', about childcare, appeared on the same page in the *AJ* as Fortune's poem 'Canada'.

Fern became a feminist through force of circumstance. When widowed with three young daughters, her family pressured her into a second marriage of convenience. It proved disastrous, ending in divorce. In her bestselling novel *Ruth Hall* (1854), she settled a number of scores autobiographically: her brother N.S. Willis, also an author, who had offered her no help financially and disparaged her writing, appeared as Hyacinth. Nathaniel Hawthorne, no great fan of female authors, famously commented: 'The woman writes as if the devil was in her, and that is the only condition in which a woman ever writes anything worth reading.' Fortune, too, could write as if possessed by the devil and, like Fern, would protest women's inequality.

Yet Fortune's 'Fourteen Days on the Roads' was utterly original. At a time before female journalists went undercover, Fortune travelled without any protection but her wits and spirit. In order to transport her household goods to Melbourne, she accompanied them in the carrier's wagon, sharing her space with 'green' (untanned) hides and their attendant flies. Such journalism is now called 'colour pieces', a perfect vehicle for Fortune. In Benalla, she took the opportunity to observe a local election on 19 October 1868. With sarcastic relish she depicted the enfranchised men voting (and boozing) at the Commercial Hotel, becoming almost too drunk to ride their neglected horses home.

For a woman to write such a scene in colonial Australia was unusual. How many female journalists were then working is unknown, as they concealed their names and gender. Ellen Davitt appeared in the *AJ* for several years, then chose anonymity while still being 'connected with literature' through the colonial periodicals. Poet Mary Hannay Black (later Foott) freelanced in Melbourne from 1869 while studying art. She contributed to Melbourne and Sydney papers, attending balls and covering society. Both Davitt and Black left journalism in 1874. The uncertainty of freelancing compelled Davitt to return to teaching, and Black left to marry in Queensland. Black would return to newspapers when widowed and had a long career. But otherwise, these early 'scribesses' tended to be anomalous and anonymous.[10]

Ron Campbell, a twentieth-century *AJ* editor, described Fortune as 'one of the first women freelance-writers of these parts'.[11] She innovated, both with fiction and journalism, creating a recognisable brand. Not only the *AJ* bought her work. In late 1868 she entered a competition by the Melbourne printer W.H. Williams, responsible for *The Australian Monthly Magazine*. She won the fiction section with the novelette 'Wongawarra'; Henry Kendall won the poetry prize.

Williams published the winners in book form, a first for Fortune. In his *Christmas Annual* she appeared with the Austral colonies' finest writers, men who would become canonical, such as Marcus Clarke. Williams or his editor had no idea of Waif Wander's real name, else he would never have begun his introduction with a stanza including the line: 'Those who up Fortune's ladder crawl.' Others arguably did: Hal Walstab, younger brother of George and also an *AJ* writer, would the same year refer to 'fickle Mrs Fortune.'[12]

'He's Behind You!'

Fortune wrote any form that paid, and theatre was the most lucrative. Her fellow *AJ* writer Robert Whitworth would recall that 'poverty had forced him out of literature into the drama.'[13] He was both actor and playwright. Yet theatre was fraught for women. Actresses might be stars, but their public display placed them only marginally above sex workers. Indeed, when Marcus Clarke married actress Marian Dunn, his social standing suffered.

The nineteenth-century stage employed women as actresses, singers and dancers. Far less opportunity existed for women writers. Theatre historian Kate Newey describes 'a misogynist obstacle course'. If Fortune was a rarity in crime fiction and colonial journalism, she similarly invaded a male-dominated preserve by playwriting. Here she was even more anomalous, but she did get one play performed.[14]

Again she collaborated with a man, actor James Patrick West (1838–1914), aka Devine. He began his career in 1858, working in New South Wales, New Zealand and Queensland, mostly in comedy. He boasted that he never needed to leave Australasia to get work, with over sixty years on the stage.[15]

How did they meet? West did not perform in Victoria until the 1880s. There was one possible rendezvous. In 1866 West travelled by sea to Melbourne, arriving on 21 April. He is not recorded as appearing on stage, but as a professional he would likely have checked out the theatre scene. That night the major attraction was a benefit performance, a memorial for G.V. Brooke, an Irish-born actor who had successfully toured the colonies and who had drowned in a shipwreck earlier that year. West, who declared that Brooke had 'not talent but genius', almost certainly attended. The performers included several professional actresses, with the male parts taken by Melbourne journalists, including the *AJ*'s Walstab and Whitworth.

Fortune's *Dora Carleton*, serialised that July and August, has scenes set in Melbourne's theatres. If Fortune made a business trip to Melbourne during her year of novels, she may well have done some research. A possible scenario is West approaching Whitworth, who was familiar to him as a dramatist and actor in Sydney, and proposing a co-authorship arrangement. Whitworth being too busy (he had three plays performed the following year), did he or Walstab suggest instead a promising newcomer, even if she were similarly busy?

Waif Wander and James West went on to cowrite a Christmas pantomime, a form hugely popular. Although pantomimes were fare for all ages, the involvement of a woman dramatist was most unusual. Only one other contemporary instance is known, by Mrs Eliza Keating in England.

Pantomime in Australia was then dominated not only by English imports, but also by a Melbourne bohemian who had cornered the market. William Akhurst (1822–1878) managed to combine subediting and music criticism for *The Argus* with a busy dramatic career: he wrote fourteen pantomimes in as many years, becoming the first notable dramatist in Australia.[16]

The pantomime form had conventions – the principal boy (usually played by a woman), the Widow Twankey (played by a man) – and familiar plots, mixed with song, dance and topical jokes. In the colonies it incorporated local references, from cockatoos to goldmining. Garnet Walch's original pantomime *Australia Felix; or Harlequin Laughing Jackass and the Magic Bat* (1873) even had cricket (W.G. Grace's XI were touring Australia at the time).

Of Fortune and West's production only the title remains: *Harlequin Little Bo Peep, King Sing a Song of Sixpence; or, The Witch, the Giant & the Good Little Fairy of the Golden Valley*. It was performed at Sydney's Clark's Varieties for Christmas 1868. The advertisement was typically exaggerated and alliterative:

> grand, gay and gorgeous glittering, great and glorious Christmas Local Extravaganza, glowing with glimmering, though generous gleanings, from all the local institutions of the day, popular, and otherwise. The joint production of J. P. West and Waif Wander Esq., and written expressly for this theatre […] No expense has been spared by Mr Clarke [actually John Clark, the ex-publican proprietor] in order that his numerous patrons shall have a special Christmas treat. Look out for our glorious pantomime.[17]

The 'esq.' suffix rendered Waif Wander male, but anyone reading 'Fourteen Days on the Road' (published in late November) would have known her gender.

For both Fortune and West, the production was a one-off. West would work in theatre into his seventies, as a respected actor and manager but not as a playwright. He was most celebrated for Shakespearean roles and melodrama. An 1889 interview and profile detailed West's career, but the pantomime was not mentioned at all.

Behind this omission was an ugly crime. John Clark, proprietor of the Varieties, went on a three-week drinking binge, beating his wife Susan so severely that she died in August 1869, the marks of his rings visible on her face. Due to the bad publicity, the Varieties was quickly renamed the Adelphi, redecorated and relicensed. West, who had been acting in Brisbane at the time of the killing, returned briefly to manage the theatre.[18] In November, Clark was sentenced to three years' imprisonment for manslaughter. That Christmas the Adelphi's pantomime featured West as actor but not playwright.

Harlequin Bo Peep is the only known instance of Fortune's writing for the stage, although she does record attending later pantomimes. Instead, crime writing and increasingly journalism would be her focus.

11

—

IN BOHEMIAN MELBOURNE

I see a good many things in the streets during my peregrinations,
and generally something new every time I go out. I am not an old
habitué, you see, so that many sights, old and wearied of by the
old town resident, come to my eyes with the freshness of things
new born. —'The Ladies' Page', December 1869[1]

BACK IN MELBOURNE AND WITH SECURE work, Fortune became a
flâneur. This journalistic sub-genre involved taking a city walk, note-
book handy, and although initially a male preserve, it drew women – the
flâneuses. Applying her observational and writing skills to the bustling
metropolis suited Fortune perfectly. She was making a name: the *Bendigo Advertiser* described Waif Wander as 'that somewhat well-known
writer', and named her as Mrs Fortune.[2] Her identity was not then
secret, and the leak probably came from writer Donald Cameron, who
contributed to both that paper and the *AJ*.

In Melbourne, Fortune began by seeking housing:

Had you ever the misfortune to be looking for lodgings, and to be
driven to that painful necessity on a broiling summer day, with the
thermometer at ninety-nine, or so, in the shade, and a wind blow-
ing in that aggravating way that utterly defies location? If you have,

120

read and sympathise; if you have not, read, mark, learn, inwardly digest, and – don't look for lodgings under similar circumstance, if you can avoid it.[3]

Middle-class women did not generally admit to wandering the streets unprotected. She also made fun of herself and those around her, including prospective landladies. The street to her seems a companion, as she negotiates urban life. In the same article she notes her 'impecuniosity', to her 'the worst of all diseases'. It afflicted her writing peers, including Henry Kendall, who nigh starved in Melbourne, Adam Lindsay Gordon and Marcus Clarke. Their struggles are described in Michael Wilding's *Wild Bleak Bohemia*, which does not mention Ellen Davitt at all, and refers to Waif Wander only as a name. Yet both women faced worse pay than their male counterparts; and while Davitt was neither wild nor bohemian, Fortune certainly was.[4]

Fortune was sometimes accompanied by her young son George. Other times she walked alone, and proudly:

> nor are my slumbers one bit less sound on that identical Christmas night in consequence of the fact I do not owe a single 'thank you' to one of my kind friends (some of them famous promisers, too) for an offer of treat or hospitality; nay, for even an expressed kindly wish during these festive times. God bless ye all, my dear friends, and grant me continued independence![5]

It seems a truly lonely life.

She had written before in quantity, during the year of novels. Now she exploited the *AJ*'s change from weekly to monthly format in early 1869. The reason for the shift was competition: the postage for colonial periodicals was higher than for imported journals, and so the magazine went from a sixteen-page weekly to a monthly of eighty pages. Fortune would write between three and five articles or stories each month under different pseudonyms, sometimes even using her real initials, M.H.F. The *AJ*'s precarious financial position meant they were desperate to succeed. If that meant giving a woman free rein, then they would do it.

Certainly she was appreciated, the editor describing Waif Wander as 'sagacious and shrewd'.[6] This man was never named, except as the magazine's 'present conductor' – a Dickensian synonym for editor. The *AJ* could be secretive, never revealing *The Detective's Album* was written by a woman. At various periods in its history it also had editors who were not officially credited, working as assistants, subeditors or stopgaps. Several sources say that Richard Egan-Lee (1809–1879) was employed at the *AJ* as subeditor, or even editor, for eight years. His tenure seems to have begun after Walstab's and Borlase's departures in late 1866.[7]

Besides editing, Egan-Lee was a printer, inventor and radical journalist. He led a complicated and wild life, in England being sued successfully by Dickens for pirating *A Christmas Carol*. Emigration to Australia in 1863 led to more trouble, including being tried and found guilty of stealing type. That would have been sufficient reason for the *AJ* not to name him.[8]

While the identification of this editor as Egan-Lee is not completely certain, his editorial comments and the *AJ*'s 'Our Whatnot' column do fit: he wrote favourably of older men as opposed to 'sophomores', of the radical writer Tom Paine, and of educated, capable and witty women. He was a rare Victorian man who did not feel threatened by a talented, strong woman: during his tenure he would have approved *The Detective's Album*, and Waif Wander's first journalism. He was important for Fortune.[9]

Now he bestowed upon her a new column. It came with another pseudonym: Sylphid, referring to a spirit of the air, sylphid being the feminine form of sylph and the subject of several contemporary ballets. Certainly it fits her breezy irreverence and her invisible observance.[10]

Sylphid wrote the Ladies' Page. Women readers were nothing new; the *AJ* covered female fashions in its first issue. Other colonial magazines saw the business opportunity, but most of their efforts were perfunctory: a column of snippets from English magazines regarding etiquette, household hints and dress. The *AJ* dedicated more space, which Fortune took in some unusual directions.

In June 1869, Sylphid began, in the direct, confident, conversational style of a flâneuse, thoroughly enjoying being a roving reporter:

> Well, it shall be just as you wish. I shall take a monthly ramble on your behalf, and jot down my observations and personal opinions on all I observe during that ramble, whether down town or up country, on visits to assemblies or distant excursions. Moreover, I shall keep my eyes open at all times, and my ears also.[11]

Her subjects ranged from public meetings to the Masonic Ball, a visiting naval squadron and the Exhibition of Fine Arts. Less enthusiastic was her coverage of fashion trends: 'I have not a single word to tell you about fashions this time, as I see no change whatever this last month.' Sylphid encountered a woman at the cemetery who feared a prospective operation would kill her. Sylphid's response expressed frustration at being confined to female frippery, fabrics and lace: 'I carry sad memories of the grave with me at every footstep; and yet it is mine to live in an ephemeral atmosphere of blond, and silk, and tulle, as it were.' She was a crime writer, not a fashionista.[12]

She went furthest with an attack on corsets, responding to a debate in *The Englishwoman's Domestic Magazine*. Tight-lacing signified virtue and self-restraint, but she objected to women subjecting themselves to such 'excruciating torture', affecting their health and, worse, that of their daughters.

Sylphid was not completely outrageous. She stated that she did not 'set my face against *all* corset[s]'. Rather she suggested a garment providing less intrusive support – although the brassiere was decades away. A woman should 'leave her figure in the shape which God intended that it should remain.'[13] Natural femininity and practical clothing recur in Fortune's writing.

Sylphid enabled Fortune to comment politically on events affecting the freedom of the public, particularly women. She may not have been a crusader or reformer, but she sought to influence readers, notably regarding conventional morality and material goods. The radicalism of the goldfields still informed her, with its clarion call for freedom and basic rights. She also took up other issues, such as the cabmen of Melbourne, whose monopoly made lone women vulnerable to overcharging and even assault. Sylphid reported on a meeting protesting against the competing omnibuses. When a draper threatened to sack any omnibus users from his employment, Sylphid speculated as to his workers' response:

> I wonder if any *men* did remain [at the meeting] one minute after this bombastic speech; or if they did not bodily charter a whole omnibus the next day, and drive before the 'establishment' for six consecutive hours, as a public protest against the possibility of being serfs, and afraid of the knout [whip]? I declare I think that, had they been women, they would have 'struck' to a *man*.[14]

A horse-drawn bus packed with striking textile workers, clip-clopping for hours in front of their workplace, would have been a very effective protest, if tedious work for the horses.

A battle raged between what Fortune wanted to express and the expectations of the *AJ*. When she mentions this editorial pressure, her tone varies between cheery and tense. 'Now let me set to and write a lively, cheerful article for the JOURNAL, one which will exhibit the greatest faith in human nature, you know, and lead young readers to believe that there is not one bit of selfishness on earth. Ha, Ha!' Later she protested in the third person that 'her whole existence [corrected in the next issue as interest] is concentrated in the fiat of an editor as to the suitability of her mss [manuscripts]'.[15]

The Ladies' Column also offered a shopping service for its remote readers, clever marketing by the *AJ*. It may have been an initiative of

Fortune, who knew the difficulties of supply in the bush. In practice it increased her workload, as she traipsed around town seeking the desired articles. Was she adequately paid for the labour? Probably not. As her contemporary Mary Ann Colclough, a New Zealand feminist journalist, wrote: 'it is a notorious fact that fallen women find it easier to make a living than honest ones do.'[16]

Fortune needed extra income, and in Melbourne she worked as a housekeeper or governess. In 'My Advertisement', she advertised for respectable employment, as P.Q. (Ps and Qs). Although this urban parody is tinged with bitterness, it is also very funny. A correspondent writing as Q.R. sends her a questionnaire:

1. What is the age of P.Q.?
2. Who or what was her husband? What was her position in society during her early years?
3. Does she wear a crinoline?
4. Is music one of her accomplishments?
5. Can she write well?
6. Is she quiet and domesticated?

These questions are markers of social place and female respectability. The narrator responds:

1. It is insolent in the extreme to ask any female her age.
2. It is none of Mr. Q.R.'s business whether or not she had any husband at all, and she's very glad that her position didn't throw her into the society of Q.R., during the early years at all events.
3. Q.R. deserves to be garrotted for the indelicacy of his question.
4. Find out.
5. Examine this and see.
6. Ha, Ha![17]

Here, and in 'The Spider and the Fly', which describes a job interview for a housekeeper (read mistress) held in a pub, she showed the vulnerability of a lone woman seeking employment.

She was also vulnerable in other ways. Of all the writers of colonial Australia, none had more in common than Mary Fortune and Marcus Clarke. They were brilliant, vital, witty and self-destructive. Their range and literary interests coincided – flânerie, the Gothic and the crime casebook.

Clarke made his name as the Peripatetic Philosopher, his panoramic urban journalism based on that of Dickens and, particularly, George Augustus Sala. The more coverage Fortune's distinctive flâneuse voice got, the more she excited interest, not always friendly. She might protest that she had 'not the most distant intention of trespassing upon the ground of our friend the Peripatetic' but the comment was defensive: she most certainly was.[18] Venturing into male domains was her speciality, but here she met someone who on the available evidence resented the incursion.

Waif Wander challenged Clarke directly with 'The Key of the Street', which rewrote Sala's famous 1851 flâneur story of the same name. In the original, Sala spends a night on the London streets, observing revellers, night-workers and the homeless. 'The members of this last class – a very numerous one – are said, facetiously, to possess "the key of the street". And a remarkably disagreeable key it is.'[19]

In her adaptation, Fortune uses a male narrator to express experience otherwise verboten for a middle-class woman. She sets her tale in Melbourne, with her usual preoccupations: lack of funds, looking for lodgings and alcohol. Her story celebrates the joy of getting shickered in the streets and even anticipates a famous line of Oscar Wilde's:

> I was lying in the gutter.
>
> I wish they had let me lie there in peace; it was so delightful to lie there and look 'up among the stars', where no human influence, I gospelly believe, shall ever prevail; doubtless there are no troubles

up there; doubtless among the *moony* people, do they exist, no weight of purse indicates the *man*.[20]

As the leader of literary bohemia in Melbourne and a gifted enfant terrible, Clarke had a domain to defend. He and Fortune increasingly coincided, for instance at the Grand Masonic Ball in July 1869. They both reported on it. Clarke wrote: 'Everybody that one cared to meet was there.' Did that include Fortune, or did he avoid her?[21] Clarke was also at the centre of a network, the Yorick Club. This key institution was founded in 1868, the year Fortune moved to Melbourne. It represented the intelligentsia and professionals, including journalists, politicians, lawyers, doctors and public servants. The clubroom gave members access to wining, dining, games and witty conversation.

A founding member was Andrew Semple, brother of Fortune's friend John, who was both a writer for *The Argus* and a country newspaper editor and proprietor. Others included Clarke, Walstab and Adam Lindsay Gordon. The membership book was a veritable who's who. It included newspaper editor, barrister and parliamentarian Butler Cole Aspinall, *AJ* writer Thomas Harrison, playwright William Akhurst, bon-vivant police commissioner Frederick Standish, Melbourne Gaol governor John Buckley Castieau, doctor and theatre critic James Neild, and George Coppin, an actor and entrepreneur.[22]

In his diary, Castieau recorded gossip and cribbage at the Yorick. Aspinall, Walstab and Gordon could drink all night, and anyone who passed out risked Walstab blackening their faces.[23] Yet there was more to the Yorick than bohemian conviviality. Here information could be exchanged, journalists unofficially briefed and tips passed on. In this exclusive community privilege abounded; introductions were made and job opportunities shared – something not available for women such as Fortune and Davitt.

The literary Yoricks promoted one another. Walstab namechecked *His Natural Life* in his novel *Double Harness; or, Pierce Charlton's Wives*, only to be reproached by a New Zealand newspaper for creating a 'literary ring'.[24] Undeterred, he went on to elevate Clarke, Whitworth and himself as novelists above Anthony Trollope in an anonymous editorial in *The Herald*.[25] Yet no self-promoter surpassed Clarke, who inserted favourable self-references into his anonymous journalism, describing himself 'in glowing colours', as Kendall put it.[26] Fortune never used her pseudonyms for self-praise and seldom got kudos from other writers.

The men of the Yorick Club were typical of their time. They had dependent wives and large families, and while they could express approval of progressive women, they did not really consider them equals. When Ellen Davitt was one of three women to have her work hung at the first exhibition of the Victorian Society of Fine Arts in 1857, with a large and ambitious painting of St Cecilia, Neild reviewed it as 'a tremendous thing for a lady to do, but it had much better have been undone'.[27]

Clarke, in his 'Noah's Ark dialogues', which featured colonial wits chatting, depicted only one woman, Mrs Sweetwinter, reportedly based on Margaret Whitworth, the wife of his friend and fellow *AJ* contributor Robert Whitworth. When she speaks of women joining the professions, like becoming doctors, her husband cries: 'Stop, stop, my dear', and another man argues that 'the proper study of womenkind is children'.[28] When Castieau went to dinner at the Clarkes', his wife Polly stayed home with their seven children. Clarke's wife Marian presided at the dinner table but afterwards left the men to talk over port and cigars. In 1871, when the Yorick held a dinner for Anthony Trollope, Davitt was not invited, despite being his sister-in-law. Neither was Fortune: women were not allowed.

Sylphid protested:

I often envy the gentlemen the privilege, denied to us women, of having clubs for needful and amusing purposes. They have their Garrick Clubs and their Chess Clubs, and what not, and we have crochet and tittle tattle. Bless us all! why can't we originate some friendly and instructive clubs of our own? If there are any ladies in Melbourne who believe in the possibility of establishing a ladies' chess club, I shall be most happy to co-operate in my small way.[29]

In one column she described seeing two women arrested for drunken fighting in the street and dragged to the local watchhouse – practically on her doorstep, she said. She knew how women drank: sneaking down the 'right of way' (dunny lane) to the pub with a bottle for spirits or a jug for beer. At the time she lived in the inner Melbourne suburbs of Fitzroy and Collingwood, the haunt of Vandemonians[30] thanks to the cheap rent. Even cheaper was the liquor, adulterated and addictive. Two months after 'The Key of the Street' appeared, the Police Court columns in three newspapers reported that Mary Fortune had been locked up for being drunk in public. There was no mention of her being a writer.

What had happened? Her journalism cites money and accommodation worries. She did not openly complain about being the single parent of an adolescent boy. The previous month, while describing the Grand Masonic Ball, Syphid alluded to 'one of the many influences, troubles to ourselves and to others, that we meet in life'. It limited her enjoyment of such a lavish event.[31]

Her experience in gaol can be reconstructed from an *Age* journalist's account of the central Melbourne lock-up in 1870, which they described as 'a little stone cage'.[32] As prisoners arrived – forty over five hours on a Saturday night – they were charged and their particulars and any previous charges noted. They were relieved of their possessions – women by a female searcher – and locked up. Each cell had an asphalt floor and a wooden ledge along one side for a pillow. Drunkards, the great majority, were usually left to sleep it off, with a blanket and coarse bread. If they could sleep, that is, amid complaints and inebriated song.

The gaol stank; *The Age* described it as foetid despite the use of carbolic acid as a disinfectant. The reporter wondered how the women and their babies avoided illness – their cell smelt the worst. The women's cell had a wooden door but privacy was minimal. One woman arrested for habitual drunkenness tried to hang herself with her bonnet ribbon, looped around the door hinge; she was revived with a tot of brandy. A male prisoner nearby then tried the same trick for the sake of the alcohol. If not bailed, the prisoners remained in the lock-up until their Police Court appearance.

The East Collingwood Court met twice weekly, on Tuesday and Friday. When Mary Fortune appeared, on Tuesday 10 August, she could have been locked up for days. Four out of the six cases tried that day involved drink. Sentences and fines ranged from five shillings or twenty-four hours' imprisonment to ten shillings or forty-eight hours for being drunk in charge of a horse and cab. Fortune, the only woman to appear that day, was described as 'drunk and disorderly', 'a hard drinker' or 'habitual drunkard'; it was not a first offence, and the police knew her already.[33]

She did not get the option of a fine, one reason being that she was still affected by alcohol. It seemed more than a hangover, for *The Herald* noted: 'she seemed to be still suffering from the effects of the quantity of intoxicating liquor she had imbibed'. Three days in gaol would induce alcohol withdrawal symptoms in a heavy drinker, at worse delirium tremens, with confusion, hallucinations and even seizures. In order 'to recover herself', said *The Herald*, Fortune got a week's gaol. That was time enough for the symptoms to abate, though severe cases were sent to the Yarra Bend Asylum.

The same week, ten Melbourne women got custodial sentences for offences ranging from brothel-keeping (six months) to insulting behaviour (forty-eight hours), but their prison records are elusive. The worst offender, brothel madam Mary (Mother) Caffrey, had form, with various charges detailed on her prison file – but not this one.[34] It seems that no gaol record for Mary Fortune exists.

Once sentenced, the women returned to the lock-up (for short periods), or to Melbourne Gaol or Pentridge if they were sentenced to hard labour. Melbourne Gaol suited a week's imprisonment, with its separate block for females. Here women, if unable to maintain themselves, laboured at tasks at half the male pay and without the privilege of tobacco – smoking signified the sex worker. They cleaned the gaol and did the laundry. Mostly they sat in the yard, idle, with scanty meals that left them hungry. If stroppy, they were punished with solitary confinement in a dark cell, or even a straitjacket. 'The female prisoners give me a great deal of trouble but after all, considering the number we have & the limited space, we get on wonderfully well & quietly,'[35] wrote John Castieau, who arrived at the gaol as governor the following year, 1870. Fortune's prison records may be missing, but her writing offers glimpses of her time there. In 'The Ghost in the Garden', Detective Sinclair describes the Melbourne Gaol uniforms for women: a 'coarse' red-striped petticoat and a cotton checked jacket 'made and shaped anyhow'.[36]

She missed September's *Detective Album* deadline, and her place was taken by 'The Detective's Note-book', an overseas story by Charles Martel. Worse, the *AJ* celebrated its fifth anniversary that month – miraculous given the risks of colonial periodicals:

> we may point with allowable pride to the success of the departments severally superintended by THE COOK, THE DOCTOR, THE LADIES' PAGE, and THE DETECTIVE. In each of these, it will be satisfactory to our readers to know that the arrangements have been made for a vigorous continuance of the respective articles by the same writers, and that their best energies will be devoted to sustain the interest and favour with which their productions have hitherto been received by our readers.[37]

The Doctor was L.L. Smith and the Cook Frederick Chambers of the Melbourne Club, but the Ladies' Page (Sylphid) and the Detective (W.W.) were one woman, who had just been gaoled. The article went on to list the magazine's contributors, beginning with Clarke, the most famous writer in Melbourne. Kendall came third, next Whitworth. Waif Wander was seventh, followed by Hal Walstab. Twelfth was Mrs Davitt, and then further down the listings, Mrs Fortune appeared. Was this section typeset before her arrest?

A different hierarchy occurs in the contents pages. In January 1870, the Ladies' Page appeared halfway through the journal. The latest instalment in *The Detective's Album*, 'The Convict's Revenge', was the second story, behind the lead serial. 'The Convict's Revenge' contained yet another version of Percy Brett in Pyne Rollington, a mounted policeman lazy but fond of kangaroo hunting and novels. In the story, a woman, Anne Rath, is violently raped. Detective Sinclair dislikes the victim, betraying his patriarchal and police duty to protect women. He is more concerned with Rollington's safety, despite knowing that the villain, Conway, has threatened to bring Anne 'lower than ever a woman was brought on this earth'.[38] Conway and his cronies abduct Anne from her family home and take her to a hidden cave with a sandy floor, recalling Melville's cave and other locations around Kingower. In this era, writing about rape was considered indelicate even in newspapers, but it is very clear what has occurred, even without using the accepted terms of outrage and violation.

> 'Don't be hiding your face there all day. You ought to be d___ glad to have three such fine chaps waiting on you! Come, turn up!' And the wretch gave the unfortunate woman a kick which still further disarranged the tatters around her limbs.[39]

When captured, Conway boasts of '[a]ll the details of the indignities [Anne] had endured at the hands of himself and his drunken mates' – in other words, gang rape. Anne, having suffered a fate worse than death, duly dies. The *AJ* accepted the story several months after Fortune's stint in goal. Perhaps being dragged off and incarcerated provided inspiration – or set off a painful memory.

Painful, too, was what happened next at the *AJ*: Marcus Clarke became 'conductor'. He had previously edited *The Colonial Monthly* (formerly *The Australian Monthly Magazine*) and the humorous *Humbug*. Both had failed – not a good omen. His appointment is usually dated to early 1870, when *His Natural Life* began serialisation. Precisely what Clarke did at the *AJ* is open to question, as well as the dates.

The *AJ*'s masthead formally named Clarke as 'conductor' only between March and August 1871. For Clarke to write a serial and edit a magazine (and, from June 1870, work at the public library) seems an onerous workload for a man with a busy social life. The journal reflected his tastes and featured his friends' work, but could he perhaps have had more of a directorial role and left the hard yards of actual editing to another: Egan-Lee?

The evidence is that Clarke and Fortune did not work well together. They were competitors, and rather too alike in personality. And there was another important factor: Fortune was a strong-minded (then a pejorative term) and ageing woman. Historian Barbara Minchinton notes that Clarke had a 'privileged male view of the world'. His 'language brands him clearly as a misogynist, and he especially disliked women who were too old to attract … Woe betide any woman who ignored him. These were not people to the Peripatetic Philosopher, they were mere props.'[40]

Clarke was twenty-four in 1870 and Fortune thirty-eight. During that year, Fortune's contributions to the *AJ* declined. As *His Natural Life* began its serialisation, Sylphid vanished, despite previous promise of a 'vigorous continuance'. For two months *The Detective's Album* did not appear. Fortune's small income was heavily cut, and in April Waif Wander referred to 'our mythical friend the Peripatetic Philosopher'.[41]

The 1870 Sands and McDougall's street directory locates 'Mrs Fortune' at 19 Westgarth Street, Fitzroy, a single-fronted terrace. In 'My Lodger', she described thriftily furnishing one room to let. It seems she became a landlady. However, in the *Detective's Album* story 'Unlucky

No. 58', which featured the dipsomaniac wife of a policeman, she wrote: 'She talks of making her own living with lodgers or boarders, or what not, but neither lodger nor boarder would stop the second week with poor Mary.'[42] The Ladies' Page now comprised cut-and-paste overseas fashion, facetiae and scraps. The likely compiler was evident from a long paragraph quoted from 'that amusing writer', Marcus Clarke. Yet Sylphid's function as remote shopper persisted for some months, for in June 1870 she was described as 'too indisposed' to obtain a writing case for a lady reader in Benalla.[43] Had Fortune simply refused, her personal strike in response to bad treatment? She was not too ill for *The Detective's Album*, now moved to twenty-five pages in.

The serial's avid audience ensured it survived, and so did she. Despite her trials she could still write vividly, informed as ever by her personal knowledge of true crime. Also in June 1870 appeared her 'Down by the Yarra', in which police are ordered to arrest rough sleepers among the wattles on the banks:

> the fog was but beginning to lift off the Yarra when we commenced our raid. The dew was lying heavy on the long grass at the back of the scrub, and at every step we brushed it off, each leaving a trail behind him as though in a light fall of snow.
>
> It was an easy task ours on that particular morning. Lying, helplessly intoxicated, with bottles around them, or just waking up, cold and trembling, with the debauchee's horrible thirst, and the misery of disease in their bones – it was the easiest matter in the world to lead the wretched beings to the watch-house. Men and women – dirty and degraded, ragged and bloated, some quietly, some profaning the morning air with the most horrible language – they were marched over Princes' Bridge in bands, and yet our task was not completed.[44]

12

THE WAYWARD BOY

IN 1871, MARY FORTUNE BEGAN A serialised novel as part of *The Detective's Album*. She also published her only book, a collection of short stories reprinted from the series. That year, her fourteen-year-old son also got into serious trouble.

George Fortune had grown up fatherless. In 'To My Little Son on His Birthday', Fortune rated herself a good mother and the boy intelligent, healthy and happy. Unlike her firstborn, he was not timid, or 'too strong to go astray' – an ominous remark. At eight he was:

> … a strong and bold
> And rude and wayward son;
> But not without a germ of good,
> My kindly little one!

George Fortune followed his mother from diggings to farms, and from the bush to Melbourne. She would have overseen his education, including in Christianity, and he attended the nearest schools:

> you come upon a foot-track, it may be worn by the children's pattering feet trudging to and fro from the nearest Common [State] School, and if you follow it for miles through wattle bushes, tall

and drooping peppermint trees, or stout and gaunt Eucalypti, you will come upon a rude home, so suited in its appearance to its surrounding loneliness and bush, that you cannot help admiring its locality; although one might find a long residence there like banishment from the outer world.[1]

Mary loved the bush, but it gave her son little opportunity beyond agricultural or mining labour. Worse was the glamour of bushrangers:

Many a truant from school has stolen to Melville's Cave, and searched with a beating heart for the buried treasure; although there are not many little chaps brave enough to venture alone. Many twos and threes have consulted and whispered around the heaped up boulders, and then separated to creep and climb and root into every corner; but vainly, for Melville's treasure has never yet been recovered.[2]

Other rural boys became bushrangers' apprentices, like the young Ned Kelly, only two years George's senior.

Scattered throughout Fortune's writings are mischievous boys. They swim in the Yarra, improvise bathing costumes using their waistcoats to avoid penalties for indecency, or hire the new craze of velocipedes (bicycles) with money shaken from 'mother's till'.[3] Significantly they walk Melbourne's streets, as truants, working at trades or odd jobs, or homeless. In 'Down by the Yarra', a detective notes:

Well, I spent all my own time nearly in hunting among the little *gamins* of Melbourne. What funny chaps those same little ragamuffins are, to be sure! And even if they are *not* ragamuffins, but decent little b'ys going to school, with a bag of books, and a 'clane' collar, an' the like, I'll back 'em against any young scamps between this and Nova Scotia for cheek and devilment of all descriptions.[4]

The *gamins* had an ambiguous relationship with police. Their networks, their street presence, had uses: surveillance and information gathering. As such they were under-age informers, paid in petty cash and quid pro quo. At story's end, a street kid is rewarded with an office job and a suit of clothes. More likely, useful boys remained where they were needed on the streets, with some immunity from arrest.

Bourke Street East on a Saturday night, The Australian News for Home Readers, *December 1863.*

In 1872 Victoria mandated free, secular and compulsory primary schooling, a first in Australia. Yet further education was only for the moneyed elite. Working-class children were expected to be self-supporting from the age of thirteen, if not in a trade, then in whatever employment could be found. Charles Dickens never overcame the trauma of the blacking factory, and George Fortune's lot could have been similarly menial: 'In town I ran messages, or blacked boots, or helped with horses, but I had to take to the matches at last, and I couldn't live on it.'[5]

Marcus Clarke records, with satirical exaggeration, how an advertisement for a 'willing boy', pay 10 shillings a week, caused an overflow of applicants. He added:

> a friend of mine who, having hired a willing boy, lost the plate-basket one night, and found it (with the assistance of Detective Jennings), at the willing boy's widowed mother's, who lived in a right-of-way of Little Bourke Street, and drank brandy out of a tea-cup.[6]

If this remark was not a dig at Mary and George Fortune (Clarke was also an allusive writer), then it was eerily prophetic.

In February 1871, Fortune published 'What Passed', recording the street life.

> Poor little lads! If I had any tears left to weep for my own troubles, I should weep them for you [...] I wonder if I might ask the Editor not to blame any spots he may see on this page to such a weakness as tears. Tears for a couple of dirty little boys, with a little dirty hand-truck, perambulated by their joint exertions! Why, Melbourne would deem 'Waif Wander' mad! Weep for two little, ragged, unkempt, almost shoeless rag-gatherers! A pretty pass we should have come to indeed! Little homeless and houseless beings, why don't they – hem! – why don't they – go to the Immigrants' Home [Melbourne's equivalent of the workhouse], eh? What business have they with small ideas and liberty and a full – stomach?
>
> [...] If, as I said before, I had any sympathies that the hard world had not driven out of me; or if I had a moiety of the wealth that vice and ignorance parade around us, not one of you but should be housed and clothed and fed, ay, and kissed, until you felt gratified that there were kind hearts in the world, and became good and honest men. But as it is, my poor lads, whom I have

often seen sharing your crust or your penny with a 'pal' less fortu-
nate than yourselves – as it is, I can only wish you may return a few
hours hence with such a load of rags and bones and bottles, that
you shall have had work to drag and push your truck up the hill;
that you will do so with happy hearts I do not doubt.[7]

That year George Fortune took a similar path. His mother, while mostly
keeping her deadlines, was unreliable in other ways. Who looked after
her son during her drinking bouts, or gaol? Evidence suggests that Mary
Fortune had de facto partners; not to mention the brotherhood of *gamins*. If her son was on the street, he was vulnerable.

In July 1871, George got arrested for stealing a hat, either for hijinks
or out of need. He appeared before the Fitzroy Magistrate's court and
would have gone to the nearest watchhouse, like the adults. The Melbourne lock-up journalist witnessed a gang of boys, aged between ten
and sixteen, arrested for insulting passers-by. Some whined for release,
others defiantly swore at the constables.[8]

Like his mother, George seems to have been known to the police.
Probably he was part of a gang, the rest of whom evaded arrest. Under
the English Bloody Code, petty theft could mean hanging or transportation, even for children. Colonial law was more lenient, but still harsh
for this boy, less than five feet tall and looking younger than his years.

'What Passed' provides a biting remonstrance before the fact:

Public of Melbourne, I wish I might venture to say one or two words
to you about these poor strays and waifs in the world of rags and
bones and bottles. If they are thieves – some of them – who made
them so? If you have money, what do you do with it? Hard-hearted
and selfish, miserly and distrustful – the very opposite of the 'Faith,
Hope, and Charity', which ought to be our motto through life. Is
there one of you who could go into our streets and select from among
those ragged children a face you think you could 'take to', and feel

that you had not one grain of sugar less for your tea to enable you
to do it – is there one of you in such a position, and fails to do it?[9]

The word 'larrikins', an English dialect term, from 'larking', had just
begun appearing in colonial newspapers. It expressed a major moral
panic. The Larrikin, thundered Melbourne's *Punch*, was dirty, ill-educated,
lazy and drunk. 'What a pity he cannot be hanged at once!'[10] Larrikins belonged to the generation born after the goldfields. Their parents
enjoyed opportunity but the children faced low-paid work in an osten-
tatiously wealthy colony. Small wonder they became trouble.

In 1874, Commissioner Standish applied the term to junior members of criminal families, boys getting rowdy after work and simply
mischievous youths. Historian Melissa Bellanta redefines the larrikins as a working-class urban youth culture, fond of smoking, dancing,
tattoos, street fighting and petty crime. Larrikins formed gangs and
aggressively invaded public street-space. They made fashion statements:
bell-bottomed trousers, high-heeled boots, short jackets and broad-
brimmed hats, all in sombre shades except for bright neckwear or a sash
around the waist. The 'home of the larrikin' was Collingwood, where
George and Mary lived.[11]

In her 1879 story 'Constable Dyason's Defeat', Mary Fortune gave
her son's name to a boy in inner Melbourne. She distinguishes between
larrikins and larking, even if the two adolescent apprentices in the story
play pranks upon the police.

> But, being as I am, and always was, very partial to boys, and inclined
> to take their parts, even when I must acknowledge they don't deserve
> it, I must 'stick up' for George and Sam.[12]

This George goes to court but gets off, unlike her son.

The legal category of juvenile offender did not then exist, and children could be sent to adult prison for serious offences. A key issue

was parental respectability: a child of respectable parents might be discharged with a caution or a lecture from the bench. A child whose parent was known to police, or who appeared 'incapable, slovenly, or inarticulate',[13] would be taken into care as a state ward. Mary Fortune was articulate, but the police knew her as a drunk.

Another issue was that in George Fortune's entry in the Children's Registers of State Wards, Mary was said to be 'at present an inmate of the Melbourne Home'.[14] That did not mean the Melbourne Immigrants' Home, which catered for paupers, but the Governesses' Institute and Melbourne Home. This charity housed healthy and 'respectable females, governesses, needlewomen, shopwomen and servants'. It assisted with employment; prospective employers could pay an annual £1 subscription for access to the roster of employable women. In 1871, twenty-two potential governesses were registered, but only thirteen received engagements.

To enter the Home, Fortune had to provide references or testimonials of good conduct. She paid in advance for her registry entry and for board and lodgings. These fees could be waived at the Home's discretion, for deserving cases. Accommodation was limited: inmates could stay for no more than three months each year. While there, they were expected to obey the matron and the Home's rules. The bylaws included lights out at 11 p.m., with reading in bed 'absolutely prohibited' for fear of fire, and only female friends could visit.[15]

Despite these strictures, the place was 'a rightly-called Home', as a group of resident governesses described it in 1875. The 'expenses of everyday lodgings' were otherwise beyond their means.[16] But as it housed single females only, George Fortune was excluded.

What was Mary Fortune doing in a charity for distressed governesses? In 1871 she was the most published woman in Australia, with four serialised novels, poetry, journalism and over sixty short stories. Yet her earnings from writing provided a meagre living. *AJ* editor Ron Campbell said of Fortune's drinking: 'God knows, she probably had every reason, as she wrote more, and doubtless got less for it, than any other Australian writer of the time.'[17]

Marcus Clarke and his friends could be upper bohemians without great censure, but a woman acquainted via her son and lovers with lower bohemia – the criminal classes – was compromised. With George facing court, did Mary Fortune ask literary Melbourne for help?

The men of the law and of upper bohemia were Yorick clubmates, and sometimes their professional lives intersected. In 1872, Castieau – governor of Melbourne Gaol – was confronted at the Yorick Club by George Walstab, accompanied by a policeman. Walstab had just been arrested for unpaid maintenance and asked Castieau to notify his employers at *The Daily Telegraph*. Castieau obliged, then received Walstab at the gaol. He ensured his fellow clubman had clean bedding but judged it prudent to do no further favours.[18]

Fortune could also have appealed to the police. She was familiar with mounted troopers, but to write about the town police she needed informants. In February 1871, her 'A Woman's Revenge' included an authorial note apparently printed by accident: '(*memo.*, to ask D. O'C what a detective card is!)'.[19] Only one D. (detective) fitted the initials: Thomas O'Callaghan. He would later become a police commissioner, but in 1871 he was only a young detective constable, third-class.

Even without the theft, by being on the streets George was subject to the 1864 *Neglected and Criminal Children's Act*, which applied to juveniles without lawful means of support and found begging or sleeping rough. This act had been occasioned by the sheer number of homeless children in the colony: runaways, orphans or children whose parents were simply too impoverished to keep them.

Although George was found to be clean and literate, he had been caught stealing. His sentence: two years as a ward of the state, primarily to keep him out of trouble. He was sent to the Industrial School at Sunbury, forty kilometres north-west of Melbourne, where neglected children were fed, housed and trained to be useful members of the community. The boys learnt trades or farm work while the girls learnt domestic skills, equipping them to be servants or good wives. Both were served with lashings of morality.[20]

In the capitalist, Christian society of colonial Victoria, government charity was controversial, not only because of its cost, but also because the new system might be exploited by those weak in family values if not actually depraved. To make the schools more economically viable and to inculcate good working habits, the children toiled for their keep. In her story 'Jack's Villa', Fortune had a *gamin* comment: 'Bill is sent to the skules where they works.'[21] From the age of nine, these children's days were spent half at school and half at work; from age thirteen, schooling comprised less than two hours. Industrial schools were not Dotheboys Hall, the abusive boarding school in Dickens' *Nicholas Nickleby*, but absconders were advertised for in the *Police Gazette*. To modern eyes, they seem a juvenile workhouse.

In 1867, the *AJ*'s columnist 'The Sketcher' visited the Industrial School at Sunbury. The Institution had impressive bluestone buildings, set atop a hill, but significant health problems. The site suffered extremes of heat and cold, water supplies were poor, and in the early years epidemics occurred, notably conjunctivitis, which without antibiotics could leave a child blind. Between these and other diseases, the mortality rate at the school was higher than in neighbouring communities.

The Sketcher found the place grim, despite small playgrounds with swings. The school's official capacity was 500 students, but in 1871 it housed 714. The boys wore a uniform, including a tweed jacket and moleskin trousers. They ranged from infants to seventeen-year-olds. The Sketcher found them lacking physical stamina, with 'ill-shaped features' and poor skin. 'Their amusements are few in number, their mischievous propensities highly developed, and their morality, as might be expected, of a very undisciplined kind.'[22]

Not surprisingly, given their diet and environment, many were undersized. But behind the reporter's words was the common opinion that criminals were born, not made, as expressed in the pseudosciences of phrenology and physiognomy. These beliefs anticipated eugenics.

The schedule was tightly regimented, beginning with prayers at 7 a.m. School or work followed, the former ending at 3.30 and work an hour later. Little time was allowed for play, apart from one afternoon a week devoted to a walk or games. An hour's religious instruction every day was compulsory. All books had to be approved, and relatives initially could only visit once a month, under supervision. Food comprised equal amounts of bread, meat and potatoes, with smaller quantities of cheese and sugar, and even smaller rations of tea, coffee and salt. There were seasonal vegetables but no fruit.

The industrial schools kept their young inmates clean and fed, if overworked. Yet the cumulative effect proved punitive, for the children and their parents. The Sketcher concluded that despite good intentions, the children led 'dreary lives [...] entirely at the mercy of their overseers, and the red-tape serpent of authority'.[23]

State wards could only be released with the approval of the highest colonial powers, the Governor in Council. Parents trying to retrieve their children faced a long, uncertain and complex process. In the Public Record Office survive records of family devotion battling bureaucracy. Fortune was a fighter; she appealed.

She tried to get George out in September, two months after his committal.[24] Twenty-eight such applications were made that month. Of these, more than a third were approved, including six by women. Support from powerful men helped; George Oliphant Duncan, Inspector of Industrial Schools, was cited in five successful cases. He was a conscientious man, an evangelical Christian who recognised that the law was not always black and white.

A modern joke asks what the difference is between welfare and a Rottweiler. The answer: the dog will let go of a child more easily. A single mother faced difficulties, and police reports proved crucial. Surviving examples show these reports were written by men who were scrupulous, pragmatic, judgemental – and hard on women. In 1870, Constable Francis Dobson of Sandhurst [Bendigo] wrote: 'Maryanne Francis is living in adultery for the past three years with Robert Woolley, a brickmaker [...] she is not a fit person to take charge of the child and properly provide for it.'[25] Her daughter Sarah remained in Sunbury.

Nonetheless, a determined woman could succeed. Harriet Huxley belonged to a convict family, with a gaoled husband and a criminal record of her own – including for assault with a saucepan. Yet when her sons John and Edward got into trouble in the 1860s, she enlisted George Duncan's support. While agreeing with police that Harriet was 'saucy and has been very impertinent', he cited her merits. She was a street hawker, hard-working, even if she did sell to brothels, as the police alleged. (Behind this comment was the common ruse of disguising a brothel's trade with a display of fruit and vegetables. Fortune herself noted the 'extraordinary number of so-called small greengrocers' shops' in some streets, with their 'stale dried fruit and limp vegetables'.) Duncan deemed Harriet honest and sober. That second factor seems to have been crucial. Her applications succeeded despite the negative police reports.[26]

Like Harriet, Mary Fortune was hardworking, and in her journalistic persona brutally honest and certainly impertinent. Yet she had no settled home and a reputation for drink. To get George discharged, Mary had to prove her respectability. She had already admitted in her journalism that there she cheerfully failed: 'By a considerable stretch of the imagination I might be considered a respectable woman, although I needn't tell you, who know the shallowness of my purse so well, that I have no claim whatever to the term.'[27]

She also had to provide a clean and furnished home. Her domesticity would be judged, and the cost of keeping up appearances could be fearful. In her police persona, Fortune commented:

human nature is the meanest of institutions. What does it matter if your parlour chairs are shabby, or you have got two sofas when your legitimate employment cannot afford you to pay for one? Or what business is it of yours if I choose to put myself in the hands of time payment people, and regret it for twelve months after? Faugh![28]

Her application has not survived, but the process can be reconstructed. The first step was to write an appeal. Then the case would be referred to the police, who would investigate and report back. In Fortune's 'The Dead Man in the Scrub', it was the police's business 'to know as much as possible about everything and everybody'.[29] Whatever the police said about her, the application found favour: 'if facts stated are correct he may be discharged.' Then, heartbreakingly, something happened. Did she get sacked from a day job, evicted or, in her anxiety, drunk in public? Whatever the reason, George Fortune remained in Sunbury. His mother had no option but to keep writing.

13

—

A VERY RARE AND
VALUABLE BOOK

IN 1871, W.W. PUBLISHED HER ONLY book, *The Detective's Album: Tales of the Australian Police*. This small paperback comprised 114 pages and sold for one shilling. It is unprepossessing but an important first for Australian and women's crime fiction. Only two copies are known, one in the British Library, another in the Mitchell Library in Sydney. *The Detective's Album* is thus one of the rarest and most valuable items for book collectors of the crime and Australiana ilk.

Some years ago, on ABC radio, its worth was estimated as $25,000. An elderly man in rural Victoria was listening and nearly drove off the road in response. The reason? He was certain a copy was among some old books he had taken to the town tip. Rare book dealer Kay Craddock gives the current value as $60,000. That *The Detective's Album* appeared at all was a minor miracle. The market for colonial literature was small – of the many *AJ* serials, few appeared in book form. Selling overseas was rare, although Borlase and Catherine Helen Spence achieved it.

Colonial Melbourne was then the centre of the emerging Australasian book trade. The main publishers were George Robertson, a Melbourne bookseller turned publisher, and Clarson, Massina & Co., publishers of the *AJ*. Neither business archive has survived, and evidence largely comes from the books themselves. They tended to be small and cheaply produced, printed on pulp paper. Publishing in the colonies was expensive, with high production costs.

In this period, publishing a book usually required a subscription list, with the author effectively crowdfunding from their friends. The alternative was publishing on commission, with the author funding initial printing costs and publicity. If the book was a success, the profits would be shared between author and publisher. Rarer was when the publisher bought the copyright from the author, taking all the risks and, if the book sold, the profits. George Robertson famously lost £90 on Henry Kendall's *Leaves from Australian Forests*. He could afford such a loss, unlike most colonial writers.

There were other obstacles to publication. The pious Robertson rejected Fergus Hume's *The Mystery of a Hansom Cab* (1886) for its 'coarse language' and 'scenes of low life'. Mary Fortune's seedy subject matter would also have counted against her, even if Robertson did not know about the woman behind the pseudonym.[1]

Clarson and Massina printed Fortune's book. It does not appear in the Copyright Register for Victoria, which had only existed for two years, and in which entry was not automatic. Even Fergus Hume took months to copyright *The Mystery of a Hansom Cab*.

The Detective's Album reprinted seven stories published between October 1870 and March 1871. 'The Hart Murder' (in which the detective is outwitted by a squatter's daughter) and 'The Last Scene' have had modern reprints. The other five were less adept. At their worst, they showed an author racing to meet a deadline, making up the narrative as she went.

Fortune could write quickly, as shown in her Sinclair persona:

I was going in for a regular night's writing in peace.

    Some people would find little pleasure in such employment, but I know none to equal it, when there's not too much of it. It's far from being the thing if you're already tired of your day's legitimate employment, and that's the worst of having more than one iron in the fire, the best being that one has more than one pound in his purse.

However, I was not tired on this occasion, and wanted nothing but to be let alone to perfectly enjoy myself [...] First I folded my margin down, and then I selected a pen, and dipping it in the ink, wrote manfully [the author snickers], 'The Detective's Album, by W. W.,' and having done so much, I laid down the pen and lay back in my chair to admire the well-known heading.

'I wonder how much copy I'll get up tonight,' I pondered. – 'Let me see, it's not half past seven, yet, and I might easily manage ten or a dozen pages.'[2]

Her book's rarity suggests a small print run, but the cost would still have been high for her. *The Detective Album*'s popularity did not mean Clarson and Massina, 'straightforward commercial men', risked their own money on the book.[3] An indication of the costs is given by their quotes for the 1870 printing of Adam Lindsay Gordon's *Bush Ballads*. For a book of 104 pages (ten fewer than Fortune's book), the firm quoted:[4]

250 copies . . . . £31 pounds 10/-
500 copies £38 18/-
1000 copies £49 10/-

How could Fortune afford such a sum, even for only a few hundred copies? It is a bibliographic mystery, suggesting real ingenuity.

Nineteenth-century printing differed little from Gutenberg's days. When a handwritten manuscript arrived at the printworks, the compositors set it into type. Individual metal letters formed the words. When a line was complete, it would be added to a galley (a long tray) until the page was finished. A metal frame called a forme held all the page components, negative and positive space, wedged tightly together and stabilised for printing. The completed forme was set in the press and inked, with the paper pressed over it to create the imprint – the printed page.

Usually, when the print run was completed, the formes would be unlocked and the type returned to its boxes, provided no further demand was anticipated. Sometimes a book did find a larger market than expected. One instance was *The Mystery of a Hansom Cab*, which is famously claimed to have sold out its first edition, meaning the type had to be reset, expensively.

When it came to printing *The Detective's Album*, a comparison of the magazine with the book reveals that the seven stories were typographically identical in both publications. There was no change in size or line length, and damaged type appears in exactly the same place in both texts. The only difference is that in the book, the two columns of type from the *AJ* have been rearranged into one.

Letterpress printer Caren Florance observes that the book was produced by

> just reprinting from the same setting. I reckon [Fortune] would have asked the printers if they could do a run-on [an extra printing] after they did the journal. It wouldn't have taken anything more than physically moving the same lines into different blocks rather than columns.[5]

Serialised novels by English authors such as Thackeray and Dickens were printed in a similar way. After each instalment was printed, the formes would be put aside and 'stashed in a corner', says Florance, rather than broken up. Once the serial was completed, cheap paperback books could be immediately printed, bound and issued, with no need for further typesetting.

How common was the practice in colonial Australia? Large metropolitan newspapers, which often produced both daily and weekly editions, could reprint from the same type – for example, to compile that week's serialisations in the Saturday issue.[6] New technology also facilitated reprints. From their third issue, the *AJ* advertised stereotypes, via a papier-mâché mould of the forme, called a flong. Clarson and Massina sent flong from Melbourne to Sydney to print the *AJ*, and also supplied customers with reprints.

Fortune was not the only colonial author taking advantage of the stereotyping process. William Carleton Jr was the son of a major Irish novelist but is now more forgotten than Fortune. He produced one book, *The Warden of Galway*, containing poems which first appeared in the *AJ*. In September 1868 the magazine touted for subscribers for the book, and it was published the following month in both Melbourne and Sydney. The typography in magazine and book is the same, including the damaged letters.

The Warden was a good-quality production, with better, more expensive paper than Fortune's book, retailing for five shillings. The *AJ* advertised it heavily, but reviews were mixed. Critic Alexander Sutherland said the book didn't contain any poetry.[7] *The Detective's Album* was produced without a subscription drive and received no known reviews. It was advertised in the October issue of the *AJ*. The accompanying illustration suggests it was advertised with bill posters, for which Fortune would have paid. In the November issue it was advertised as 'now ready'. By then her efforts to get George released had failed. Had Fortune hoped the publication of a book – a powerful and prestigious object and a source of cultural capital – might have helped her case? She was writing detective stories, after all, on the side of law and order. Could it provide a kind of moral balance to her child's petty crime? If this was her hope, it was not realised.

A first book is a rite of passage. Here it would have been bittersweet; the book did not get George freed and she never published another. In September she started a new serialised novel in the *AJ*, *The Bushranger's Autobiography*, suggesting she may have been paying her printing debts by taking on extra writing. Her pay would not have compared with Clarke's, who sold the serial of *His Natural Life* for £100 pounds with an advance of £50. George Walstab received less stellar terms. During his maintenance dispute, it was revealed in court that his serial rate was £50 for up to eighteen months' work. We do not know what Fortune was paid for *The Bushranger's Autobiography*, but it would have been less than the men.[8]

In producing her book, Fortune took advantage of the fact that her work had already appeared in print form, allowing her to cheaply reuse the same typeface. Given her scant budget, her book might not have appeared otherwise. Thus she avoided the kind of large bills from Clarson and Massina that are said to have been a crucial factor in Adam Lindsay Gordon's suicide.

Fortune and Gordon did not compete, but in 1868 Gordon was commissioned by Borlase to write a weekly serialised novel, *The Mysteries of Sydney*. The title suggests crime, perhaps drawing on Gordon's experience in the colonial police, but the work never appeared. Gordon had recently suffered the death of his infant daughter and several horse-riding injuries.[9]

Gordon's fame came from verse, which was then more prestigious than novels. He published both with George Robertson and Clarson and Massina. In 1870 Gordon, although unwell physically and mentally, contracted with Clarson and Massina to print *Bush Ballads*. On 23 June, he met with the firm and discovered his cumulative debt: between £50 and £70. He would have also owed George Robertson for previous publication. Gordon had no prospect of payment. Kendall had written a laudatory forthcoming review of *Bush Ballads* and showed it to Gordon that afternoon. The book was to be published the following day. Early in the morning of 24 June, Gordon shot himself on Brighton Beach.

What followed shows how cut-throat the colonial book trade could be. Alfred Massina rushed to exploit the publicity and recoup Gordon's debt. Gordon's work had not been copyrighted, and Massina visited the bereaved widow to secure the copyright, paying her 'much less than the poems were worth'. They were entered in the new Copyright Register the day after Gordon's death.[10] The investment proved sound: *Bush Ballads* became a bestseller and Gordon a posthumous literary icon, with a bust in Poet's Corner, Westminster Abbey.

The Bushranger's Autobiography

Clarke's conducting of the *AJ* would be described by proprietor Alfred Massina as disastrous, with a dramatic drop in circulation. The serialisation of *His Natural Life* was also fraught. Clarke sometimes sent in scanty copy, with the instalment for January 1871 having to be printed in larger type to fill the space. In December that year he sent nothing at all. Massina claimed Clarke had to be locked in a room to write. Egan-Lee's descendants recall it was his office, which must have been inconvenient.[11]

Clarke's departure was marked by an editorial dig: 'everyday talent, with TACT, is more valuable than even GENIUS without it.' Gradually Clarke's innovations, such as the 'Literary Table' – cheap piracy from overseas writers – disappeared. The readership preferred local content, such as *The Detective's Album*, now returned from the rear of the magazine. *The Bushranger's Autobiography* began soon after his departure. Egan-Lee knew Fortune's worth.

Lists of the *AJ*'s contributors, while giving Clarke precedence, consistently put Waif Wander in the top five. Fortune's previous novels had opened the *AJ*, but not *The Bushranger's Autobiography*. Clarke still dominated, with half-page engravings accompanying *His Natural Life*. The *AJ* promised in October 1871 that *His Natural Life* would end four months later – time enough for Fortune to get into narrative stride and assume the chief serial position. Instead, *His Natural Life* lasted twenty-two months. In early 1872, however, it lost both the engravings and the prime position.

His Natural Life and *The Bushranger's Autobiography* can be seen as rivalry, a literary pissing contest. Clarke's serial started as a murder mystery, Fortune's speciality. From October 1871, he ventured into another of Fortune's territories: the goldfields. In the final part of the serial, Rufus Dawes survives a lethal hurricane and arrives at Port Phillip. The serial even included Eureka.

Both novels feature a vendetta between two men. The struggle crosses hemispheres, and the rivalry finds expression in the possession of women: Sylvia in Clarke, Mary Greville in Fortune. In *The Bushranger's Autobiography*, Eber Pierce encounters Myra Shelford, a young woman ruined by villain Howard Britton. She assumes drag to avenge herself, becoming mounted trooper Basil Carew.

In content and form, *The Bushranger's Autobiography* was an adventure novel with crime content framed by *The Detective's Album*: Detective Sinclair 'edited' the memoir of an outlaw. Again Fortune mined her past, with the narrator, Eber, based on Percy Brett. She thus wrote through a fictionalised version of her estranged husband – strange psychologically, but consistent with her gender shapeshifting. It could get creepy, as when a character comments of Eber: 'Father, does he not put you in mind of our own dead Percy?'

The novel begins in Ireland, following the early biography of Brett. The vendetta originates here and drives the narrative, with the victim pursuing the villain and then becoming wanted himself. The chase follows Fortune's own progress in Australia, from Melbourne to the goldfields, Castlemaine and Buninyong. Pierce encounters three women, two of them love interests, all with similar Christian names: Mary Greville, Myra Shelford and Maria Waterton. The name George recurs too, often in connection to the three women.

The pressure of serialisation had caused Fortune to forget details before, and in March 1872, the penultimate instalment, Myra inexplicably became Julia. In this instalment Britton escaped from gaol, to enact a very personal revenge with Mary Greville, Eber's first love. As in 'The Convict's Revenge', Fortune describes a brutal gang rape, using similar details:

In a deep wide cave, lighted by a dozen torches, a band of wretches were gathered around a female, who was experiencing the most inhuman outrage at their hands. Most of these brutes were in a state of mad intoxication, and some of them were rolling on the floor tearing at each other, like wild beasts, for the possession of that helpless woman.

[…] At the moment of my entrance, the woman had escaped from all of the brutes, but two, whose united grasp held her almost helpless. Her dress was torn to rags from her person, and hung only in shreds that vainly endeavoured to screen her nude limbs, and she stood at bay against the perpendicular end of the cave, like an animal whose courage had lasted until the very end.

Mary calls to Eber to shoot her attackers and dies in the ensuing gunfight. Her last words are: 'Don't grieve, Eber! I'm so thankful to escape from a world so full of horrors.'[12] The scene was unprecedented for a woman writer of her era. Only the male pseudonym permitted Fortune to write it.

In June, *The Bushranger's Autobiography* finished with an afterword from Sinclair. It concludes: 'If you are as tired of it as I am, you will be glad to read the words, "THE END".'[13] Serialisation was a hard grind. *His Natural Life* ended in the same issue, both serials limping rather than racing to their finish line. Massina had tired of Clarke and declined to publish the novel in book form. Clarke took it to George Robertson, for a £25 pound advance. *His Natural Life* would go on to sell to the English publisher George Bentley, making Clarke's name internationally, but not improving his finances in the long run. He had a strong public persona, and the admiration for his work would ensure he became as canonical as Gordon. Fortune, anonymous and not self-promoting, never achieved such fame.

The sheer size of *His Natural Life* made it too costly for colonial book publishing, and the consequent revisions contributed to it becoming a classic. The beginning and the extended conclusion were cut; these contained mystery, then associated with the sensation genre, of which Robertson disapproved. Frances Cashel Hoey, an Irish novelist and journalist, was one of the novel's revisors. She wrote to George Bentley: 'What a horrid, powerful, clever raw book it is! What admirable narrative and ludicrously bad dialogue! What forcible language, and creaky grammar.'[14]

That first remark also applied to *The Bushranger's Autobiography*. It begs the question: if *His Natural Life* only made it into book form after massive revision, what might have happened had *The Bushranger's Autobiography* received the same editorial scrutiny?

14

———

THE MISFORTUNES OF
GEORGE FORTUNE

IN JANUARY 1872, WITH GEORGE IN Sunbury, the *AJ* published Fortune's 'Our Colonial Christmases', a memoir. It ends with a striking self-description:

> if there is any comfort in being 'a rolling stone that gathers no moss', surely it must be found in the variety of objects and scenes over and through which we roll. If we get knocked about sometimes in rattling through rough pebbles, and bumping against some of our more settled fraternity, don't we roll pleasantly over green spots at times, and crush perfume from the flowers as we pass?[1]

The Fortunes were soon to face some rough spots, disrupting Mary's writing and doing worse to George.

In mid-January, George absconded from the Sunbury Industrial School.

> '[…] I was in the [industrial] schools for some time then and after.'
>
> 'Poor lad! You've had a hard life.'
>
> 'Oh that's nothing. I've just come out of Pentridge, though it ain't that I think that worse than the schools.'[2]

He fled with John Strang (aka Strong) and John McConachie, aged fourteen and eleven. The trio were followed several days later by George Bird, also eleven. They appeared in the *Police Gazette* on 23 January, with Strang and Fortune both described as four feet ten inches tall and of 'stout build'.[3]

Absconding from the Industrial School was common, despite the penalty of caning. The escapees could walk to Sunbury and the train, or else trek twenty miles to Melbourne. Of the four boys, the orphaned Strang disappeared – likely evading the police. Bird hid his Sunbury uniform in the Carlton Gardens, changing into rags received from other street kids. When he was arrested after a month, he gave an alias, a common practice. Identities were commonly swapped between young offenders, who were not officially photographed.[4] McConachie was also arrested after a month, only to abscond again. After arrest for larceny he was committed to the Reformatory, the worst destination for a young offender: they became convicts.

If the police knew Mary Fortune's address, they would have visited in case George had returned home. In 1878, police sought James Alexander Spence at his parents' home, which was located in a city laneway with several brothels. His mother Rosalinda denied he was there, but another woman in the house silently pointed to a cupboard. Both son and mother resisted, and later the constable concerned was attacked by the boy's father, John Spence, a convicted criminal. The parents got three months' gaol and James went to the Reformatory.[5]

In March 1872, George was part of a gang of boys who entered James Allan's barbershop in Fitzroy. George enjoyed camaraderie, and his unstable childhood likely meant he longed for company: any lark for approval and acceptance. On the counter were eighteen pounds of tobacco. Fortune, who was short but strongly built, picked it up and handed it to his accomplices, who fled. The tobacco was abandoned in the street, but Fortune was arrested, left behind to take the rap. He refused to dob – a badge of honour.

the very name of an informer 'stinks in the nostrils' of the criminal classes. To be an informer was to be hated and to be loathed of all men.[6]

George thought quickly at the police station and gave a false name: James Davidson. He took a year off his age – perhaps partly to disguise his real identity, but also to avoid being tried as an adult. His new entry in the Register of Wards stated that his father, also given as James Davidson, was 'dead'. It could have been the name of his mother's boyfriend, or a fiction. George was described as clean, healthy and wearing 'good' clothes. That would suggest he was probably living with his mother. In giving the police an alias, he saved her from charges of illegally harbouring a fugitive, even if he was her son.[7]

When the police interviewed Mary, at her home or at the watchhouse, she concurred with his lie, giving her name as Mrs Mary Davidson, of Collingwood. She did truthfully state her employment: 'writer for the *Australian Journal*'. The arrest seemingly explains why Fortune went AWOL from *The Bushranger's Autobiography* for two months.

George appeared in Fitzroy Police Court as James Davidson; nobody recognised him nor gave his ruse away. An organised gang of thieves being a serious matter, he was remanded while his accomplices were sought. One did appear in court, a Samuel M'Intyre. The victim, Allen, was out of town, so M'Intyre could not be positively identified, and his co-accused said nothing. M'Intyre's father being both present and respectable, the boy 'was discharged with an admonition to be more circumspect for the future'. Guilty, but don't do it again?[8]

George pleaded guilty and was sentenced to a year in the Reformatory aboard the Sir Harry Smith, a hulk for juveniles. Thus he gained a permanent black mark against his name. Reformatory boys could join neither the navy nor the public service (which included the police).[9]

In 'The Stolen Deed', Mary Fortune depicted a street urchin who does odd jobs for Detective Sinclair, like a Baker-Street irregular:

Jemmy Dace was a gem among the Melbourne *gamins*, and devoted to my service as long as he was appreciated, that is, well paid [...] I daresay he was fifteen years old, but didn't look twelve, and was the cheekiest young vagabone that ever smoked a cigar, with his hat on one side and his hands in his breeches pockets. I have admired that fellow many a time, and predicted a career for him. The inimitable way in which he will set up his pug nose and chaff anyone who tries to get illegal information from him, or the owl-like visage he will assume to deceive when necessary, will be worth money to him when he gets among us, as he will one day, or my name's not Sinclair.[10]

The Sir Harry Smith, *circa 1870.*

Jemmy resembled George, but George had no opportunity to become a detective. Had George had Jemmy's relationship with the police, he would not have got into so much trouble.

The *Sir Harry Smith* provided less opportunity to escape than Sunbury, although the boys could swim to shore, risking drowning and sharks, or steal a rowboat. A photograph held at the Royal Historical Society of Victoria shows the boys aboard, in dark sailor suits and hats, marked with the ship's name and their ID numbers. As in 'The Dead Witness', this small image enlarged reveals extraordinary detail. The youths look undersized and wan, their expressions glum or defiant; one boy grimaces at the camera. Also shown are a drum and a small cannon – not toys, but for work.

The Reformatory had a strict routine:

The boys rise early in the morning, stow away their hammocks, and wash down the decks. This over, they go down to a breakfast of hominy; and afterwards they are inspected, to ascertain whether they have washed and cleaned themselves properly for the day. They are then handed over to the naval instructor, who keeps them employed during the morning holystoning the decks, polishing brasswork, and in the general cleaning operations sailors are put to. At twelve o'clock they are mustered for dinner – soup, the soup-meat, potatoes, and bread – and the meal over, they are allowed half-an-hour's play-time. At one o'clock they go to school, where they remain until half-past three. They can all read, more or less, it may be remarked, and many of them write very fair hands. School over, another half-hour's play is given, and then comes supper. When the meal has been partaken of hymns are sung, and word is passed to trice-up hammocks. The next half hour or so the lads are allowed to converse freely; but after the ringing of the sleep bell silence is strictly enjoined.[11]

What benefit existed in two and a half hours of schooling and less play?

When George Oliphant Duncan, the Inspector General of Penal Establishments, appeared before the 1872 Royal Commission into Penal and Prison Discipline, he noted: 'unless boys are intended for the sea, a ship is a bad place for them', with their tendency to 'abominable practices'. By that he meant homosexual acts.[12]

In August 1872 the Royal Commission published its findings, recommending the *Sir Harry Smith* be abandoned. The industrial schools were also declared a failure, to be replaced by a system of foster care. Sunbury and the other schools would close within the decade – too late for the Fortunes.

Mary had put aside *The Detective's Album* after George's first arrest, in favour of *The Bushranger's Autobiography.* When the latter ended, George was in the Reformatory as James Davidson, and Mary duly returned to Detective Sinclair. But art and life were becoming too close for Fortune to write in the persona of the police, who were now her son's enemies. In late 1872 she started a new series entitled *Navvies' Tales: Retold by the Boss.* She depicted lower bohemia in the striking 'Lost in Town', which would prove to be her last *Detective's Album* story for several years. It was realistic, anticipating noir. Two goldminers, Tom and Matthew, come to town on a spree. After a drunken party with Tom's wife, Matthew awakes alone in a gutter, bloody fingerprints on his clothes. Fearing for Tom, he asks Sinclair for help. The detective sets up a sting, disguising Matthew as a moneyed bushman, bait for the lowlife.

The pair enter the slums. They meet Ben Harris, 'a noted thief, burglar and fence [receiver] of the lowest order' and also Tom's wife. Her alias is Nell Parsons, 'one of the lowest, most unscrupulous, and notorious women'.[13] At Nell's cottage, furnished with little more than a mattress and a gin case, Sinclair and Harris hide in a cupboard, only to find Tom's body. At story's end, Nell throws herself in the Yarra, another of Fortune's drowned women, with a 'sad white face' and her long black hair 'like tangled seaweed'.

If Fortune felt similarly lost in town, she still found a new market: *The Advocate,* a Catholic weekly founded by printer and journalist Samuel Winter. He was a friend of Alfred Massina, of Massina & Co.,[14] and his brother Joseph edited *The Advocate*. The fact that she was an Ulster-born Protestant was quite outrageous, but apparently not a hindrance. Waif Wander was anonymous, and if the Winters knew her identity, then she had the advantage of a Christian name that suggested a Catholic, coupled with the Gaelic-derived Fortune. She could use her Irish experience to write for the diaspora audience, necessary extra income. If she deceived, it was by performative mimicry, as with her first-person detective stories.

'Mary Reardon's Christmas Eve' was self-referential, set in what reads like the Kingower area. Unusually, she also provides an exact year for the setting of the tale, 1871, and the month, late June, corresponding to when George was first arrested. The story features a boy who loves his mother and is led astray by a young friend – but his fall is from a tree rather than into crime. One detail is the cutting of 'chestnut curls' from the injured boy's head – reminiscent of the routine shearing of state wards.

The *Sir Harry Smith* boys were moved to Coburg in January 1873. At the time, Coburg was a village north of Melbourne, most notable for Pentridge Prison. Begun in the 1850s as a primitive penal stockade, Pentridge relieved overcrowding in Melbourne Gaol and provided a captive workforce for the nearby bluestone quarries, from whence came its masonry.

Within Pentridge's walls was the new Jika Reformatory for boys. It included five acres for them to cultivate as market gardens, supplying the prison and other institutions. Despite the green space, Pentridge was a dismal fortress. The *Sir Harry Smith* might have been uncomfortable, but it moored in open waters without the taint of prison. Jika, by contrast, offered a punitive existence, confinement and monotony, prayers and violence. The young inmates rose at daybreak and had four hours of school, trade instruction or work in the grounds. From 5.45 p.m. they were locked into their dormitories, where they could read or do homework until lights out, after which talking was forbidden. Punishment included floggings and confinement in cells with bread and water. For play they had the exercise yard except on Saturday afternoons, when ninety minutes of cricket or football were permitted. Access to the library and to letter writing was dependent on good behaviour.[15]

Escaping was difficult, as there were armed sentries. The threat did not daunt Edward Huxley, son of Harriet, whom we met earlier. A seasoned absconder from Sunbury and from the *Sir Harry Smith*, he declared he would willingly risk a bullet. Ten days after his arrival in Jika in February 1873, he and four other boys tried to scale the high stone walls. Not even the adult prisoners had been so bold. Inspector Duncan forgave the culprits without penalty, provided they did not do it again.[16]

George was not involved – a sensible decision, as his release was nearing. A month later he left Jika. What happened next is indicated by notes on his Ward record, unfortunately obscured by tight binding. On 9 April 1873, George (still known as James Davidson):

Left

    Ran away from the C [constable?]

    In West Melbourne

    Looking for the boy's M [mother?]

It seems George had been licensed by an employer, as occurred with state wards over the age of twelve.[17] Here was yet another means by which the authorities tried to make juvenile detention pay. Girls got domestic service, boys apprenticeships or – more usually – manual labour. In principle it was a stepping stone to freedom, while reducing prison housing and other costs for the state. Licensing was subject to abuse, despite police scrutiny of the placements. Efficient volunteer committees of ladies were also empowered to report back.

George might have been mistreated, or perhaps he found the taste of freedom too much. He could have been looking for Mary, for parents considered dubious by authorities were not given their children's new addresses. George probably located her via the *gamins*, or through the *AJ*.

In March, Mary sent the *AJ* 'Yatalonga', which was published in June. The story features Melburnian mother Maria Wyville and her son. It is autobiographical and sentimental but also a fantasy of what George might still be. She wrote him into a better future.

> George Wyville was nearly sixteen, and he was not what is usually called a handsome lad; but there was something far more attractive than mere regularity of feature in his bold and frank-looking bronzed face. He had light brown incorrigible hair that would tumble up in waves and tangles in spite of all the pomatum and brushing in the world, and dark blue eyes that looked you full in the face from under such a broad high forehead, as any one must have been proud of in a son. He was not tall for his age, but he had the chest and shoulders of a young Hercules.[18]

This description fits the surviving photographs and descriptions of George Fortune. Wyville longs for his old country life, of riding and shooting possums. 'Mother, shall we *ever* get out of this hateful town!' A letter from 'the dear delightful old Labour Office' arrives, offering Maria an interview for a housekeeping position in the bush.[19]

Bigamy features again, with a lost husband remarried. He is now a wealthy squatter living under the alias of Shelford, his real name Barthwayt (both names Fortune had used before). The story becomes a revenge fantasy, with Shelford dying in an accident. Maria proves her prior marital claim and inherits his property for their son, dispossessing his second wife, Mrs Shelford, the type of arrogant and overdressed woman Fortune despised. The story ends with Maria remarried to her employer, the family secure in the colonial squattocracy. How unlike the home life of Mary Fortune! Her audience had no knowledge of her son's criminality. If they had, they would have judged her harshly.

In May 1873, the month after George absconded from his work place-ment, Mary began the series *Navvies' Tales: Retold by the Boss* (W.W). The tales feature men yarning after work; the notion seems derived from George Wilson's and Joseph Fortune's work on the Canadian rail-ways, but transplanted to Australia. The early tales were accompanied by handsome half-page engravings, beginning with 'The Dog Detective', set on the diggings.

These tales are not Fortune's best but they have humour. She could still send herself up: 'I'm sick an' tired ov yer stories! It's nothin' but blood-shed and hangin' an' murther wid ye from wan week's end to another, until I'm a'most afeared to go to sleep ov a night at all, at all!'[20]

They also express anxiety about conviction and its consequences. In 'Charley Evans's Story' a mother cannot protect her son from bad com-pany and he is transported to Australia. The accompanying engraving shows Charley melancholy on a ship's deck with other convicts, as in the photograph of the *Sir Harry Smith* boys. 'The Convict Son' reintroduced Mark Sinclair. The detective is investigating the case of a father with a wanted son; the father hides the boy from police. Sinclair observes the fugitive with sympathy: 'His face in the moonlight looked whiter than that of a corpse, and every movement betrayed a wild hunted look.'[21]

The story appeared in October 1873, and was prophetic: that month George was arrested for burglary, for stealing £4. Again he had com-pany: Francis Holmes, another ward and an associate of Edward Huxley.[22] Both were sentenced to two years in Jika. George gave his real name but lied about his age: he was seventeen but said he was fif-teen. He was: 'lousy & dirty. Clothes unfit to be kept. Eruption on skin.'

Where he might have been staying is suggested by 'Jack's Villa', an 1891 story by Fortune set over twenty years previously. It describes 'a small, tumble-down tenement at the back of Jack's wretched home', sublet to 'a class of poor boys who were fast hastening on the road to ruin. Any boy who could muster sixpence a week was free of the shelter of Jack's shed either as a lodging or a temporary place of refuge from parents or police.' With this sanctuary came friendship, but at a cost: 'God help the boys who are driven from their homes to herd in such places with those older in sin than themselves!'[23]

Following George's arrest, Mary Fortune received another visit from the police. They recorded: 'Mother Mary Fortune, a governess, No. 8 Grey Street [East Melbourne], in poor circumstances. Mother is a drunk.' Fortune on this occasion did not mention her writing. She lived with Mrs Charlotte Bryson, whose children were grown. Fortune seems to have been a lodger, an arrangement organised by Walstab, to whom Bryson was related by marriage. He had an appalling few years, illness and family deaths, yet he could still help Mary Fortune, trouble though she was.

Within four months, Mary herself was wanted by the police:

Information is required by the Russell-street police respecting Mary Fortune, who is a reluctant witness in a case of rape. Description: – 40 years of age, tall, pale complexion, thin build; wore dark jacket and skirt, black hat, and old elastic-side boots. Is much given to drink and has been locked up several times for drunkenness. Is a literary subscriber to several of the Melbourne newspapers. Stated she resided with a man named Rutherford, in Easy Street, Collingwood.[24]

Easy Street was a misprint for Easey Street, later an address of Squizzy Taylor, the notorious 1920s gangster. Rutherford appears to have been Fortune's de facto partner, his name an alias, as no lowlife of the name can be traced with certainty.

Unlike George, Mary Fortune left no surviving photographs. The police notice is her only official description. Other clues to her appearance, as to so much else, survive in her fiction. In 'Yatalonga', Maria Wyville seems as much Mary as her son is George Fortune: 'She was above the middle height, with the same fine forehead inherited by her son, and a pair of thoughtful brown eyes. She had fine brown hair, a figure everyone admired, and the hands and feet of a lady [i.e. small and shapely].'[25]

In stories in which variants of Percy Brett appear, he is usually paired with a dark lady, with hair rippled or curly like George's.

'Yatalonga' continues:

In the street you must involuntarily have been struck by the air of calm self-possession and perfect elegance exhibited in every movement, and she was a woman who always looked 'dressed', even if it was only a print dress that draped itself around her. To conclude, Mrs Wyville was thirty-five, but looked every day of forty to a stranger, while in the unreserve of animated moments among friends you might have doubted if she had reached even thirty.

When Shelford the squatter meets George Wyville, he comments: 'there is a something in your face that seems familiar to me.' George replies: 'I am sometimes said to be very like my mother.'[26] Could an artist then take the surviving photographs of George Fortune, and morph them into a fair likeness of Mary? Add a dress, darken his hair and eyes, photoshop women's ringlets onto his head, and even add a bonnet? Will we then gain a visual image of Mary Fortune?

The fact that the police sought Mary shows they took the rape seriously. The victim could have been badly injured, or even a child. A reluctant witness meant a hostile witness: Fortune did not want to testify. In news reports and the *Police Gazette*, 'reluctant witness' sometimes referred to the victim, but it seems unlikely the police would have taken the crime so seriously if Fortune were the victim: a woman with Fortune's history of drinking would have been regarded as culpable.

If she was the victim, Mary Fortune knew how the law treated victims of sex assaults. As her income depended upon anonymity, she eschewed publicity. A major court appearance might have blown her cover and career. She also knew how informers were despised. In her fiction she punished rapists, but real life was different. If her evidence could get a man hanged, then she could be in danger. Her flight from police suggests she feared the accused.

The advertisement appeared intercolonially, a further sign of the case's importance. She would evade the police for four months. Somehow she kept up her contributions and the *AJ* paid her. Only on 29 June 1874 was she found.[27] The case never apparently came to court. Was Mary Fortune's silence a factor?

Another writer in difficulties was Ellen Davitt, who was sent as a teacher to a rural school so dire that it destroyed her health. She fought for compensation, which was declined. She had no pension and was obliged to keep teaching, first privately, then in the Anglican denominational system, which was not sectarian about her Catholicism.

The magazine that had published both women was also struggling. The *AJ* had not fully recovered from Clarke and was 'dying on its feet'. That year, 1874, the cover price reduced from one shilling to sixpence. In September, Robert Whitworth became editor, but his literary versatility, from plays to gazetteers, did little for the journal. Richard Egan-Lee had left to start in 1875 his *Police News*, a sensational and highly successful true-crime weekly.[28]

Having George in Jika for the second time was a burden for Fortune, but less worry than having him on the streets. A journalist from *The Spectator* found Jika more piteous than vicious. He saw boys, 'many of them gentle and bright-faced', variously engaged in boot-making, drilling or working a sewing machine. He sought signs of childhood: 'One touch of nature relieved the grimness of the whole scene – a group of youngsters at one side cheerfully playing at spinning tops.'[29]

After sixteen months, in March 1875, George was again licensed. David Brown farmed Castle Glen, 370 acres at Bylands, near Kilmore; his house was described as the best in the district. He was a former policeman, and by most accounts kind and a good friend. That George stayed out of trouble while in his care suggests a positive influence. In this rural district, with the farms a considerable distance from each other and from the townships, it was harder to get into mischief.[30]

Mary Fortune would mention Bylands twice in her fiction. In 'De Lunatico Inquirendo' it provides the setting: the small township surrounded by a 'well-to-do farming population', predominantly dairy. The inhabitants tended to large and interlinked families of Irish Catholics, some not unacquainted with the Kellys. The hub was the large Union Hotel, opposite the racetrack, where Adam Lindsay Gordon had competed in a steeplechase. Bylands also supported a doctor, parson and lawyer. The latter, Thomas de Courcy Meade, made a 'very good living' from both his practice and a farm. Fortune called him Mr Sharp and spoke from experience.[31]

In 'The Waif of the Slums', a former industrial schoolboy recalls:

'When I was old enough they sent me out to work with a farmer – that was two years ago.'

'And then?'

'They were good to me, but I ran away.'[32]

This time, art was not drawn from life: George Fortune did not abscond.

FIZGIGS

GEORGE FORTUNE'S RELEASE ALSO FREED HIS mother. *Navvies'
Tales* ceased in May 1875, and the following month she resumed *The
Detective's Album*. Said Sinclair:

> I am very glad to get back to the old Album. It has lain in my office
> drawer ever since "the Boss" took my monthly story-telling out of
> my hands, nor have I opened it since I had the pleasure of doing it
> on your behalf.[1]

'The Boss' was the persona behind *Navvies' Tales*, but an editorial
or even proprietorial decision could have been a factor. The *AJ*'s sales
demanded the popular series return.

Mary also began writing for another outlet: *The Herald*, the Melbourne evening newspaper. That she sought work elsewhere was canny,
given the *AJ*'s difficulties. Walstab worked for *The Herald*, and Massina
was part of its controlling syndicate along with Samuel Winter of *The
Advocate*. As 'W.W.' she provided short fictions, chiefly 'Police Stories'
of only a few thousand words. She wrote four that year and sixteen in
1876. Almost all were printed in two parts. If readers wanted to know
what happened, they had to buy the next issue.

Her 'Police Stories' featured a narrator in uniform rather than a detective. He is known initially as 'A15', referring to a police number, but later becomes Martin B. This character is depicted as working-class and presented without condescension. That he appeared in an evening paper, which workers had time to read, was no accident. B. walks his beat in a 'dawdling stroll', keenly observing the streets just like a flâneur.[2] 'Beat books' from this period show how this mobile surveillance system mapped the city's crime.

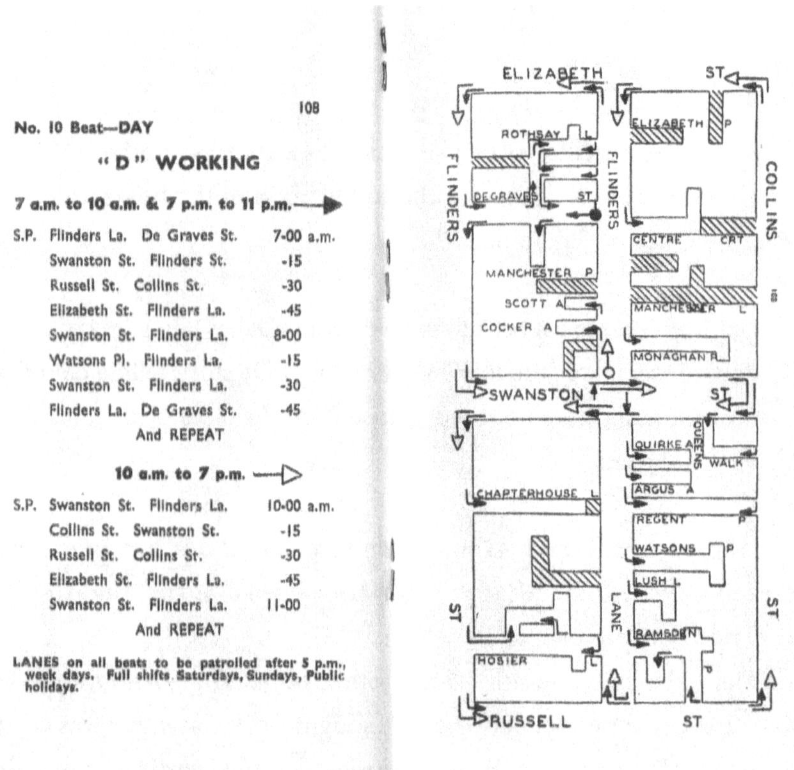

A beat book.

B.'s voice is somewhere between Detective Sinclair and Fortune in her autobiographical journalism. These short, realist police procedurals provide a slice of Melbourne life. The work of the urban constable involves petty theft, rowdy drunks, and free perks from small businesses, such as hot grog after closing time. B. comments: 'there is no member of the community who has more opportunities for the study of human nature, and for serious speculations upon its proneness to evil and its probable future, than a policeman, especially on night duty.'[3]

In these stories Mary depicts constables gossiping on their beats, particularly with women. Gossip relieved what could be a tedious and lonely job and provided information. The exchange was two-way. Fortune gained story matter, and the force got fictionalised. The Police Stories were sometimes not fictionalised enough: in 'The Stolen Brooch', a thief is employed by a high-class draper, and the firm took offence at being named.

Fortune's return to *The Detective's Album* was initially rusty, but she soon regained form. 'The Stolen Deed' mixed high and low life with humour. Sinclair dressed in drag for a disguise, a multi-layered personal joke: a woman impersonating a man impersonating a woman. In it appears a cant word: 'fizgig', said to derive from a police constable stumbling over the word 'physiognomy' in court.[4] The word's meaning, then little known beyond police and criminals, was a paid informer. In using it, Fortune showed how well she knew these intersecting worlds. Her use of the term predated its appearance in newspapers.

Fizgigs played an important role. When the police force was instituted in England in the early 1800s, 'police espionage' was decried (it was seen as a bad example from the French) and detectives were banned from associating with the underworld, particularly informants.[5] This restriction soon proved impractical. When the English and Irish models of policing were imported to Australia, they came with a perceived need to keep crime and political dissent under control through surveillance and informers. This approach produced results, particularly with a large ex-convict population. Detectives learnt on the job the value of a good 'fiz'. Each detective cultivated a network of informants who were their sole property, paid in cash and reimbursed from police funds. Rivalries among detectives were reflected in their use of informers, who were often associated with different gangs and dobbed each other in. Fizgigs not only supplied information; they also trapped their criminal associates into committing crimes while escaping arrest themselves. They were invaluable to the police.

In her stories, Fortune depicts the grey area between thief-catcher and thief. In 'The Stolen Deed', Sinclair comments: 'We have many acquaintances, and *all* of them rather a seedy class, or they wouldn't be acquaintances of ours, you know, for we make them simply to be useful, and we don't find "fiz-gigs" among the Upper Ten [high society].' He admits the association could contaminate: 'as if one could touch pitch, not to say live and breathe among it for years, and not carry some sensible emanation of its perfume!'

The fizgig in the story is female:

the owner, or rather resident of that cottage had been known to me for years as a most amiable woman who was open to treat for information possessed 'for a consideration.'[6]

The amiable woman, Mrs Gorman of Carlton, even lets Sinclair use her back parlour, with spyhole, all the better to observe villainy. In doing so he evicts a lodger, whom he describes as the 'inevitable daughter' – a code understood by the detective and Mrs Gorman for sex worker. Mrs Gorman may sound improbable, but there really was a Carlton fizgig, Charles Graham, whose hairdressing salon was established and subsidised by Inspector Secretan, head of the Detective Department. It was a 'focus and rendezvous of criminals.'[7]

In 1881, Graham was arrested for stealing boots by a constable who did not know he was a fizgig. For character witnesses he called upon the detectives. The Prahran Magistrates Court duly and diligently subpoenaed Secretan, who declined to give evidence 'unless absolutely necessary'. Magistrate Dixon then castigated Graham as a fizgig and sentenced him to gaol – a dangerous place to be, now his cover was blown.[8]

Did the detectives who knew Fortune draw on her knowledge of the criminal world? She was perennially short of money, and a stipend would have been handy. She knew O'Callaghan, and detectives considered a fiz their sole property; if she was his informant, she belonged to him.

She would likely have had a code name. Daniel Kennedy, who informed on the Kelly gang, was code-named 'The Diseased Stock Agent', and Mary's was probably similarly evocative, although perhaps not as much as Waif Wander. Her crime writing may have been a useful cover – another informant with literary aspirations, James Wallace, a schoolteacher in Kelly country, gained information from the gang's associates by claiming to be writing a book.[9]

A modern Melbourne detective, former detective superintendent Sandra Nicholson, was interviewed for this book. She agrees that Mary Fortune would have been a fizgig: 'If Mary wanted money or knew something, she could sell information to police.' In Nicholson's experience, women fizgigs could also be motivated to inform by mistreatment or by having been scorned. Female fizgigs had their advantages: 'Men would speak freely to and in front of women where they might not have with men.' It was not unusual for women with criminal children to inform, although it did not necessarily protect their wayward offspring.

Nicholson states that Fortune fits the psychological profile of an informer, even to the alcoholism. 'I'm in no doubt she would have been a fiz for O'Callaghan either willingly or naively.' Mary knew the risks and denounced informers in her fiction as strongly as she did female alcoholics. If she protested a little too much, it protected her.[10]

Likely Mary's ambiguous relationship with the police began earlier. If so, it explains how she knew far more about the force than her brief marriage with Percy Brett would have provided. 'The Wages of Sin', from 1907, shows mutual attraction between a mounted trooper and a young woman, in which flirtation becomes transactional. When handsome George Rigdon meets pretty Mag on the road, she gives him directions, for which he is 'greatly obliged':

> 'Oh! Greatly obliged be hanged!' she said, with a toss of her dark, glossy head; 'I'll expect you to pay me in some more acceptable manner one o' these days!'
>
> 'Indeed, I hope we shall be better acquainted. You must be very lonely here – such a girl as you is lost in the bush;' and George's eyes pointed the compliment.

He gives her a bag of sweets, innocent 'payment for the information'. Mag soon sees the advantages of Rigden. She has designs on another young man, who already has a sweetheart: 'if he gives her that ring I'll have some payable information for the young trooper!'[11] The information is that the other girl's father operates a still. It would take a fizgig to know that women could inform for motives of love. Although the story is melodramatic, Mag is perfectly realistic as a female informant. Fortune depicts the exploitation of sexuality in the relationship between police and informants – a tradition that continues, as in the case of Melbourne lawyer Nicola Gobbo, known as Agent X, who represented gangland criminals while sharing information about their activities with police.[12] However, the fact that Fortune was wanted as a hostile witness in 1874 does indicate that the relationship was complex. Did she give O'Callaghan information that she was not willing to put on the record or testify to in court? She was no Mrs Gorman, endlessly acquiescent, even allowing Sinclair to borrow her dress for his disguise.

'The Stolen Deed' also contains a self-referential statement of literary intent. Sinclair encounters a suspect's poetry:

> They were neither more nor less than 'effusions' [...] of the style classed by a literary friend of mine, not troubled with sentiment, under the head of 'mush and milk' [...] from the magic words

'competitive' marked in one corner of one fairly copied string of verses, I concluded that the gentle companion was to become a competitor for the prize offered by the proprietors of the AUSTRALIAN JOURNAL; and being pretty well acquainted with the paying style of literature of the present day, I feel certain she will win it. The lines commenced 'Lost love among the breathing lilies,' and ended with something about 'a soul in sweetness dying,' or 'sighing,' I'm not sure which, but you will know when you see them printed.[13]

In real life, Fortune won the prize in question with 'Work with a Will', under the byline Nessuno (meaning 'nobody' in Italian). The poem reads as masculine, and the message of the dignity of labour reads retrospectively as Marxist. The judges were *AJ* editor Robert Whitworth, poet George Gordon McCrae and Marcus Clarke. They awarded the winning guinea without knowing who Nessuno was. Again Fortune had shown her worth in a blind contest, her gender disguised.

Fortune admitted that the freelance life could be lonely. In December 1876, she wrote a Christmas article, 'My Friends and Acquaintances':

I am what my friends – ahem! – two-legged acquaintances call 'a very eccentric person,' and 'a *rather* peculiar creature,' and, I suppose, that is the reason I am so chummy with all the dogs of the neighbourhood; for my friends and acquaintances are mostly of the canine species.[14]

People had let her down, among them George. The Reformatory had damaged George, in the world's eyes and perhaps also psychologically. He had found bad company and developed worse habits. Mary's stories would increasingly consider prison and its effects. In 'John Fowler's Sin' (1877), a young prisoner, Harry, is released from gaol after two years. But he is melancholy, as his father observes:

the one expression in the young face was a sad one to recognise with its years, and it was just what the father had seen and dreaded – a despairing heartlessness, as if the world had nothing good to even promise the young man.

His father remarks: 'they've crushed all the life out of you.'[15] Harry had made a bad friend at school, for whose robbery Harry was blamed. The stolen goods were hidden in Harry's belongings by his friend's father, a wealthy squatter. The story is a revenge fantasy, with the true villain eventually convicted. Harry becomes a man of property in the bush.

Another source of anxiety was the *AJ*. Massina seriously considered closing the magazine until in 1878 William Smith Mitchell, a new partner in the firm and overseer of the printing works, asked for the editorship. Mitchell knew popular taste well and did not interfere with *The Detective's Album*. Under his editorship, circulation rose again.

Fortune also found extra work, chiefly via syndication to country newspapers across Australasia. The practice had begun with Borlase in the 1860s, and from 1877 the Cameron & Laing Literary Supplement appeared. Donald Cameron (1845–1888), like Fortune, had been involved with the *AJ* since its earliest issues. He later worked as a journalist and wrote mysteries. By the time the Cameron & Laing supplement appeared he was also a politician in the Victorian Parliament and a renowned drunk. For colonial newspapers, the supplement was cheaper than material from overseas and provided local content, which meant colonial authors benefited. Literary historian Elizabeth Morrison estimates the supplements reached an audience of at least 90,000 people.[16]

Mary now had more security in her writing career. But 1879 would prove eventful, not least for George, with consequences for them both.

THE STONE JUG

ON 6 JANUARY 1879, ELLEN DAVITT died in Melbourne of 'cancer and exhaustion', aged sixty-seven. She was buried with her husband Arthur in Geelong, under a handsome monument she designed. That she was transported the distance shows she had friends, but there were no funds to inscribe her name on the memorial.

The major dramas in Fortune's life that year would be due to George. On 17 January 1879, Hugh Mulqueeny, a Bylands farmer and hawker, was burgled, losing a purse with 100 gold sovereigns. For a fortnight police had no leads. Then they charged four people with housebreaking and robbery: Eliza Britten; her son James, aged thirteen; farmworker Henry Toogood, aged sixteen; and George Fortune. He was now twenty-three, although he took four years off his age when giving his details to police. Mrs Britten was released on bail of £25 with a surety of the same amount and the others were remanded.[1]

Sergeant D. Deasey (a surname that recurs in Fortune's work) first arrested Henry Toogood, who had a troubled history as a neglected child and runaway and had been licensed from an industrial school. He denied any involvement in the robbery. Next Deasey roused George Fortune from bed at Michael Ryan's farm. For nearly four years George had been a law-abiding farmworker at Bylands. Deasey did not know his history but had information that George had hidden the stolen money. That proved persuasive, for George took Deasey to Ryan's paddock, where the 'plant', the missing purse, was unearthed among the ti-tree. It contained only £59. Where had the rest of the money gone?

Deasey's testimony to the Kilmore Police Court records their conversation. George said he first saw the purse late on the night of the robbery. 'It was just as I got it,' he told Deasey. The Sergeant put the two in separate cells, then arrested the Brittens. George would not inform, but after a night in the cells Toogood confessed, weeping.

Fortune and Toogood were charged with the theft, James Britten with aiding and abetting, and his mother with feloniously receiving. Toogood's confession was read aloud, omitting anything that incriminated others. Young Britten was discharged and put into the witness box. He testified to seeing Mulqueeny depart, then meeting Toogood in the township's slaughter yard. Toogood left and returned forty-five minutes later with the purse. He gave James 1½ sovereigns, which the boy returned to him the next day, lest he 'get into trouble about it'.

While talking with George, Deasey

[m]entioned a certain name, and then said 'You see I know all about it.' [George] replied, 'Did she split [confess or inform]? If I get into it and get lagged, by — I will do something worse, and I will have the plant when I come out.'

'She' was Eliza Britten, as indicated by testimony from local shopkeepers. After the robbery she either paid off her accounts or bought new goods. The defence lawyer Thomas de Courcy Meade argued she had merely 'been rash enough to pay her debts'. Magistrate Wyatt retorted that it was curious she had repeatedly paid with gold sovereigns. When the three accused were committed for trial in Melbourne, he set her bail at a surety of £100. That suggests she was suspected of having been behind the crime.[2]

George had upheld the thieves' code of not informing, but still Toogood and others had dobbed him in. Betrayal is hard to take. Did no one hold him in high enough regard to protect him? Was there no honour nor loyalty?

At the trial, Eliza Britten avoided prosecution. George and Toogood pleaded guilty and were sentenced to two years' hard labour, for receiving stolen goods and theft respectively. A newspaper would later recall George Fortune at Kilmore as 'a hard-working and industrious young fellow. But he did not continue long so, for he fell in with bad companions, and thereafter into a life of depravity and criminality.'[3]

At Pentridge Prison, George Fortune and Henry Toogood were photographed and added to the prison record – a genuine Detective's Album.[4] In 1875, a journalist described it:

> I confess this book of photographs seemed to me one of the saddest
> things I ever looked upon; the countenances were such as an angel
> would weep over. And to think that once they slumbered peacefully,
> in all the guilelessness and sweet unconscious beauty of infancy,
> under a mother's smile.[5]

Toogood's photograph shows a sad-faced child with a scar over his left eyebrow and soulful brown eyes. He was only 4 feet 8 inches tall, and the prison records note that he had tattoos on his hands and arms. In the following year he was given three days in solitary confinement for adding to his tattoo collection. George Fortune, not much taller at 5 feet 4 inches, appears personable and chubby-faced, but his eyes are startling in their intensity. He looks like someone who felt things deeply. In the prison record his name is recorded as Eastbourne Vaudrey, for the only time.

Also in 1879 occurred another, more famous, encounter with the law. In February, Percy Brett, respected Jerilderie citizen, entered the Royal Mail Hotel for a drink. He found himself taken hostage by the

Kelly gang, who were robbing the adjoining bank. Witnesses reported Brett displayed real courage. When Kelly threatened to shoot a hostage

> Mr. P.R. Brett coming forward in a determined manner and stating 'There will be no shooting here Kelly. If you shoot Rankin you will shoot the lot of us: but in the end they will capture you. You have had it all your own way and nobody has interfered, and you have got what you wanted: but there'll be no shooting.'[6]

Brett used his police experience to assume authority via strength of personality. He de-escalated a dangerous situation: Kelly calmed down. Brett later conversed with Steve Hart, regarded by the hostages as the most terrifying member of the gang. Brett would later appear in Douglas Stewart's play *Ned Kelly* and be the subject of a sketch by Norman Lindsay. Coincidentally or not, Mary Fortune published a Kelly story in the May issue of the *AJ*. 'The Misfortunes of "O'Shicer of Ours"' featured an incompetent and vain policeman, thoroughly bested by Kelly.[7]

George's imprisonment in Pentridge caused Fortune to return to Melbourne after 'an absence of some years', as she described it in 'Ladies' Column: Visit to the Library'[8]. His gaol record notes that she lived in Lilydale, now an outer suburb of Melbourne but then a township in the Yarra Valley; her occupation was recorded as 'newspaper and journal writer'.

In August 1879, Mary gained a new job at *The Herald*. The paper had realised the potential of women writers to attract new readers, which meant hiring female journalists. They followed the lead of the colonial magazines and weeklies such as *The Australasian*, whose 'Lady's Letter from London' started in 1873 and was written for thirty years by Frances Cashel Hoey.

The Herald published six times a week. It ambitiously aimed for feminine content every issue, not only a Ladies' Column but also women writing 'Social Sketches and Interesting Chit Chat'. While fashions and embroidery still appeared, *The Herald* created a space for women to write about their lives. A staff of aspiring 'lady contributors' was sought. The first 'Social Sketches' column was credited to Mignon – 'being myself a woman'.[9] The column began tentatively but then became more vital, the phrasing and style indubitably Fortune's.

The brief was to be lively rather than frivolous, eschewing moralising and politics yet sending female reporters into the colonial parliament. The columnists could, within the limits of female decorum, write about what they pleased, which suited Fortune perfectly. That same issue, an editorial note stated that the staff of women was being organised and requested applications, a sure way to create an enormous slush pile. Shortly afterwards 'Mignon' became 'Nemia', who asked her lady readers for patience while the column found its feet.

The first contributors wrote under initials or Christian names. Some are known: E.A.C. was Ellen Augusta Chads (1837–1923), and Louise was Teresa Louise Grace Dumas (1855–1888). The name Mignon vanished, perhaps at Fortune's request – in French it meant small and cute, neither of which applied to Fortune. Nemia, a female variant of Nemo (no one), was a variation on Nessuno and Mrs Nemo, names Fortune had used before.[10]

The experiment proved successful, and in September, the following month, 'the entire charge of that department' was given to a 'literary lady' – essentially the paper's first women's editor.[11] As Fortune/Nemia happened to be the most experienced female freelancer locally, she was most likely the lady in question. The job involved not only writing but wrangling a staff of freelancers, responding to letters from readers and reading imported magazines in search of material to cut and paste (as Sylphid had done). Fortune took to the role gladly. It meant associating with young women seeking 'a purpose that would give a salt to life, and more of a career than matrimony', to quote her contributor Catherine, writing about women's jobs.[12]

Massina agreed. Around the same time, the *AJ* employed a small number of women typesetters, predating Louisa Lawson's 1880s initiative with *The Dawn*. The *AJ* and *The Dawn* met similar opposition from the printing union; the women were kept separate from the men and paid less.[13] Yet Victoria was progressive, with new notions about women's roles. In 1883, Bella Guerin became the first woman graduate of Melbourne University; in 1884 the Victorian Women's Suffrage Society was founded.

Did Fortune go dress shopping with two of her staff, as described by Nemia in October 1879? If so, it was a rare instance of her enjoying the company of younger women. She bought fawn cashmerette (a soft fabric with a glossy finish, in imitation of cashmere) for a short spring walking dress, 12 yards at 1/9 per yard. That she needed so much fabric was due to the prevailing fad for drapery. Cannily, she bought extra in case of shrinkage or 'a required change of style'.[14] As a lady journalist, good yet practical clothing was required.

Nemia was Fortune's flâneuserie revived: vital, feminine, engaging, irrepressible. Yet like Sylphid, Nemia was not strictly autobiographical. Sylphid had referred to writing for the temperance movement, which was acceptable experience for that new and outré thing: a lady journalist. That was certainly possible. Nemia went further, claiming to have attended classes with women famous for qualifying as doctors in America, Elizabeth Blackwell and Mary Walker. That she got their names wrong made the claim harder to believe.[15]

In creating these backstories, which Fortune also did for Sinclair, she was using not so much a pseudonym as a heteronym. The term was originated by twentieth-century Portuguese poet Fernando Pessoa, who created an extraordinary collection of varied personas. Fortune had at the least Waif Wander, Mark Sinclair, Sylphid and Nemia, masks she could don to enable her writing in different genres.

Nemia visited landmarks including the Public Library, although not to visit Marcus Clarke in his office, where he entertained his raffish mates. For bigger stories, such as Hospital Sunday, various of the *Herald* lady contributors covered different aspects of the charity drive. They provided respectful copy about the music and the theology, such as

Anglican Bishop Moorhouse's sermon at the Town Hall. Nemia wrote 'Outside the Hall', concentrating on the crowd's crush, in which children fainted and women damaged their clothes.

Fortune may have had no great interest in Moorhouse, but Clarke had. That November, Clarke wrote an article criticising Christianity in *The Victorian Review*. Moorhouse responded, and a battle via columns followed, which generated enormous public interest. Clarke succeeded in exposing the weaknesses in Moorhouse's argument but he was tarred with atheism. George Robertson withdrew the magazine containing Clarke's riposte from sale.

Clarke's rocky financial status made the controversy foolhardy. Money-lender Aaron Waxman had paid off Clarke's most pressing creditors, but now Clarke was paying him back, with interest. He had his library salary, but needed to write furiously as a freelancer to support his growing family. Fortune had less financial burden: the government housed and fed her son in Pentridge.

In late 1879 she wrote *The Detective's Album*, ran the women's columns, including contributing at least sixteen items herself, wrote short fictions for *The Herald* and syndicated Christmas stories for other outlets. And then she made a bad decision: she let her personal life disrupt her new job by introducing George. He had made appearances in her fiction and journalism before; he was her beloved subject. But using him to provide copy for a newspaper was transgressive.

The ladies of *The Herald* had ventured into institutions such as orphanages before. Visiting a prison was more daring. Four years previously, the crusading Mary Ann Colclough got access to Pentridge, including the notorious 'A' Division, where the worst prisoners were kept in solitary confinement and masked outside their cells. Her account in *The Herald* was scathing; Fortune likely read it.

Now, Nemia reported on George's prison life – and did not conceal it as fiction. Christmases with her son had always been important, and she wrote up her Boxing Day 1879 for *The Herald*.

LADIES' COLUMN

A Visit to Pentridge

There are doubtless in this great city of Melbourne many women to whom a visit to Pentridge is a matter of frequent occurrence, but there are not many who would care to acknowledge the fact by detailing their experiences during one. This is the reason, however, that I decide on relating mine – this and the knowledge that the subject possesses a deep and painful interest to many who would not venture to acknowledge or speak of it.

Circumstance made it expedient for me to visit Pentridge on Friday last, to a young man sentenced to a term of imprisonment, and for whose release on petition steps were in progress. Having found out by application in the necessary quarter that I should require an order from the Inspector-General of Penal Establishments [George Oliphant Duncan], on producing which at Pentridge I should be able to see the prisoner 'between one and three o'clock', I made my way to the King street offices at ten o'clock on a Friday morning, and after waiting for some little time, the Inspector not having arrived, I was at length shown into his office and made my business known to a middle-sized, middle-aged gentleman, who, after a few questions, gave me the order I had applied for. I asked him if there were any stated hours for an interview with a prisoner on order, and he replied 'No you can go straight out now if you like, any time before four o'clock.'

And before I proceed I should like to record how favourably I was impressed by the grave and quiet manner of the gentleman who furnished me with the order I required. It is pleasant to meet with and acknowledge a perfect absence of the pompous self-assertion and want of courtesy unfortunately too characteristic of the Government servant and official of the present day and generation.

I made my way to Brunswick by omnibus and thence to Coburg also by the same class of vehicle; and I thought afterwards that if anything could reconcile one to the loss of liberty it would be such a drive and through such scenery. Almost the whole way it seems a perfect flat for such miles; a flat, it is true, with many cottage homes scattered thickly across it, as the city spreads out its feelers wider and wider and encloses in its embrace more of the level green fields. A long, tedious, dirty road it is, with a depressing view of level, far-stretching fields and enclosures on either hand; and it was not until we reached Coburg itself that the neighbourhood of the road became country-like; and over green grassy slopes and verdant foliage one could see a line of blue hills bounding the horizon.

It was not quite twelve as I alighted nearly in front of the gloomy looking dark stone building, which it was not necessary to inform me was the prison itself; but not knowing the entrance and noticing a man whom, from his dark blue policeman-like frock coat I guessed to be a warder, I asked him how I should proceed. He was evidently off-duty and told me that I should not be permitted to see a prisoner until after one o'clock.

'Well, but,' I said, 'I was told by the Inspector-General himself that I could come straight out if I wished, and one would think that *he* ought to know.'

'May-be, but I don't think you'll see anyone until after one, but you can go and inquire inside,' and he pointed out the entrance very civilly.

There was a wide open carriage gate in the high iron railings, and a wide open small gate for foot passengers beside it. I entered by the latter, and as I did so I noticed a couple of warders standing talking to two mounted-troopers near the kerbstone. They were talking with seeming interest, and I afterwards learned that the troopers had just escorted out the prison van with Laurence, the murderer of Mr Finlayson, in it, and they were waiting to escort it back again. I was not so closely occupied with my own business but that I had a moment to speculate on the feelings of this wretched man. That they were those of the deepest relief who can doubt; yet, were it not for the manner of the felon's death, and its awful disgrace, who would rather not die it than suffer the living death of the life-imprisonment to be faced by the miserable being who has been saved to suffer a life-long remorse by being adjudged a lunatic?

[James Laurence, a railway clerk, shot dead Thomas Finlayson in an oyster saloon after being suspended for drunkenness. He was first sentenced to hang, then reprieved as insane.]

In the principal entrance to Pentridge there is a small grating, which I was not, however, obliged to make use of, as the door was wide open, and I entered to find three or four warders looking at me as if to question my business. Having told it, and parted with my order, I was again informed that I could not see a prisoner until after one o'clock, and I again repeated my ancient formula, 'I was told by the Inspector-General himself that I could come straight out if I wished, and one would think *he* ought to know.'

One warder looked at another and handed him the order with a few whispered words, and the one in possession of the paper turned again to me. 'It's against the rules entirely ma'am, but as we'll see what can be done, will you take a seat here for a bit.'

'Yes,' I returned, 'only please remember that the Inspector General said I could see the prisoner any time before four o'clock and that time is money with me. Surely the Inspector General knows the regulations of this place.'

'Yes ma'am I – a – of course. But you see here's how it is. There's school from eleven to twelve, and then there's dinner, and it is a very awkward time, but we'll see what can be done;' and then he whispered to a young warder who disappeared, and I took the opportunity of inspecting my present *locale*.

The sort of hall I stood in was simply an open space between two heavy stone buildings and this open space was roofed with the second storey above. At the end, which opened to the front, was a huge door pierced by a small grating, as I have previously told you, and at the opposite end a strong high railing with a small wicket gate in it permitted a view of a great quadrangular yard enclosed by the prison buildings. At one side of this hall was what I guessed to be an office, and at the other a door leading to the room which I after discovered to be devoted to the interviews of prisoners with their friends.

As you know, I am naturally of an enquiring disposition, and not at all likely to be cowed by any one's rules and regulations but my own; and though I knew, or at least thought, that visitors were not supposed to look through that railing into the yard beyond, I nevertheless went and looked through it observingly. I didn't stop long, for I saw that the kindly disposed warder was uneasy, and that only my sex and position saved me from the hint that I should doubtless have got had I lingered longer where I had no business to be. What I did see was, first a thermometer hanging against the dark stone in the shade outside the railing, and that it, even in the gloomy shadow of sheltered, heavy stone walls, registered 76. You will remember what a close day Friday last was, and this was just before some heavy peals of thunder, and before the rain came down with a will.

And then I saw 30 to 40 boys, apparently of from 16 upwards, crossing the yard towards one of its outlets in a straggling and apparently jolly party. The aspect of these lads surprised me, for though they were dressed in prison clothes they seemed to be moving as carelessly as though going to work, or leaving it with the liberty of home. Indeed they were 'larking' with each other, as I distinctly saw one lad turn round a laughing face to another, who had pulled his ear, or played some practical joke on him. And then I caught a distance glimpse of a man with a warder on each side of him, moving away in the distance, and I heard a whisper that it was Laurence, just arrived from Melbourne gaol. Having caught this glimpse of prison life, I drew back, and enquired where I should see my young friend whom I had come to visit.

'Here, ma'am, if you please,' said the warder, as he mounted the one step leading to the side door, and opened it. 'He's just coming now,' and having said this, he drew back a form to permit my entrance, and went out, closing the door behind him.

I naturally turned my face towards that end of the room where the man had made a comfortable way for me to pass, and I saw before me an iron rail about three feet high, with a broad banister of polished wood on top. This rail ran from side to side of the room, and behind it, with a space of two or three feet between the two, was another iron railing, only the second one reached from floor to roof and had again behind it a screen of wire netting that would scarcely permit the passage of a little finger between the meshes. Behind this screened iron railing again there was a space of say five or six feet, and then the wall, and high up in it an iron railed window with a yellow holland blind behind the rails.

Standing behind the rail and wire netting as I entered were two figures, one the young man I had come to see, the other the young warder I have already alluded to. The prisoner was comfortably dressed in white moleskin trousers, and dark cloth jumper; he had a straw hat on his head, and a neat checked tie under the collar of his striped shirt. I only saw one brand on his clothing and it was on the left leg of his trousers, a broad arrow, and a number. He looked well and rosy, and had, I am bound to say, a far happier expression than the not much older warder who stood at a little distance from him.

Well, I need not detail a private conversation to you, in which you could not be expected to feel an interest; but I may say that the conversation went far toward doing away with all my preconceived notions of prison life. My young friend expressed a great anxiety that I should know how far from uncomfortable he was, and how determined he was not to be released on petition. 'He was well and contented so far, a stone heavier nearer than on his committal, and he had good food.' 'Good food!' I interjected scornfully, 'Gaol diet of course.' 'No better than gaol diet for we have plenty of vegetables. I work in the garden and I'd just as soon be here than in a situation on a farm. You just ask the overseer if I am not one of the best workers he's got' this triumphantly 'and we've got a splendid library, all Scott's novels and hosts of others.' 'And what time to read them in?' 'Oh lots of times, an hour at dinner.' 'And as till eight o'clock,' the young warden volunteers. 'And what kind of a bed?' I ask, in my depreciatory way. 'Oh a first rate bed,' with a laugh, and a sly look; 'three first-rate pairs of blankets. I sleep as well as if I were on down.'

Ah! I daresay. He was young. 'Well,' I said, 'you may be, as you say, contented, or you may not. You are very like a boy I knew once, who would tell any amount of lies to prevent his mother from fretting.'

'True, I don't want her to fret; don't let mother fret'; and, in spite of the screen, I saw the tears fill up the young bright eyes. 'Indeed, I am comfortable, and in a few weeks more I shall be on tobacco.'

The grand desideratum! Making, with fears that 'mother' would fret, all the young man's trouble; and I came away with the full belief of the observation I made to the warder outside, which brought the reply: —"Contented! An' well they may. Faix, only that they can't get out, they're better off than fifty out of every hundred outside!'

And I believe it. It seems a strange thing to say, but I should rather like to have a boy in there, than with his liberty to spend in horrible larrikinism at every street corner. We know the worst at least when we have reached that.

Coming out I saw the hearse-like prison van moving townward with its trooper escort. No wonder it looked like a hearse; it had been bearing a living man to a living grave: that is all the difference. Perhaps it would have been better if the late occupant had indeed been a corpse before he was hidden for ever by those bluestone walls. I saw, too, a warder on his elevated perch, at the corner of the gaol; he was sitting down, with his broad back towards the road. And then I regained the omnibus, and, as well as the jolting permitted me, tried to analyse the information I had gained concerning young prisoners at Pentridge.

In the first place they were released (if they behave well) about a quarter of the time short of their period of imprisonment; and when about half the time is served they are 'put on tobacco'. This, as I understand, means that they get a certain daily of weekly amount of that weed, of their own earning. Then a few months previous to the terminus of their time they leave the gaol, and are sent somewhere down the Bay (I am not very clear where) and their friends are at liberty to visit them often, and take them tea and sugar, etc. All this was quite new to me, as it will be to many of my readers: and I think that it may be as wonderful to them as it was to me that there may be one prisoner in Pentridge who refused to be released on petition for such a reason as that he would owe nothing to the law that had unjustly convicted him.

NEMIA[16]

This extraordinary piece united Fortune's social and personal agendas. George was not the subject of a petition – that was her inking the waters like a squid, to hide. The article reveals two disturbing things: that George quite liked prison, preferring it to working on a farm; and that she preferred him inside rather than running wild. Or was George trying to protect his mother from the brutal truth of Pentridge? He had trouble keeping his promises, but he could still shield her. She would worry less if she thought he was safe.

Soon after, Nemia vanished from *The Herald*. Likely somebody dobbed her in. Walstab knew her secret, but he had helped her in the past. Was she exposed by an old foe, or by gossip from that den of pressmen and police, the Yorick Club? Was it coincidental that Marcus Clarke was selling reprints to *The Herald* at the time, and would have been dealing with Winter, the owner and editor of *The Herald*?

For *The Herald* the news could have been a considerable shock. Melbourne pressmen were not saintly, and Winter (nicknamed Stormy) was notably foul-mouthed and blasphemous. But women were always judged more harshly than men. The key issue was how it would affect *The Herald*'s readership if Nemia's secret was made public. Mary was sacked. Waif Wander and W.W. would not return to the newspaper for several years, and then only with fiction.[17]

Nonetheless the Ladies' Column survived, covering Melbourne life and even describing an opium den. Mary Fortune had been denied a newspaper job in 1855, but she helped create a space for Australian women journalists.

17

—

MARVELLOUS MELBOURNE

IN THE 1880S, MELBOURNE BECAME THE largest and wealthiest city in the Southern Hemisphere. George Sala declared it Marvellous Melbourne. Buildings grew high and ornate, and capital and speculation ruled, with white collar crime as rife as the petty thefts and violence of the poor. In this milieu the *AJ* enjoyed prosperity again, with new premises, extra compositors and new publications added to its list.[1]

Of Fortune's contemporaries and rivals, some had died, while others had failed or ceased writing. Henry Kendall suffered poverty and ill-health until a day job saved his life and muse. He published his third book of poems in 1880. Walstab reconciled with his wife, worked for newspapers and the public service, but wrote no fiction. Kendall called him indolent but also 'brilliant, wayward, unlucky'.[2] The same words applied to Fortune and Clarke.

In May 1880, Fortune received a rare critical appraisal. Henry W. Mitchell was a freelance journalist who was unable to walk and was confined to his home. This did not stop him editing periodicals, subediting for a newspaper and writing articles, fiction and pamphlets with titles such as *Diseases Peculiar to Men*, which he sold by mail from his home. In 'A Well Known Contributor', Mitchell wrote:

I am sorry that I am not in a position to place before my readers full details of the life and work of this popular author, but as her very name is shrouded in mystery, and as no one knows who she is or where she lives, I do not think that I ought to bring her forth from her obscurity, but simply content myself by criticising her writings, and congratulate the proprietors of the AUSTRALIAN JOURNAL on their good fortune in having so gifted a writer on their staff.[3]

Mitchell's words hint at restraint: he sounds like someone in the know who, like the Waif herself, played a referential game. The *AJ* guarded her identity, which was vital given George's continuing crimes. That October he was released into a city obsessed with Ned Kelly, whose trial began on 19 October before Justice Redmond Barry. It was the end of the age of bushranging and would cast a long cultural shadow, which is felt even now.

In November the *AJ* reprinted Mary's radical goldfields poem 'Climb Up the Hill' under a new title, 'Excelsior', revised 'with changes that redeemed them from the Republican taint'.[4] That month *The Detective's Album* returned to Green Hills, Buninyong, where George had been born, with another story about rape. George celebrated his birthday on 3 November as a free man. Ned Kelly was hanged eight days later.

On his release, George returned to Bylands, like an unwelcome homing pigeon. He stayed in the Union Hotel for two days, seeking employment or old friends and evading the police scrutiny that he would have faced in Melbourne. He told the hotel's proprietor, James Robinson, about his role in the Mulqueeny robbery, which was still locally famous. Was he boasting, seeking sympathy or simply being honest? Robinson remembered George, and George cased the joint.

In his mother's story 'Mag Braban's Share', a young felon is released from Pentridge. 'Who would trust a "gaol-bird"?' he bitterly declares.[5] Another story, 'The Deed Done in the Scrub', features a city lad 'on the tramp':

he was ragged and tired and hungry, but even then no one could mistake the cut of the cunning town-lad about him.

I was sitting outside the door smoking, when I saw the dusty-looking and wearied boy coming along the road, picking out the bits of grass at the side to walk on, for his shoes were worn to uselessness; and I think he would have bolted when he saw me, a policeman, if I hadn't called him.

'Come on here!' I called. 'What are you going to run for? Come on here, boy!'

He came limping, and stood before me, the very picture of misery. As I have said, his clothes were tattered and dusty, and his bare toes were sticking out of his shoes. An old straw hat on his head let his dusty hair through in more places than one, but, with all, the boy had a good face and a pair of intelligent eyes …

'I can't tramp much farther, sir,' he cried, as he burst into tears and began to rub his dirty hands all over his dirty face. 'I've tramped all the way from town, sir, on the look out for a job, and I can't get nothing to do.'[6]

The story ends benevolently, as does 'Mag Braban's Share'. It did not with George. In April 1881 he and a companion returned to Bylands. While ascending Pretty Sally Hill (now Big Hill), a hawker named Walter Constable saw George larking, 'rolling up a German [luncheon sausage]'. What he was doing was unclear: pretending to smoke it? Again George made himself memorable, and aroused suspicions. When George asked Constable for a lift in his cart, he was refused. At dusk Constable arrived at the Union Hotel, where he and proprietor Robinson saw a man emerging from scrub opposite. Constable recognised Fortune. Robinson and the hawker had tea but were disturbed by a slamming door.

Robinson checked the bedroom where he kept his money and found over £20 missing. He went to Kilmore for the police, but canny farmer Richard Johnston rode his horse to Wallan train station. There, he and a local policeman arrested Fortune and crony on the platform, shortly before the Melbourne train arrived. *The Kilmore Advertiser* described both as 'well known ruffians'.

The other ruffian was James Williams, a violent larrikin with a longer record than George's. Later George claimed he had been the 'dupe of an older criminal than myself'. It is unclear if he was referring to Williams or to someone else; perhaps 'the bad companions' that he had in Bylands.

Both George and Williams were charged with larceny. When they were caught, £20 was found on George and another £2 in his purse, of which he remarked: 'Mind, that money don't belong to the other.' He would not explain his meaning. If he had money, why rob the hotel? En route to the police station Fortune told Williams: 'We have made a mess of it.' Williams replied: 'It's all right, it can't be helped now.'

In Kilmore Police Court, again before Magistrate Wyatt, George and Williams appeared, apparently unrepresented. They confidently engaged with witnesses. George objected to Robinson mentioning the Mulqueeny robbery and queried whether he could have been recognised by twilight. Wyatt, losing patience, cautioned Fortune against self-incrimination. What proved conclusive was that one of the pound notes found on George had writing on it, which a customer of Robinson's could testify to having seen before. The pair were committed for trial at Melbourne Criminal Court.[7]

In the city the charges against Williams were withdrawn, a *nolle prosequi* – he had only seven shillings on him when arrested and could not be positively identified at the Union Hotel. George pleaded guilty and was sentenced to another two years' hard labour, this time in Melbourne Gaol. Mary had written in a story in 1877: 'When he returned to his evil ways, and evinced such hopelessness of reformation, how could I respect him any more?'[8] That story concerned a husband; a mother could not abandon all love for a child.

Somebody else unable to reform was Marcus Clarke. In 1882 he adapted the play *Happy Land* by W.S. Gilbert, shifting its setting to

Melbourne – it was deemed so effective a political satire that it was banned. But Clarke had greater troubles. He could never manage money and was nearing bankruptcy for the second time, despite his wife Marian having returned to the stage in 1880. His only hope was that he might gain promotion from sub-librarian at the Public Library to Chief Librarian.

Clarke was gifted but louche, bohemian and uncontrollable. He had been tolerated while he had powerful protectors, Sir Redmond Barry and Sir Charles Gavan Duffy, both Library Board trustees. But they could not help now: Duffy had retired to France and Barry famously and quickly followed Ned Kelly in death.

In mid-June 1881, Clarke's estate was sequestered and he failed to get promoted. In a new anonymous freelance venture with Walstab, the syndicated 'Metropolitan Echoes' column, he deplored his plight in the third person:

> I hear that he purposes to resign altogether, and return to journalism and romance [novel] writing. The public will be a gainer by this proceeding, but I doubt if Mr Clarke is not more courageous than prudent to tempt the stormy billows of Bohemian seas without ballast. His friends, however, will throw him a tow-rope if necessary.[9]

Clarke was asked to resign from the library in July. A fortnight later, 'Metropolitan Echoes' reported that 'Mr Marcus Clarke, the well-known author' was ill with 'lumbago [back pain] and internal inflammation'.[10] He died the next day. Even as he lay unconscious, his hand moved, as if inscribing his last words.

Though Clarke had his rivals, enemies and those who regarded him with a mixture of exasperation and affection, his death at thirty-five aroused widespread and sincere shock. His wife and six children were left destitute, and his friends now rallied round to fundraise. Of Clarke's many obituaries, perhaps the best was Kendall's. He wrote that Clarke was too good-natured, too careless in money matters to succeed in this selfish, grasping world. The career that commenced under a morning sun of brilliant promise ended in the deep shadow. I have no desire to lift the veil, no wish to say any more. One by one my friends are all wearing away.[11]

Kendall died himself the following year.

Far from wearing away, Mary Fortune remained productive, proving herself tougher and more persistent than nearly all the fellows. In 1882 she wrote twenty-five crime stories for *The Herald*, besides *The Detective's Album* as usual. That September she began her memoir 'Twenty-Six Years Ago' in the *AJ*. The publication claimed copyright, indicating the hope of book publication, but it was not actually registered.

She had written in *Bertha's Legacy*:

One week we are punished by the present – tortured by fear and anxiety, or overwhelmed by unexpected disappointment; the next we are grovelling among the memories of the past, which should be dead, but which is *not*, and our hearts are mangled afresh with recollections, and remorses, or loves, as the case may be, that we have writhed under before, in this present, and that we shall writhe under a hundred times again in the future.[12]

Painful though the past was, it provided fine copy. Yet the memoir soon stumbled, with the second instalment not appearing until January 1883. She also suspended her *Herald* stories and, briefly, *The Detective's Album*. What happened this time? The answer lies with the police.

The Kelly outbreak had revealed significant failings in the Victorian police force, with Commissioner Standish forced to retire. In 1881 the Longmore Royal Commission into the Police began, chaired by Francis Longmore, MP, a political liberal and a tough idealist. The inquiry would prove long, thorough and inquisitorial. For Mary, who made a living from fictionalising the police and had a son in gaol, following the commission would have been more than research.

The commission produced sensational revelations, and from September 1882 these involved the Detective Branch. Henry Mitchell had praised Fortune's crime realism: 'She exposes all the nefarious arts, tricks and dodges adopted by [detectives], who are undoubtably the authors of more crime than they prevent.' The commission found them 'little less than a standing menace to the community'.[13]

These twenty-six men included O'Callaghan, now a senior detective and prized thief-taker. Inspector Secretan, described by several witnesses as 'useless', presided over some rogue cops. The word fizgig had by now begun to appear in the press, although Secretan claimed he did not understand its meaning. In fact the practice infested the force, and in its secrecy was open to exploitation by criminals.[14] The Royal Commission noted that the practice could involve entrapment:

A 'fiz-gig' is paid to start the prey which the expectant detective captures without trouble or inconvenience [...] He is supposed to receive not only a subsidy from the detective who employs him, but a share in the reward, and a certain immunity from arrest from offences with which he may be chargeable. He may plan robberies and induce incipient criminals to co-operate, but provided he lures the latter successfully into the detectives' hands, his whereabouts and antecedents are not supposed to be known to the police.[15]

In September 1882 appeared whistle-blower Patrick Boardman, a contemporary of George Fortune and similarly a larrikin. By his own account he had a reckless youth. It culminated in his 1871 arrest with other larrikins, including girls, as they made merry in a quarry – what he would describe as 'immoral conduct'. As he was known to the police as an 'incorrigible young thief', he was sent to the Reformatory hulk. Boardman had pretended to be an orphan lest his parents find out, but when they did, they acted quickly. His father Thomas was a state-school teacher of unimpeachable respectability. He retrieved the boy by petition within weeks.[16]

Patrick remained under continuing police surveillance, so in 1874 his father sent him to New Zealand. When he returned to Melbourne in 1877, he got into bad company again. He took part in the Hotham (North Melbourne) bank robbery, which featured, with engraving, in Egan-Lee's *Police Times*. That gained Boardman a three-year sentence. Out early for good conduct, he went straight, but was still of interest to the police. Their behaviour brought him to the commission.

In 1882 Detective John Duncan approached Boardman to become an informant. Boardman neither liked nor trusted the detective, who had arrested him at Hotham after a violent tussle. He temporised – implicitly agreeing but not openly refusing. The carrot had been proffered; now came the stick, with police surveillance and an attempt to incriminate Boardman in a robbery.

Detective Charles Forster saw an opportunity. Although near retirement, he could still expose his rivals – Secretan's favourites, including Duncan and O'Callaghan – and reveal his workplace as a 'nursery of crime'. He needed Boardman to support his evidence, and the young man judged that he had nothing to lose in going public. Boardman sent a statement to the commission via Castieau. The very next day Boardman was charged with vagrancy, although he was working as a bookmaker.[17]

When summoned to appear at the commission, he told a damning tale, being supported by witnesses including his father. Duncan had offered Boardman £3 a week, protection from prosecution and half shares in rewards. Not only that, but Boardman was to go to the Prisoners Aid Society (set up by George Oliphant Duncan and Castieau) and befriend newly released prisoners. Boardman produced a list of prisoners due to be released from gaol, given to him by Detective Duncan. O'Callaghan had also been involved. The fizgig would tempt the ex-prisoner with an opportunity for crime, pretending that he was seeking accomplices. When they offended, the detectives would get an easy arrest. The informer would be allowed to escape; his partner in crime got gaoled again.

What drove Boardman was that his 1877 conviction had been due to a fizgig, Charles Britchener, an ex-convict from Western Australia. The evidence is that Britchener was Duncan's fiz. The Royal Commission heard that the police knew about the Hotham robbery in advance, even hiring rooms in a nearby hotel. Following the robbery, Britchener avoided arrest. Before Boardman's trial for the robbery, Duncan tried to enlist him as an informer: if he revealed the identities of two others involved, he would get only six months for being on premises illegally. Boardman refused and Duncan warned that the evidence given against him would be 'ten times worse' than the charge itself.[18]

During the Royal Commission's examination of Boardman, O'Callaghan was suspended for impertinence and withholding evidence. Boardman capably defended himself, and the commissioners believed him.

For Fortune this evidence was personal: in November, George Fortune would be released. Once out he was vulnerable to fizgigs. Unlike Boardman, Mary Fortune had everything to lose by going public. However, that would not stop her writing to the commission anonymously, as was her wont.

Brian Hardiman, whose distinguished career has included the Office of the Ombudsman (Police) and the Office of Police Integrity, comments:

> Although most Royal Commissions seek to have as many of their hearings as possible held in public, In Camera Hearings are an inevitable feature of Police Corruption enquiries.
>
> What you might not quite appreciate is the extraordinary level of hidden investigation that goes on behind the scenes which only rarely sees the light of day [...] The public hearings and evidence

of only a few witnesses are conducted/published to provide the public narrative and case studies to back up the eventual conclusions and recommendations.

[...] In summary, I would not be surprised at all if Fortune was involved in public or secret enquiries and/or used material gathered and provided to inform such enquiries.[19]

If so, she ran the risk of retaliation, not least via George, who was released from Melbourne Gaol in late November 1882. Common procedure was that when a prisoner with a sentence of over twelve months was released, they would be escorted to the detective office and paraded in the muster room. Thus the detectives' memories were refreshed, and they knew who was out on the street. George had offended twice at Bylands, so could not return there. Now he was known by the police in Melbourne and they would target him whether or not he committed a crime. He had seventeen shillings and sixpence in prison pay, and the option of charity from the Prisoners Aid Society, but as Boardman had testified it was a magnet for fizgigs.

Ten days after his release, George got arrested again, for vagrancy. This time he was accompanied by George Ford, aka John Gardiner, who had only been released a fortnight. Newspapers described Ford as a 'bag hunter' (mugger of drunks) and pimp.[20] The pair had suspiciously loitered near Bishopscourt, home of Bishop Moorhouse. Neither could give 'satisfactory account' of their presence, and their reputation damned them. Were they led there by a fizgig, or followed? We can never know but the result was that George was back on charges without actually committing a crime. This scenario of release and rapid re-incarceration was so common that Mary included it in a poignant 1902 story of a son's need to escape Melbourne lest he suffer the same fate.

I met Detective Long and he advised strongly to get out of town or I'd be arrested on a charge of vagrancy.[21]

On 1 December they both pleaded guilty and were sentenced to twelve months' hard labour.

In 1878, *The Herald* had commented that an ex-convict had 'the feeling that, in the eyes of his fellow men, he is less than a human being. He comes into the world cold and cheerless, unable, it may be, to obtain work.'[22] Boardman had testified that detectives actively worked against a marked man – especially one refusing to dob. Secretan had sent Boardman's photo to New Zealand, with his history and details of his 'bad character'. The Otago police took this information to the factory where Boardman worked and he was sacked. Yet as he showed no signs of offending, the local Commissioner of Police helped him to find alternative employment shearing.[23]

In another case, cited by an anonymous writer to *The Herald*, a boy gaoled for stealing apples found work in a shop after release. A detective visited to tell the proprietor he was employing a 'gaol-bird'. The boy was not sacked, but he felt the stigma and left: 'his life is blighted.'[24]

The same writer described the fizgig tempting the released prisoner, inevitably resulting in arrest:

At the trial it comes out that the prisoner was just discharged from Pentridge, the judge is more severe on him, the jury more ready to find him guilty [...] and severe moralists point to the fact of the man's re-committal to prison as proof strong as Holy Writ of the truth of their theory that the criminal cannot be reformed. It never seems to strike these people that that man had no chance of reformation.[25]

The two Georges' capture suggests that despite the Royal Commission, detectives continued with corrupt business as usual. The aim was punishment rather than reform, easy results and full prisons, justifying government's expenditure on the penal system.

While awaiting George's sentencing, Mary wrote a story for *The Herald*, 'Little Peepshow', about a girl street hawker. She supports her ill mother as her father is in Pentridge, where he is dying of injuries suffered in the bluestone quarry. Accidents were not uncommon – a source of anxiety for Mary Fortune. Both the dying man and George had been convicted six times. The story ends with the prisoner's wife commenting, dry-eyed: 'Surely any future must be better than the living death of a hopeless prisoner.'[26] 'Little Peepshow' appeared the day after George's conviction. Fortune wrote out her sufferings, caught in a twisted dance between the law and her son.

In January 1883 the next (delayed) instalment of her memoir covered the period when George was conceived, an agonising recollection. That month, the Royal Commission delivered its report on the Detective Branch. Shortly afterwards Francis Longmore lost his seat in a general election, though from an unrelated cause: he was an Irish nationalist sympathiser.

In her memoir 'Twenty-Six Years Ago', Fortune wrote:

What fate was to be for me and mine in this land of gold over which the shadows of night were slowly dropping? Could the question then been answered, would I have stopped and retraced my steps? Alas! It is impossible to say, for human nature is a strange thing and the unknown and untried has always attractions for the sanguine and young.[27]

Her fate had been adventure, a writing career and independence, but also grief: deaths, the failed marriage to Brett and the ongoing disaster of George. She continued the memoir, but its quality dipped. The penultimate episode ended abruptly, and was followed the next month by only a few thousand words. They were no conclusion, instead reading as if she was simply unable to progress further. Either something horrible was happening in her current life, she felt crushed by the weight of memory or she had been contacted by someone from the past unwilling to be her subject matter.

Also in 1883 Standish, the former police commissioner, died at the Melbourne Club, the causes including cirrhosis of the liver. He had lived to see the Longmore Royal Commission castigate the police he so proudly led. Its recommendations included that the Detective Branch be disbanded due to its rampant corruption. Secretan retired; he was just one of 300 to depart the force. O'Callaghan, despite having been suspended during the Royal Commission, was kept on, too valuable to lose. Duncan also remained. The Detective Branch was not reformed as suggested, although it lost some of its autonomy.

George Fortune had been sent to a country gaol in Maryborough, a town he had first visited as a babe in arms. By mid-October he was free and sensibly stayed outback. The main difficulty of avoiding Melbourne was finding employment. Ford had been released from gaol the same day – no good influence. For six months the pair avoided arrest until, in April 1884, they were both charged in Shepparton for being in a public place with intent to commit a felony.[28] This time George Fortune gave his name as George Millege; one of Ford's aliases was Thomas Millidge, the name of a real and charismatic young villain. They got six months' hard labour at Beechworth Gaol, about forty kilometres south of the New South Wales border.

From 1884 through to early 1885, Mary wrote for the firm Cameron & Laing a serialised novella, *Dan Lyons' Doom*. It was widely syndicated, followed by a run in the *Melbourne Journal*, which was edited by Cameron. The work was Fortune's longest fiction since *The Bushranger's Autobiography*, and it was a dark melodrama of murder and revenge. Fortune again featured goldfields content, colonial boyhood and the sandy caves near Kingower. New was the emphasis, in the authorial voice, on religious faith. Unlike Marcus Clarke, Fortune was conventionally religious, although she did not always express it. Now she commented on a bereaved boy:

but Daniel had no words to put his heart's cry for help into – do you think that Daniel's aspirations went not up to Him, whose ears are ever open to prayer, as strongly as though they had been shouted from a platform to a chorus of Hallelujahs from men and women who do not often enough recall that – 'BUT THOU, when thou prayest, enter into thy closet and SHUT THE DOOR?' Well, you see, that may be a matter of opinion, but *I* believe that such unspoken aspirations as Daniel's on that damp spot of grass go straighter to God who 'seeth [sic] in secret' than any irreverent shouting will ever do, no matter in what words of eloquence the unseemly noises may be made.[29]

In her journalism Fortune had decried evangelicals, but here she also expresses her habitual privacy. In 1885 it would be breached again, and she would need all the consolations of faith.

18
—

THE BANK ROBBERY

ON 3 JUNE 1885, FIVE MEN robbed the National Bank on the corner of Shelley Street and Simpson Road, Collingwood (now a coffee shop in Victoria Street, Richmond). As far as planning and execution went, the gang pulled off a major heist, a perfect crime. What happened afterwards, when egos met alcohol, proved another matter.

Police scrambled to solve the robbery. *The Weekly Times* reported the command: 'Arrest the thieves – Spare no effort.'[1] Various detectives assisted, with four dedicated to the case: Henry Cawsey, William Napier Considine, Peter Lovie and Michael Ward. All had reputations for efficiency without being tainted by the Royal Commission.

Two had investigated the Kelly gang. Considine had been partners with Ward after Glenrowan: prior to that Ward had been the only detective assigned to the Kellys, recruiting informers and spending time undercover, with his hair and beard grown as disguise. Historian David Dufty calls him the real hero of the Kelly outbreak.[2]

While police and press swarmed around the crime site, a key perpetrator sauntered by, attending to business as usual. William Parker was fifty-five and a 'marine store dealer', meaning he had a small rag and bone business – although technically he was an uncertified insolvent and his wife the proprietor. He wandered the streets, collecting goods for the couple's two store yards, one of which was in Simpson Road.

Marine stores often figure in court reportage as sites for stolen goods. If Parker was a fence – someone who knowingly bought and resold stolen goods – he would not have been unusual. He knew criminals, and as a man whose livelihood depended on observing the streets, evaluating opportunities, he realised the two-man bank had a weak point. In thieves' slang, Parker 'put up' the robbery: if he was not the organiser, he originated the idea.

Parker had observed how the bank secured its money. Cash was not kept in the safe, but taken morning and night between Simpson Road, a sub-branch and the main branch in Bridge Road. Parker passed the information to a good friend who had lately emerged from Pentridge.

The friend, an experienced thief, listened to Parker and then watched the bank himself, to verify and to formulate a plan. He also gathered a band of ex-felons, who noted that only the bank's ground floor was used, while the upper floor was seldom if ever entered. They watched Mrs Robey, the charwoman, collect the keys from a hotel nearby and return them after work. Then either the manager, James Bywater Humphries, or his assistant, Alfred Nairn Bradshaw, a teller and accountant, would get the keys and open the bank. The gang planned to waylay them in the street – until realising that Humphries carried a revolver, along with a sword concealed in his walking stick. They revised their plan.

In the early hours of 3 June the gang met, all wearing two sets of clothes and a cap. The top layers would be discarded after the robbery to thwart identification. They drew straws as to their roles. Three would enter the bank and one would take delivery of a horse and cart, the getaway vehicle. The owner would be paid £2 if they failed and £20 if they succeeded. At 4 a.m. they tried the outside door with a skeleton key but found an impenetrable Chubb lock inside. Instead they broke in via an upstairs window and hid on the top floor, chewing and spitting tobacco to pass the time. Mrs Robey came and went, oblivious to their presence. The man outside watched until they safely entered, then went to collect the cart and arrange a place to rendezvous after the heist. Returning, he waited nearby.

That morning, as usual, manager Humphreys entered the building, followed by Bradshaw. He felt a slight touch on his hat and turned to find three masked men, each carrying an iron bar and a revolver. In the tense, terse banter that followed, the robbers cited the Kelly gang – whether as a joke, inspiration or association depended on the reporting. That may explain why Ward and Considine were assigned to the case. The intruders relieved Humphreys of his revolver, his walking stick and the cash, then bound him and Bradshaw. A contemporary engraving shows the brutality of the hold-up, but Bradshaw would depose that being bound was the only violence, threats apart. He and Humphreys even negotiated that they be gagged with their own hand-kerchiefs rather than the gang's rags. That done, the robbers left the building by the back door with the extraordinary sum of £1125.

> The desperadoes had provided themselves with a fish-hawker's cart and horse, and the bag containing the booty was covered with sacks, and the lot got away bawling 'Fish ho! all alive ho! Rabbit ho!'

They had not gone far when they met Sergeant Devine, who was in charge of Collingwood Police Station.

> 'Hulloa!' said the sergeant; 'got to hard graft and honest living again?'
>
> 'Yes,' answered one, 'we've turned up the b___ game, and working honest now.'
>
> 'That's right,' returned Devine; 'stick to it.'[3]

They drove to Studley Park to divide up the booty – they must have laughed all the way. That done, they threw their guns into the Yarra.

Back at the bank, the two bound men were less helpless than resourceful. Though Bradshaw had nearly choked on his gag, he was able to dislodge it. He untied Humphrey's gag with his teeth, then shuffled to the door and unlocked it. A young man passing by untied him. News of the robbery quickly spread. Detectives sought the usual suspects and consulted their fizgigs. For four days no useful information emerged. Nobody was seen to splash out suspicious cash, and the fizgigs heard nothing.

Then came a discovery: some bank cash bags in Studley Park. Police summoned the black trackers, and while they searched, news arrived that a party of men had driven to the park in a cart. The trackers found their footsteps in soft soil, leading to a gully containing discarded clothing. Yet the detectives could discover nothing further.

Two narratives explain how the crucial breakthrough occurred, neither published for decades. The first involved luck, and the police instinct for the shady. On 6 June detectives Considine, Cawsey and Ward happened to be walking along Juliet Terrace (now Liverpool Street). It then comprised the lowest depths of Melbourne's red-light district, with Romeo Lane (now Crossley Street, home of Pellegrini's) allegedly for the male sex workers. The trio noticed suspicious behaviour from Madeline Sullivan – known to them both as a larrikiness and source of information. She combined prostitution with assault and petty robbery, although her prison photograph shows a mild-looking, dark-haired woman, under five feet tall. Sullivan opened her front door but on seeing the detectives quickly withdrew. That decided the detectives: if Madeline didn't want them to see her then they should find out why. They invited themselves in for a little chat.[4]

They sat in the kitchen while Madeline cooked what seemed to be a very large Irish stew for one person. Detective Cawsey sat near a closed door and when Madeline's back was turned, used his foot to turn the handle – but found the door locked. Madeline told him she had a lodger, who was in bed asleep ... at 3 p.m. Cawsey asked to see him and

Madeline refused. Only when the detectives threatened to break down the door did it open.

Inside they found the teenage Eva Bradley, with a man whom Mick Ward had previously arrested for jewel theft. More chat ensued, until the suspicious Cawsey grabbed the mattress and threw it back, revealing about 150 sovereigns. The man gave his name as Joseph Yates, an alias. He responded nonchalantly: 'If you'd copped me yesterday, you'd'a got more money.' Yates would turn Queen's evidence, agreeing to testify for the prosecution to gain a reduced sentence.

The second breakthrough narrative similarly emerged well after the event. A member of the gang was good-natured, and while drinking at a hotel post-heist, took pity on William (Gunny) Hughes. Gunny was a larrikin and professional prize-fighter but down on his luck. When given five sovereigns, Gunny correctly guessed their source. As a criminal and also a fizgig, he saw his chance, so went to see his handler, Detective Constable James Lomaine. Another source describes Lomaine as 'figuring largely' in the case, although he was not then mentioned in the press.[5]

Truth termed Gunny a 'cowardly, low scoundrel, and a bludger of the worst kind on women. He was living off the prostitution of a pretty dark-haired harlot.'[6] Gunny set up his 'Delilah' with a man described as 'one of the moving spirits' of the gang, to seduce and gain proof of the crime. She succeeded and Gunny earned himself £50.

Put together, these tales do not fit exactly, but they do suggest that when three detectives went for a walk down Melbourne's mean streets, luck had nothing to do with their visit to Madeline Sullivan. Police then arrested the other members of the gang. They raided a house off Spring Street, where Margaret Walsh (also known as Margaret Ryan and by other aliases) lived. At 1 a.m. on Sunday 7 June, the police entered and seized George Fortune. Five minutes later Edward Caney (born Henry Isaacs and also known as John Alcock), a dealer, knocked at the door and was arrested too. The police then proceeded to Sandridge (Port Melbourne) and at dawn they forced open a house owned by one Jackson (alias Parker, the 'putter-upper'). There they arrested Thomas, aka Tiger McMahon, described in the press as a 'half-caste' African, and Thomas Millidge (alias Buck Millidge and Charles Montgomery), said to be the man entrapped by Gunny Hughes. Both resisted arrest – they had possession of bank notes and crepe masks.

Now the police had the whole gang, all known larrikins: Fortune, Caney, Millidge and Yates the betrayer. Trial depositions reveal that Yates officially confessed on 8 June, something perhaps not unconnected with Detective Inspector Kennedy's threat of flogging. McMahon provided the cart, in which he collected rags and bones for Parker.

George Fortune had a criminal record, but not for major crime. He might have visited Melville's cave as a child, but he had never committed robbery under arms. That was the matter of *The Detective's Album*. Now his mother's writing would intersect with his true crime.

Another arrest made was that of Bernard Dunleavy, aka Delany, aged twenty-six, a case of mistaken identity for the man driving the cart. As Dunleavy sold rabbits, quite possibly the chant of 'RABBIT HO!' proved a factor. He refused to talk and remained in custody. Dunleavy had good reason for his silence. In 1877 he figured in a bizarre incident in which two saveloy vendors sped their carts down inner Melbourne lanes, pursuing welching larrikins. During the chase a pedestrian got a fractured skull, and the larrikins were blamed. Dunleavy was convicted of manslaughter. In 1885 he could prove an alibi: selling rabbits at Prahran market.

At the police court, a large crowd gathered to see the perpetrators of what the *Glen Innes Examiner* described as 'the neatest, and yet clumsiest bank robbery, that has yet taken place'. The reporter added: 'The driving off with the coin, as if it were bacon, is decidedly neat. Not so, however, the division and enjoyment of the spoil. Liquor and carousing spoiled the game.'[7]

The men were charged with vagrancy. More money had been found: £250 buried in pickle jars in Studley Park. An old adversary of George

Fortune's took part in the hearing, Deasey from Bylands, now a Melbourne sub-inspector of police. Also charged with vagrancy were three young women, either known larrikinesses or suspected sex workers. Eva Bradley had been found with the informer Yates, and Annie Murray had also been arrested at Madeline Sullivan's. Catherine Agar (alias Ryan and O'Neill), was a housemate of Murray's and arrested at Margaret Walsh's home with Fortune and Caney. The two older women, Sullivan and Walsh, were charged with keeping disorderly houses. Bail was refused for all.

The Mount Alexander Mail described the prisoners, who in court stood in a line, as 'a forbidding lot of holiday-clad larrikins and hoydens of the lowest class'.[8] The reference to good clothes indicates that they had asked friends and relatives to outfit them for the court appearance. Millidge was the most striking, determined, vigorous and muscular. McMahon's dark complexion was noted. Yates looked the most intelligent – *The Mount Alexander Mail* thought him a likely crime-planner for his 'less clever associates'. George Fortune seemed more respectable, although scowling, 'his snub nose and thick lips do not give his features an attractive appearance'. Caney fared worst in terms of physiognomy, with a low forehead and 'strong brutal lower jaw'.

'Putter-upper' Parker was charged the same day. A search of his yards did not reveal the stolen money, but merely stolen horse-harnesses. He was committed for trial on that offence, got bail and absconded.

Most of those charged had tragic life stories. Consider the women: Madeline Sullivan and Catherine Agar had both lost babies, and the latter had to identify her larrikin brother in Sydney after he died in a prize fight. She was unlucky to be arrested, having left Walsh's house for a jug of beer (illegal at that hour), only to find the police there on her return. Like Sullivan, she mixed sex work with robbery, but had a conviction for riotous behaviour.

Of the men, Thomas McMahon was born in Castlemaine in 1859, the son of a former American slave, Richard McMahon. His father had tangled with the law but managed to get well compensated for damages after a false arrest for selling sly grog saw the police dismantle his tent premises. He bought a hotel as a result and died before his son got into serious trouble. The teenage Thomas was convicted in 1876 of raping Kate O'Neal, his employer's child, aged nine. McMahon denied it, telling the court that James O'Neal had a heart that was 'a black blot'. He was sentenced to death, commuted due to his youth. Instead, he served ten years' hard labour in Pentridge, the first three years in irons. He was released early in March 1884 and went to work with his brother John, employed by Parker.[9]

The other men charged were typically thieves. Edward Caney (b. 1858) was the son of George Isaacs, who wrote the first novel published in South Australia, *The Queen of the South* (1858). Isaacs père had come from a wealthy London Jewish family but worked hard as a colonial writer with less luck than Mary Fortune. Caney ran wild in Melbourne, with a string of convictions from his mid-teens, mostly for petty theft. His first prison photograph shows a boy with a mischievous glint in his eye. He had been free since October 1884.[10]

Thomas Millidge (b. 1863), had been in trouble since the age of eleven. His first arrest made the papers, being described as 'more like a romance than a reality'. Four boys went on a crime spree, stealing anything they could, from a camp oven to hens. It sounds more like high spirits than serious crime.[11] The charges against young Millidge were dropped when he informed, but he became a rogue and vagabond. In 1882 he had briefly escaped from a road gang at Maryborough Gaol, receiving in 1883 two years for theft from a country railway station. He was an unruly prisoner, his misdemeanours filling the prison register. Millidge and George Fortune coincided at Maryborough – that both George and his accomplice Ford took aliases of Millidge/Milledge shows affinity and influence.[12]

None of the above had committed major property offences, unlike Yates, aka Alfred Henry Bisset Raingill. He had arrived in Melbourne as an unassisted immigrant from Liverpool, aged thirty, in March 1879. In court he denied any convictions prior to emigration.[13] He lied: in 1868 he had three convictions, including stealing a glazier's diamond. When released in 1870 he burgled again, resulting in a ten-year sentence. Raingill might have served further time had he not turned Queen's evidence, gaoling the rest of his gang. His informing was widely reported, which explains his emigration.[14]

Months after his arrival, Raingill was convicted of larceny: twelve months' hard labour. He would describe this crime during the 1885 trial as 'going into a house at Brighton while the people were out and taking some things' – which made the court laugh. His next conviction was five years for jewellery theft.[15] Several papers thought Raingill no henchman, with *The Weekly Times* declaring him 'the prime mover'.[16] Elsewhere Millidge was named as leader.

On 19 June the suspects appeared in court again. As the police were still collecting evidence, they applied for a further remand. During proceedings an argument occurred over whether some of the money recovered should be used to pay the defence, to which George Fortune declared: 'We shall not be defended at all unless the bench allows the money!' He also stated that no National Bank notes had been found, to which his lawyer quickly added, not in Fortune's possession.[17]

This appeal showed desperation. Not only had George been betrayed again, but the criminal justice system was treating them unfairly. His whole life had been like this – dragged from one place to another, leaving friends behind with every move, fending for himself on the streets and being pursued by police for every lapse.

McMahon was the most engaged of the accused with the trial and requested copies of the depositions (as did George Fortune). He protested about a report in *The Herald* that he had 'peached' (informed), but his complaint was shut down. The men were removed and the women tried. Sullivan, Walsh and Agar could not prove lawful means of support and were gaoled for six months. Annie Murray and Eva Bradley had a boyfriend and a brother respectively, who testified to supporting them lawfully. They were discharged. Walsh would unsuccessfully appeal, which enabled her lawyer to cross-examine Detective Lovie, who had pressured Walsh in gaol to inform. It would be claimed that the robbery was planned in her house. She may also have been a 'putter-upper': certainly, the preparation was far superior to any previous crime by the accused.

That week *The Herald* printed a phrenological article describing each accused in damning detail. Defence barrister Emerson raised objections to it in court because it 'put the prisoners down as the most criminal type'; as the paper was circulated among those most likely to be jurymen, it was prejudicial against his clients. The judge acknowledged his concern but had no control over the press. He did however warn the reporters present to note Emerson's objection.[18]

Phrenologist Joseph Fraser demeaned McMahon racially, stating he had the 'muggy face of the criminal of the hard type'. Fortune looked 'sly and trickish rather than of the brutal type', probably not the leader but an abetter, with manual skills such as picking locks. Had he 'turned', like Yates, he would have 'made use of his liberty so acquired to commit some new crime'. Millidge was the 'real criminal of this gang ... that will scruple at nothing and twist a neck as soon as not'. Alcock was little better: 'had Millidge struck Alcock would have followed suit. Fortune would have busied himself getting keys and emptying the safe.' Yates he saw as 'not at all a bad specimen of humanity' and the 'most likely to turn over a new leaf'. If Fraser was perceptive about Fortune and Millidge, then he could have not been more wrong about Yates.[19]

On 20 July the trial began in the Central Criminal Court with a crowded public gallery, including friends and family. Mary Fortune would have known the court from her research, but now she had a personal involvement. *The Herald* described the men in the dock: Fortune was 'haggard and careworn';[20] Millidge anxious; Caney 'smirked' in bravado and McMahon was impassive. Raingill was the 'star of the show'. While the others were charged with bank robbery and McMahon as an accessory, Raingill only faced the lesser offence of vagrancy. Although initially he turned his face away from the prisoners while giving evidence, as the trial progressed he became more confident, facing them and answering 'in a very lucid manner'.[21]

Raingill testified that he had met the robbers in Pentridge, where he had spoken to all of them except George Fortune. On his release, on 28 February 1885, he met Millidge, released a fortnight earlier, who took him to the lodgings he shared with Fortune above a cigar shop. Later, Raingill and Caney cohabited in a house with two young women, Harriet King and Elizabeth Bourke. These two, casual girlfriends – Bourke of Raingill and King of Caney – would be cited as defence witnesses but were reluctant to come forward. They risked being charged with vagrancy, although in court they were described as boot-machinists.

In the end they were compelled to appear for the prosecution but merely gave evidence that the accused consorted together. That was true: in March, Millidge, Caney and Fortune robbed the Vine Hotel in Collingwood, two men diverting the landlord with chat while a third, most likely Fortune, nipped upstairs with a skeleton key to steal jewellery and £20.[22]

Raingill testified that in April, Millidge told him he had 'been laid onto a good thing' by Parker, who would receive £50 for the information.[23] He also claimed he had not entered the bank and was merely the watchman and fetcher of the cart. Raingill's evidence was detailed, from the mechanics of the robbery to the division of the spoils. He minutely outlined the gang's disguises, including that Caney and Fortune darkened their moustaches with burnt cork, and details of where they had purchased their clothes. The clothier and his assistant both deposed; Fortune had been such a good customer that they had given him the cap he wore during the robbery. It all seemed conclusive, despite the defence arguing that nothing Raingill said could be trusted. Only prosecution witnesses appeared.

During the trial, McMahon took notes and even conducted some effective cross-examination.

MCMAHON: Were you ever Queen's evidence before?

RAINGILL: No.

MCMAHON: Didn't you tell these men that they were to do nothing until you put them on, and didn't you crack you were a big man and would put them on to the London way of thieving?

RAINGILL: I never was in London in my life.

MCMAHON: Ho, ho! And you never did ten years and never turned Queen's Evidence?[24]

Raingill lied under oath here, not unique in the trial.

The drama continued when a juryman fell ill and was unable to continue. Judge Charles Cope directed that the trial should proceed, and the jury found them guilty. Millidge, Fortune and Caney were convicted of robbery under arms, and sentenced to five years' gaol, while McMahon received one year. They were lucky in that the crime had previously been a capital offence; and that Cope stated he was biased against long sentences. He had previously convicted Fortune re Bylands, Caney for eighteen months for fencing, and Raingill for jewel robbery.

When asked if they had anything to say, McMahon declared that he had been unfairly tried and that his lawyer wouldn't let him give enough evidence to prove that he played no part in the robbery. Millidge said nothing, Caney requested leniency and Fortune handed up a letter to the judge. It would be published in newspapers around Australia:

Your Honor,

Let me tell you a little of my history, and hope that it will lighten the sentence you are about to inflict upon me. I had the misfortune to be left fatherless when but a child; my mother never married again, so I never had the chance of a father's counsel. I was brought up solely by my mother, whose only fault was to love me too well. When scarcely

19 years of age a temptation crossed me which I did not resist. I was arrested for receiving stolen money, and received a sentence of two years, which you yourself gave me. Your Honor, I was sent to mix with criminals of all classes, where the talk consists of little else but the best way to prey upon society. I ask, could it be expected that a lad who has mixed with hardened criminals will come from even as good as when sent to mix with them? No, your Honor, this has been the cause of my being here to-day. Some six months after I was released, becoming the dupe of an older criminal than myself, I was again arrested and convicted and sentenced to two years; was released on 20 November 1882. Since then I have been trying to lead an honest life and retrieve the past, and was doing well until I met Raingill, or 'Yates', who has led me to this crime. I resisted his urging for a long time. Eventually he said I was afraid; that did it. I had not the moral courage to say 'No' any longer. My mother is an old lady. Give me a chance to see her alive, and to be a help in her old age. Do not make my future too dark. I can write no more, and she is a widow; for her sake, if not for mine, be merciful to George Fortune.

If George was the sole author, then he was not the only compelling writer in the Fortune family. The letter focused attention upon Mary. Maurice Brodzky, a muckraking journalist and friend of Marcus Clarke's, ran the story in his *Table Talk*, most pruriently:

Social philosophers have a pet theory that the publication of the lives of notorious criminals tends to create successors in the line. It is however seldom that a parent errs in this respect and writes works of fiction which tend to foster crime, but it appears that the literary efforts of the mother of the young man Fortune one of the National Bank robbers induced him to start his criminal career. He is the son of a lady who wrote a series of 'Detective Stories' in a Melbourne publication [...] under the name of 'Waif Wander'.

It is a bitter reflection for this unhappy lady to think that some of the stories which she wrote in all innocence may have tended to mould the character of her child to such an extent as to render him a felon with a spirit as venturesome and daring as any of the criminal heroes which she pourtrayed.[25]

Brodzky did not name the *AJ*, against which he had a grudge: in 1879 they had pulled the plug on his autobiographical serialised novel *Ben-Israel*.

For Millidge, Fortune and Caney, the crime had been an escalation. That suggests it was a case of simple opportunity, presented by Parker, who was also responsible for McMahon's involvement. For the first time they received major press attention. This may have given them more status in gaol, but the crime dogged them for life: every time they reoffended it would be recalled.

The Mount Alexander Mail credited Fortune with the last words in the trial. As he left the dock, he turned and cried out: 'If any man says I gave any information in this case he lies.' Another source reported it was McMahon, which seems more likely given his earlier protest.[26]

Fortune had the slimmest criminal record and seems to have been a follower rather than a leader. Raingill mentions him incidentally:

Seems George hung around with a nasty crew … If George wasn't poverty-ridden, then it was most likely he just fell in with the wrong crowd and was easily led. I've seen that before. Young men trying to prove they are hard men to other hard men … It most likely went from playing tough to serving time and then just falling fully into the life of a crim.

George, like a significant proportion of prison inmates,[27] probably suffered from what since the 1980s has been termed antisocial personality disorder (ASPD). Now this diagnosis is often used as a justification for not attempting to rehabilitate inmates. Colonial authorities similarly thought that criminality was innate and incurable – and the public agreed, explaining the lack of outcry when ex-criminals were targeted by the police.

ASPD's symptoms include failure to conform with social norms, deceitfulness including the use of aliases, impulsivity and failure to plan, consistent irresponsibility, reckless disregard for the safety of one's self and others, irritability or aggressiveness and lack of remorse. Prisoners with this disorder also have trouble functioning outside the structured system of gaol. In fact, 'ASPD is the best at predicting recidivism'. Those afflicted can be 'intelligent and charming but exploit others for their own personal gain'.[28]

Care must be taken when applying a modern-day diagnosis to the behaviour of a criminal in the 1800s. Yet everything we know about George's crimes and prison experience fits closely with ASPD. Its 'single most common symptom among formerly incarcerated persons is the inability to fulfill promises'.[29] In his letter George said he wanted to reform for the sake of his mother – but heartbreakingly, he did not succeed.

In the aftermath, Detective Constable Lomaine, for whom Gunny Hughes worked, was promoted to sergeant. Neither were mentioned in the apportioning of the reward money, most of which went to Raingill. Harriet King and Elizabeth Bourke also put in a claim but got nothing.

The following year, William Parker returned from Sydney to his family, having grown a beard. He was arrested and sentenced for receiving. His involvement in the robbery could never be proved, as it was hearsay, based on Raingill quoting Millidge. Parker served a year in gaol, then returned to Sydney.

His significance as a major putter-up and fence in two states would not be revealed for decades:

His house was a meeting place where 'jobs' were put up by one burglar to another – where the plans were arranged and all preliminaries settled. Over all these meetings 'Old Bill' presided, and his venerable old head would shake as he would give a parting word of advice or warning to some of the 'boys'.[30]

Of the others, Eva Bradley and Annie Murray apparently went clean. Margaret Walsh's prison records end too: she or a namesake became the licensee of a Carlton hotel. Madeline Sullivan did more prison time for vagrancy, as did Catherine Agar – the latter dying at her sister's home 'after great suffering'.[31]

In late 1886, McMahon was charged with jewel robbery. He was arrested over the New South Wales border after a dramatic chase on horseback – had he had a better mount than the police, he would have escaped. Extradited to Melbourne, for the second time he met an accomplice who had turned Queen's evidence. The undefended McMahon, by now a skilled bush lawyer, cross-examined again. He disconcerted the witness into changing his evidence, which McMahon asked the judge to note. He was acquitted.[32]

Caney did not reoffend, surprising given his record. He and his wife Millie had a son in 1885. The baby died, and the couple had a daughter the next year. She survived, and after his release they had another son in 1892. Reverting to his birth name of Isaacs, he died in 1927, a law-abiding Brighton bootmaker.

Millidge was also released in 1890, despite assaulting a warder at Pentridge. He took up coining, then moved to Sydney in 1894. He and two accomplices broke into the Union Steamship Company's offices. They intended safecracking but fled, brandishing jemmies. When intercepted by police a violent fight ensued, with Millidge threatening to shoot a loaded revolver. Of the trio, one escaped, but Millidge and Thomas Carroll, also Victorian, were unfamiliar with the locale – they ran towards the Water Police Station and a handy arrest.

Millidge claimed to be Charles Montgomery, a New Zealander. When he and Carroll were sentenced to death for 'wounding with intent to murder' police, an outcry ensued. Twenty-five thousand people 'testified by their signatures', including Cardinal Moran.[33] Despite appeals, the sentence was upheld. The night before the execution at Darlinghurst Gaol a mass protest meeting and procession occurred because 'no life had been taken, and no life should be sacrificed in return'. The pair died on 3 April 1894, with their Victorian police records duly annotated. Carroll, who had previously received three years for housebreaking, suffered a bungled hanging by the usually efficient New South Wales executioner Nosey Bob Howard. He was slowly strangled, while Millidge's death was textbook.[34]

Of the two informers, Gunny Hughes died in 1889 after being severely beaten in the street. The press named him as a well-known fizgig and mentioned Simpson Road. The other informer, Yates, aka Raingill, was discharged after the trial and left for Sydney as George Shaw. He had already encountered Sydney's underworld, and within months he got three years for theft. Other charges followed, for false pretences, then for coining.

Maitland governor John McKenzie recalled that Shaw

> wrote a letter to the penal authorities asking that he might be removed from that prison to another, where his antecedents were unknown. He stated that it had become known among the prisoners that he was the man who turned Queen's evidence in the Collingwood bank robbery case ... he was perfectly sincere in the expression of his fears that his companions would do him an injury.[35]

Shaw did suffer for his informing. His New South Wales prison records list various injuries indicative of hard treatment, the worst being a bullet wound to the knee.

In July 1902, Shaw faced arrest by two Sydney policemen. He drew his gun, shooting Constable Maher in the shoulder and fatally wounding Constable Guilfoyle. Fleeing to Melbourne, he gained police attention but not arrest for sleeping rough in St Kilda. Only after he molested a little girl did Constable Richard Johnstone take to his bicycle to find him. When they met, the fugitive shot Johnstone, fatally. Shortly afterwards

Shaw avoided arrest by committing suicide with the same gun.

The dead man could not be identified immediately. His corpse was placed

> in a tank containing formalin, so that it can be preserved until it is identified. This was done this afternoon, after Dr Mollison had made a post-mortem examination, and extracted the bullet from the deceased's brain. There were no indications of insanity, but the man's skull was proved to be of unusual thickness. A cast of the murderer's head was taken by Mr. James Douglas.[36]

The Weekly Times reported that 'nearly 5000 people viewed the body'. Three people identified the corpse, significantly prison governor McKenzie, who knew Shaw was Raingill. He was driven to the morgue by Simpson Road detective Mick Ward, who was now a sub-inspector.[37]

Some ex-criminals were consulted. 'Such men had their own motives for wishing to keep out of a matter which could reflect upon them nothing but the revival of a past disgrace, and they could not be induced to look at the body except on the distinct undertaking that they would not be called as witnesses of identification.'[38] Such as Isaacs/Caney, a recent widower with two children?

In Raingill's page in the Victorian criminal register, a clipping from *The Argus* dated 27 October 1902 was pasted:

THE ST KILDA TRAGEDY

> The remains of George Shaw, the murderer of Constable Johnston, were interred on Saturday in the paupers' ground in the Melbourne General Cemetery. The service was read by Rev. A. Toomath, Church of England chaplain to the cemetery, there being neither mourner nor spectators present. Special arrangements have been made to ensure that no other bodies shall be placed in the same grave.[39]

Mary Fortune, true-crime consumer, surely followed the coverage. She might not have gone to the morgue, with which she was familiar, but the identification would have confirmed her low opinion of Raingill.[40] In her fiction she depicted many villains, some driven to crime by hard lives, others whose behaviour was inexplicable. Contemporary writers did not necessarily believe that criminals had devilish inspiration, but motive fascinated them and their readers.

The bank robbery as depicted in
The Illustrated Australian News, *10 June 1885.*

In 1885, Inspector Kennedy deposed that Raingill was a 'dangerous criminal'. Defence lawyer Townsend MacDermott described Raingill as 'a polluted, miserable, chronically inclined criminal', which proved prophetic.[41] If there is a sinners' continuum of those involved in the bank robbery, then Raingill was the worst, and the word evil is apt. Without his suicide he would have hanged, for actual murder, unlike Millidge. Raingill would have had no petitions for mercy and received no sympathy. Yet whether his offending was a matter of habit, worsened by gaol, or mental illness (as was suspected at the time), is a mystery that no crime writer could solve.

19

SAFECRACKING

By 1885, Mary Fortune had gained a major crime writing rival. Young lawyer Fergus Hume came to Melbourne from New Zealand, seeking fame as a playwright. Failing to break into the local scene, he thought to write a book as self-promotion. Hume visited a bookshop and asked what was selling. The bookseller's answer: Gaboriau, his novels now termed 'detective fiction'. But Fortune had got there first with *The Detective's Album*.

Hume wrote *The Mystery of a Hansom Cab*, citing his influences, including Gaboriau, Braddon and Clarke. Yet he could hardly have been unaware of W.W. They differed in that Hume did not privilege the police as heroes. He knew enough of the Melbourne Detective Office to depict its rivalries in his two detectives, Gorby and Kilsip. As he only arrived in Melbourne after the Longmore Commission, he missed the fizgig revelations. The novel's detection is based more on clues than on information received.

Hume self-published in late 1886, with a brilliant publicist, Frederick Trischler, who took stereotypes of the book to England the following year. There, Trischler made the novel an international bestseller, and in doing so helped to consolidate detective fiction into a profitable publishing category. Conan Doyle, who had been competing with Hume in England and received similar rejections for his first Sherlock Holmes story, 'A Study in Scarlet', famously hated the book. Yet he was a major beneficiary of Trischler's having proved that detection could sell.

What Mary Fortune thought of *The Mystery of a Hansom Cab* is unknown. She innovated in a different way. Her skilful novella 'Bridget's Locket' began serialisation within a month of the *Cab*'s first edition, in the Sydney-based *Australian Town and Country Journal*. In its pages Percy Brett occasionally appeared, even being photographed in his capacity as stock inspector.

'Bridget's Locket' was rural crime, now a major Australian publishing category, and had a woman as detective. The motif of female amateur sleuths was as old as Catherine Crowe's *Susan Hopley* (1842) and Wilkie Collins' Marion Halcombe in *The Woman in White* (1860). Here Fortune imported the motif to the colonies, as informed by her newspaper experience as Nemia, and her observation that opportunities for women were improving. Her detective is a woman supporting herself as a dressmaker. In 'Bridget's Locket' Fortune anticipated the New Women detective fiction of the 1890s.

Her depiction of the protagonist plays with physiognomy, giving her traits that in *The Detective's Album* were usually associated with a villainess. 'Jane Webster was no longer young. She was nearly 40. Her features were well formed, but there was a hard expression about the thin lips, which scarcely ever smiled.' Jane is difficult and moody, with reason: her husband left her for another woman. She is skilled at her job, her personal advertisement at a race meeting being a 'well-draped dress of fawn cashmere', the same colour Nemia bought in 1879, but in the cheaper cashmerette.[1]

On her voyage to Australia, Jane befriends Bridget McDermot, an Irishwoman joining her spouse. When Jane later sees Bridget's locket on another young wife, she investigates, harassing the husband as a suspected murderer. She triumphs: 'As if one *could* be too cruel to a wretch like him.'[2]

In her other writing, Mary continued to return often to the past, particularly to the goldrushes. During the last decades of the 1800s she produced some outstanding stories, among them 'The Phantom Hearse', about sly grogging in the Melbourne slums, depicted with what we might term dirty realism. Again she depicted spousal abuse unflinchingly.

If George liked thieving, then she liked writing. It is the privilege of a writer to imaginatively escape via their craft – and she earned her living from it too.

⁓

George Fortune was released on 1 March 1890 and left Melbourne to escape his notoriety. Rural life offered a new beginning. The relative anonymity, the help of kind-hearted locals or even police could provide ex-prisoners with redemption. Such was the message in Mary's fiction, and likely also her real-life suggestion to George. She would have continued to visit her only surviving child in prison, as she had as Nemia, and write to him too. If George had hopes for a better life outside, then she had too, although she knew that he was vulnerable, both from the police and from his criminal cronies.

If George had any chance to get his life in order, then moving out of Melbourne was probably the best idea. Newly released prisoners were listed in the *Police Gazette*, hence the need for aliases. George would change his name to avoid scrutiny, becoming Henry Lidney. He couldn't go alone – he feared that – but he only knew other ex-prisoners.

These precautions did not mean George escaped police attention. Within days he attracted suspicion: on 11 March at the Violet Town races, on 14 March at the Benalla races and on 18–19 March at the Albury races, all popular events attracting thieves.[3] George had simply taken the North Eastern train line (built by the narrators of *Navvies' Tales*) with three ex-Pentridge companions. They stopped off for the races, working as bookmakers, complete with totaliser. Had they gone north-west rather than north-east, George would have encountered a notable Castlemaine horse named Waif Wander. It was not Mary's only racing namesake: there was also a prize-winning greyhound in the late 1880s.

George Fortune as colourful racing identity? Hardly, although the quartet's activities led to complaints of swindling. Police investigation found no evidence of crime, although the four did not seem to have much idea how the totaliser worked. The suspicion was that it was being used as a 'blind'.

George's associates were all newly released. Thomas O'Brien's real name was Thomas Furlong, aka Badger, his ten convictions occupying two pages in the Victorian gaol books – rare even for hardened criminals. The photographs tell a sad tale: the first photo shows a fresh-faced youth, the second a hardened, unhappy man. William Henry's real name was John Watson, with violence against the police and housebreaking on his record. Henry Wilson was Thomas Griffiths, gaoled for offences ranging from petty theft to assault. As Fortune was the last to be freed, his release seems likely to have been the impetus to form a gang and go bush.

The night of 19 March they robbed Burrow's Mill in Albury, intending to steal the safe. They got disturbed: Constable Holder walked past the mill at 3 a.m. and noticed a light and a man standing outside. When questioned, the stranger claimed to be seeking shelter. The other three appeared and all fled, gaining only £3 in loose cash.

Next they moved to Benalla, striking at 4 a.m. on 21 March. This time they waited until the constable on night patrol had returned to barracks. They broke into four businesses on the main street. Muirhead's back door was opened with skeleton keys, with £9 stolen. Another business, Mrs Hilligan's, had nothing to steal. The real prize was the Broken River Hotel and its iron safe. The problem was how to move it to a secluded spot where it could be opened, and so they stole a wheelbarrow from the Benalla Hotel, just up the road.

Again they were witnessed, this time by a young lad, Edward Elliott, who worked at Carter's bakery, opposite the Broken River Hotel. Seeing a group of men laughing and joking with a wheelbarrow, he assumed they were merely transporting a drunken friend.[4] The four proceeded down the street to Thomas Knox the blacksmith's, where they stole tools including a pick and sledgehammer.

They then wheeled the safe about a quarter of a mile to the river-bank. There they broke it open using Knox's tools. Nobody bothered investigating the noise. This time they got £50 in cash, cheques, documents and £300 worth of jewellery.

George Fortune had used skeleton keys before, but a safe was a major escalation. The next detail of the story is the most surprising: they returned the tools to Knox's shop, now stained with green paint.[5] In 1894 George's former associate Millidge would use oil when sawing at a Sydney safe, to cut down on noise and heat. Here the oil in the paint made for a colourful substitute.

The crime raises questions. What kind of thieves risk returning their stolen tools? Were they Robin Hoods, or did they have sympathy for blacksmiths? Why were they laughing and joking in the main street? Like the bank robbery, the theft mingled sophistication and stupidity. Was there a desire to be caught because they were already so institutionalised that they were unable to function outside? Or were they just larrikins on an adventure?

As the first major burglary in Benalla, the crime was widely reported. Mary Fortune in Melbourne, reading the papers, would have recalled her earlier visit to the town. That had produced 'Fourteen Days on the Roads'. She had joked the title sounded like a prison sentence, and for her son Benalla meant exactly that.

At 6 a.m., a servant, Julia Lennox, found the hotel's doors open and its locks broken. She raised the alarm. Catching the culprits did not involve the usual suspects, nor a fizgig. Instead, police pieced together evidence through skilful detection worthy of Fortune's Mark Sinclair. First, black trackers were taken to the broken safe, but they were hindered by numerous other footprints around the area. The thieves appeared to have crossed the river at least two or three times. It seems they did so deliberately to create confusion. The police had used trackers in investigating the bank robbery, giving George Fortune some experience of how they worked. One black tracker at Benalla, named Prince, did follow the trail for some distance before losing it at a log fence.[6]

George Fortune had also learnt the hard way the need to skedaddle. By the time the alarm sounded, the four had got some distance from Benalla. All the police had at first was Elliott's description, and that the men with the wheelbarrow were not locals. All available police, with civilians assisting, scoured the countryside. Leading the hunt was Detective Sergeant Sainsbury. When the trail went cold, he kept going, heading south to Baddaginnie, then Violet Town and Euroa. He must have overtaken the thieves but missed them, because they had not kept to the road.[7] Somebody in the gang knew bushcraft, probably George.

Sainsbury criss-crossed the district via train and horse, without luck. The fugitives had caught the train northwards without being spotted. If they were heading for the New South Wales border, they apparently baulked at Albury, where they had drawn attention already. They bought tickets to head south at Chiltern, doubling back. If it was meant to confuse pursuit, it also had the danger of returning them to the scene of the crime and risking recognition.

That it also took them deep into Kelly country seems no coincidence; they seem almost like fanboy tourists. They also played fun-loving criminals, acquiring if not molls then two young female companions. The group of six was observed as the train passed through Glenrowan. At Winton, the men disembarked, watched by a suspicious station porter named Cooper.

Next morning at Winton, Sainsbury heard the news, and that his quarry had taken the Benalla Road south. They had even stopped at a public house for refreshment. Sainsbury took the midday train back to Violet Town, with Cooper accompanying him. In this game of trains and roads, cops and robbers, it so happened that Sainsbury missed the gang again, indeed passing on the railway culvert near where they sheltered.

At Violet Town, Sainsbury, Cooper and Mounted Constable Morna-ment took a buggy out into the country. Farmers informed them that four 'active-looking coves' had been seen heading back into town. The search party drove the buggy back to the bridge over Honeysuckle Creek, on the Sydney-road. Mornament went down to see if the quarry were sheltering under the bridge and saw two men run into the bush. He followed them down to the creek and came upon a camp with four men.

Sainsbury asked where they came from. George Fortune acted as spokesman. He lay on the grass during their conversation, in his last minutes of a brief freedom. George replied that they had tramped from Corowa, camping at Glenrowan and then Badaginnie. Significantly he could not recall the name of Glenrowan, but only that it was where the Kellys were shot. When Sainsbury persisted, George replied: 'I'll answer no more b— foolish questions.'

Sainsbury then informed the group they were suspected of the Benalla robbery and that he recognised one gang member from the Albury races.[8] Mornament started searching the men. George regain-ing some cheek, he asked Sainsbury for his authority: 'You might be spielers [gamblers or swindlers] as I read of a robbery having been committed up this way.'[9]

When Sainsbury showed his detective's card, George fell silent. Had he drawn his unloaded British Bulldog revolver (small, and designed to be carried in a pocket), the encounter could have become deadly. The search continued, with Henry getting mouthy. Mornament was ordered to handcuff him and when Henry resisted, Mornament knocked him down. Some accounts say two others tried to go to his aid, including Fortune. At this point Sainsbury drew his loaded revolver, formally arresting all four.

The search found about £40 in money and old coins, which Wal-lace of the Broken River Hotel could identify as his safe's contents. Also discovered were skeleton keys and a masterpiece for opening locks. The next day, a search party with black trackers returned and uncovered £100 worth of jewellery planted in the sand of the creek.

The prisoners were marched, handcuffed in pairs, to Violet Town lock-up, and then to Benalla. In custody, they were formally identified. George's bank robbery conviction proved a millstone: *The Argus* described him as that gang's leader.[10] It was not clear whether Fortune led or instigated the crime, but somebody knew about safecracking. On 3 April they were tried at Benalla Petty Sessions by the police magistrate Mr Dobbin.

Furlong, aka O'Brien, the tallest and most powerfully built, drew comment as a 'rough and uncultivated looking fellow, with all the features of an amateur fighting man'. The four, who whispered to each other in court, reserved their defence on the robbery charge. That meant they did not plead guilty or innocent, which allowed their lawyer more time to consider all the evidence against them and the legal issues involved. They were committed for trial in the criminal sittings of the Supreme Court, to be held in Benalla on 15 May. The lesser charge of rogues and vagrancy was then heard. Here the prisoners pleaded guilty and were sentenced to twelve months' hard labour. They were then removed to Beechworth Gaol.[11]

Sainsbury also pursued the two girls from the train, locating them in a Seymour hotel. As they had not accompanied the felons to Benalla and had no stolen property in their possession, they were not charged.[12]

At the second trial, some fifty police arrived in town to prove previous convictions. They included five detectives and Inspector Deasey, who had arrested George in 1879. Consequently, it was estimated the costs of the trial would amount to £200.[13] The presiding judge was Mr Justice Holroyd, with a jury of twelve.

All the prisoners pleaded not guilty to both charges:

1. Feloniously and burglariously entering the premises of
   Mr W.J.R. Wallace, with intent to commit a felony.

2. Receiving those goods, knowing them to have been stolen.

Fortune and Henry addressed the jury, repeatedly asserting their innocence – without effect. Edward Elliot could not with certainty identify the men with the wheelbarrow, but Constable Holder from the Albury robbery could. All four were found guilty on both counts. After the verdict, twenty-three convictions were read out against them: two for Fortune, five for O'Brien, six for Henry and ten for Wilson. It was a selective list.

They were sentenced the next day and the judge asked if they had anything to say. Fortune replied: 'If your Honor has not the power to give me a very long sentence, I would like you to make it as short as you can, however severe it may be, not that I dread severity, but because as I am yet capable of rising to something better, than this, I will have a chance to reform.'

Given Fortune had emerged from a five-year sentence only to re-offend seriously almost immediately, he was optimistic in the extreme.

O'Brien and Wilson did not reply. Henry asked Holroyd to bear in mind that he would receive no indulgence whatever in gaol and expressed hope that whatever sentence might be inflicted upon him would be a short one.[14]

The judge replied at length:

Prisoners at the bar, you have been found guilty of burglary. You Henry Lidney [George Fortune], have been twice previously convicted, the last time in 1885, for a very serious offence – robbery in company – and you received 6 years imprisonment with hard labor. In fact you had not been very long out of gaol before this your latest offence, was committed.

[...] Now, it is quite clear to me that the four of you are the most dangerous kind of men. If I thought there was a chance of any of you reforming – of your turning around and leading an honest life – I should not be disposed to pass a long sentence upon you. As it is, I see no hope of you reforming if I passed short sentences upon you. With regard to you Henry and you, Wilson, it is quite clear to me that you are hardened criminals. I think there is a little more chance for you O'Brien. And you, Lidney, are the most intelligent of them all. But I certainly cannot forget that it was you who carried the revolver with the cartridges.

Lidney – Yes, but there was nothing in it, your Honor.

His Honor, continuing – I cannot forget to note the last offence you committed. Your record is the lightest of the lot, but as you are the most intelligent of the four, you ought have known the advantages to be derived by leading a better life. I cannot allow you to prey any longer upon society, and must therefore pass long sentences upon each and all of you. I might not, perhaps, be so severe upon you only for the fact that prisoners of your kind have to work hard in gaol, and as I know you will learn how to work whilst there, and be plainly fed and have a clean place to live in, I can understand that the term I intend to give you in prison for the offence you have committed will keep you in check – for a long time to come at least. The sentence of the court is this: that you be imprisoned in Her Majesty's gaol at Beechworth, or any other gaol that the Governor may appoint, for a period of 10 years, accompanied by hard labor, and that the first three days of the second and subsequent years of your detention be passed in solitary confinement.[15]

The judge seems not to have been fully informed of all of O'Brien's crimes, including four years for assault and robbery, hardly a slight offence. Had he made a deal, telling the police where the jewellery was hidden? The others got ten years; he got seven.

The severity of the sentences caused a sensation. Wilson smiled in bravado, while Henry was trembling and near tears. He gazed at Wallace, shaking his head, apparently uttering a threat. O'Brien barely reacted, his eyelids drooping. And as for George Fortune, he looked 'thought-fully and regretfully about him … Those watching him closely had the impression that he was "deeply affected by the weight and severity of the sentence passed on him"'[16].

Was his mother in the court watching? Did she get to speak to him in gaol or while he was awaiting trial, or did she just read about it in the newspapers? We will never know what contact she had, but we do know George had disappointed his mother again. Was the judge right in that there was no hope of him reforming? He just couldn't seem to resist the temptation of bad company and adventure. One consolation: this time none of the gang had informed on him.

That same day in court, a man got ten years for stabbing his wife.

In an 1894 *The Detective's Album,* Mary put words into a fictional criminal's mouth: 'all I hope is that my mother will forgive me when she knows I am dying in gaol.'[17]

During his sentence, Mary Fortune wrote a number of stories about reformation for ex-lags. Her characters were either irredeemable and dangerous or weak and easily led. In 'Regan's Doom', a young man is released from prison: 'Of a merry and rollicking temperament, Bill Condy's choice of companions had been unfortunate; and it is so easy to get lower in the scale of sin.'[18] Pentridge did not improve him: 'If I had been bad before, I was a devil when I left Pentridge.'[19]

Condy recognises his weakness and leaves Melbourne:

'I'm going out of town as fast as ever I can sir!' The young man said, eagerly; 'for if I meet one of the old set it is all UP with me. I never could say no, sir; but I've got a chance now, and I mean to run for it!'[20]

Conversely, Mary also wrote of a mother's bad influence. In 'Mag Braban's Share', Edward Braban emerges from two years in Pentridge to find his drunken, slatternly Irish mother waiting.

'Night an' day, when he was a little boy, I slaved for him to send him to school clean and dacent. When his villain of a father deserted me, an' there wasn't a bite nor the price of a bite in the house, I went down on my knees scrubbin' and clainin', till he was educated like a gentleman [...]'

She wants to take her son home, but he knows her criminal connections, 'old dangerous' pals of them both, 'watching and waiting for you, to help in a lay they are on'. However, Mag proves not to be Edward's mother. Although she follows him to the country, the haven of W.W.'s fictional reform fantasies, it is fatal for her but not him.[21]

Even if George Fortune had managed to go straight, prison would still have offered a lure later in the decade, with guaranteed food and shelter. In the early 1890s Marvellous Melbourne's boom went bust. Property values had been grossly inflated, and lax banking regulations permitted wild speculation. A sub-prime crisis resulted and sent the colony into severe depression.

Among the many businesses seriously affected or closed were publisher George Robertson and Cole's Book Arcade. Writers and journalists took themselves to the wild, bleak bohemia of England. Mary Fortune stayed put. She had little choice with George in prison. She still had freelance work, from *The Herald*, *The Advocate* and above all the *AJ*, which had a big enough readership across Australasia to survive – just.

Ronald Campbell wrote:

The flow of publications dried up. *The Sporting Weekly* gradually faded. The staff dwindled. The demand for Adam Lindsay Gordon's poems ceased, but the *Australian Journal* staggered on, a thing of shreds and patches, put together with scissors and paste. The serials, mostly of the *Family Herald* variety, were bought for a song, if not quietly filched under the elastic copyright laws of the period. The early pages were lightened by a few woodcuts or steel engravings, but these too, disappeared, leaving the pages of a uniform dullness.

Fortune, he opined, was the only paid staff member during that time, keeping *The Detective's Album* 'going through thick and thin.'. Although economic recovery began in 1894, it was slow.

In 1898 the 'Personal' column in *Table Talk* devoted a paragraph to Mary 'Ffortune', a curious spelling that appears only twice. It could have been intended to distance her from George – but editor Brodzsky knew the connection. She was described as:

M.H. Ffortune, the best detective story writer in Australia, is little known. Regularly every month she produces a hair-raiser of this description for an Australian publisher. She is probably the only truly Bohemian lady writer who has ever earned a living by her pen in Australia. But she is very old now and lives from hand to mouth.[22]

By this time Fortune had been writing crime stories for over thirty years. She was now sixty-six, and despite the ravages of alcoholism, she retained her vigour and story-telling skills. In 'Grey's Gold', published that year, she rehashed the details of the Benalla heist, complete with the safe in the wheelbarrow (although not the green paint).

George Fortune was released from prison again on 8 April 1899, aged forty-three. This time he attempted a significant break from his old life. He crossed Bass Strait to Tasmania, likely with money provided by the Discharged Prisoners Aid Society. He had a new identity: Thomas Harding. But he remained under scrutiny: the Victorian police telegraphed their Tasmanian counterparts about his arrival.

20

—

THE RECIDIVIST

GEORGE FORTUNE HAD NEVER LIKED BOATS - neither from Christmas Day 1868 with his mother, nor the *Sir Harry Smith*. Bass Strait might be a rough trip, but at the end was a new start in a new colony. He looked forward to that. On the other side of the water his past would be left behind. No Victorian police officers hounding him or setting him up. He could be a new man, keeping his promise to his mother. Yet he knew his travelling companion would make that almost impossible. But better to have company than to travel alone, with his demons and worries. People didn't take kindly to released prisoners, and the years of privation in Pentridge had taken a toll. He was no longer a trusting, chubby-faced young man. His face was now thin, expressive of mistrust and a simmering anger.

George Fortune's criminal career was all about thieving for company – he seldom acted alone. Also on the steamship *Coogee* was another Pentridge recidivist. William Freeman had eight convictions for violence and theft, and even more aliases than Fortune. He travelled as 'Joseph Walters'. Freeman was only ever known as Joseph Walters while in Tasmania. George Fortune travelled as Thomas Harding and assumed a hybrid identity in the newspaper reports and in gaol – sometimes Thomas Harding, sometimes George Harding and occasionally George Fortune.

The pair arrived in Launceston on 12 April 1899. Five nights later, police pursued Walters onto the Victoria Bridge, where he threw stolen jewellery and skeleton keys into the Tamar River. When escorted back to his lodgings, he loudly warned the sleeping George of the arrest. The police could only arrest the pair on suspicion of burglary, as dragging the river proved fruitless. The charge became idle and disorderly. The two made headlines in the Launceston *Daily Telegraph*:[1]

SUSPECTED PERSONS.

TWO NOTORIOUS VICTORIAN CRIMINALS

George's guilt was by association, as Walters' keys were the sole evidence – at most, of intent to break and enter. The newspaper also reported that robberies ceased after their arrest. They pleaded guilty, receiving six months' gaol. In his first prison photograph in Tasmania, George was unshaven, his hair a little unruly. His jacket was threadbare, and he wore a pinstriped shirt and a cravat. He had shaved his beard off (as disguise?) but retained a moustache. He turned his piercing gaze upon the camera, frowning. Tasmania had not been the new start as hoped, only more worry for his mother. It was barely a month since he had been released from Pentridge.

Walters and George went to Hobart Gaol, a spartan, run down complex subject to overcrowding. While not as infamous as Port Arthur, it was similarly a monument to cruel convictism. The penitentiary was intended to be as 'unpleasant as possible', with hard work and much religion. Consider these edicts on solitary confinement:

> placed in this monotonous position, and reduced to the lowest authorised scale of prison diet, the criminal is thrown up on thoughts of the past and the penalty he is paying for his crime, and may therefore be expected (especially if religious influences are brought to bear upon him) to realise past errors and enter upon good resolutions of the future.[2]

Hobart Gaol kept detailed records, such as that George had a tattoo with the initials S.G.B. Also noted was what prisoners ate every day, information of some significance. The gatekeeper's record book notes the prison's rhythm, arrivals and departures, with times: warders, the doctor, visitors and the convict gangs labouring outside the gaol.

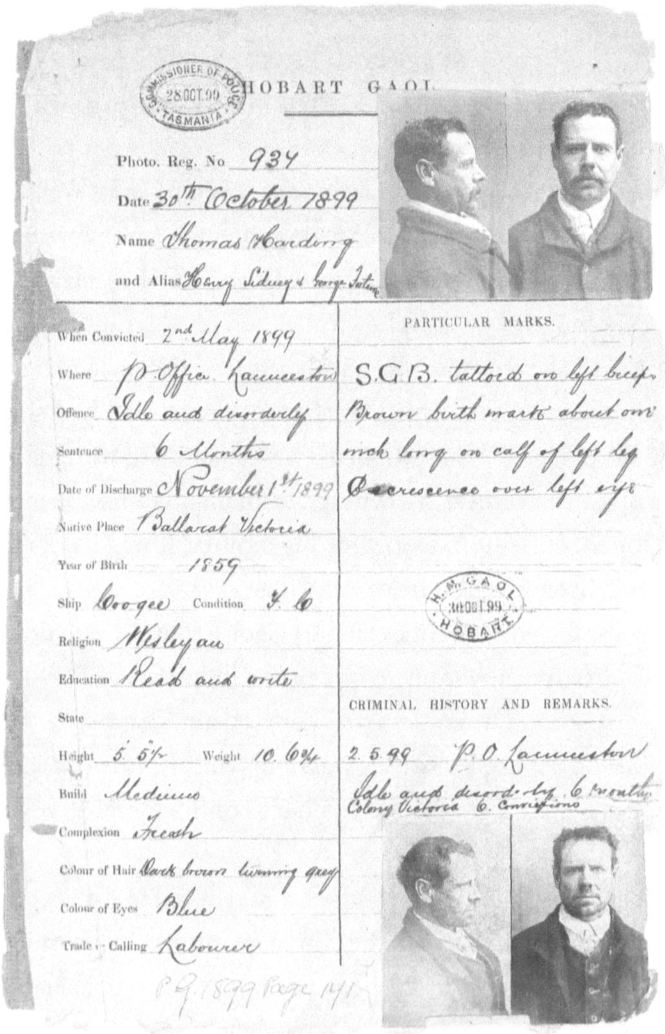

George Fortune's criminal record from the Tasmanian Archives.

On 15 May Walters appeared in the work ledger as 'finishing boots' (the Victorian Penal Register listed him as a bootmaker). George, who appeared in both Victorian and Tasmanian Registers as a labourer, was likely assigned to one of the gangs, for the Botanic Gardens, the Stone Quarry, Government House, the Domain and PW (Public Works).

At Hobart a sliding scale applied: nourishment was used in punishment. Prisoners undergoing hard labour received Diet 1, rations 'at the minimum really adequate, and no more, to empower the prisoner to complete his task, for the non-completion of which in due time the scale of diet should be reduced'. Prisoners on remand or in gaol for less than three weeks got Diet 2, much less.[3] The inmate labour generated income: small sentences meant less money, hence reduced rations.

Diet 1 comprised:

1½ pounds coarse bread, 2/5 ounces barley, 4 ozs green vegetable, ¾ pound meat uncooked with bone, 2 ozs oatmeal, ¾ pound potatoes, 1/50th oz of pepper, ½ oz salt, 5/16th of soap, 2 ozs sugar and 3/16th ozs tea, 1/200th ozs allspice and 1/400th ozs cloves. Diet 2 had ½ lb meat, ½ lb potatoes.[4]

It was a dull, hard existence, but not much different from the Victorian gaols. On 1 November George and Walters were released, to celebrate the new century as free men. It did not last long. In February they were caught stealing £3 10s. from the Shipwrights' Arms Hotel at Battery Point.

Patrol Constable Hicks encountered the pair at 2 a.m., and, suspicious, followed – only to lose sight of them at the Shipwrights' Arms. Suspecting they had broken in, he roused Constable Longman, who lived nearby. Returning to the hotel, the constables woke the licensee, David Parker, and his wife. Walters fled out the back door, pursued by Parker and the police. In the meantime, Parker's son David Jr heard his mother scream and met George rushing out of the bar parlour. The two scuffled, with Parker Jr holding the intruder down until his father returned. The Parkers tied up the hapless George with rope.

The object had been to crack the hotel's safe, but when unsuccessful the pair robbed the till. George told police he had been 'fairly caught'. The two had removed their boots to creep around the hotel – they asked for them back, a wish granted by police.[5]

In Hobart Gaol, the two were assigned Diet 2, remand rations. They pleaded guilty and on 27 February received three years for burglary. The day after the sentencing, George returned to Diet 1. He was assigned to plaiting – making cordage from dry fibre, then later mats.

In late June, George became a wardsman, reserved only for the most trustworthy. It required less physical work and another diet: no. 7, with more bread, plus milk, butter, rice and extra sugar. It excluded meat, vegetables, oatmeal and potatoes. While undoubtedly fattening, the health benefits were dubious.

George began to appear regularly in the prison's medical book from 1902. While this register does not describe symptoms or diagnosis, it does note treatments and whether the prisoner was fit for work (they nearly always were). From the records, the medical regime seems slight at best and neglectful at worst, with doctors often not visiting for days. When they did, the gatekeeper's book shows scant consultation time. George's first prescription was for bismuth, an antibacterial for stomach and gut disorders, but also used for syphilis. Later he received tussis, essentially cough mixture, with or without added opium.

George now applied for and was granted seven months' remission for good behaviour – suggesting a model prisoner. He and Walters were released in late June 1902. The surveillance continued, as they travelled Tasmania with their swags. Newspapers and the *Police Gazette* tracked their progress, making it harder for them to survive legally. Yet the pair managed to stay out of gaol for nearly a year.

On 24 April 1903 a warrant was issued, the charge being burglary at Hobart's Royal Exchange Hotel. The two were arrested in central

Tasmania in early May, in company with Alfred 'Nobby' Edwards and Joseph Cawthray or Cawthrey, both known larrikins. Although George and Walters appeared in Hobart's Police Court on 11 May, the charge was withdrawn.[6] For the first time George Fortune's stint in gaol was just a short stay in the police cells. Edwards, charged with being 'unlawfully on premises', also seems to have had his charge withdrawn.

Such was not the case for Cawthray (b. 1878), a fellow inmate of Hobart Gaol. This young man, a 'rowdy', had a father, also Joseph, with form for drunken violence. His mother, Mary Cawthray, successfully divorced her husband for cruelty in 1901, her physical abuse being detailed in court. Mrs Cawthray's barrister described it as the 'worst case of cruelty by a husband toward a wife that it had ever been his lot to have anything to do with'.[7]

Joseph Jr already had seventeen convictions. The bench noted that, for a young man, he had one of the worst, if not the worst, record in Tasmania. The charges included stabbing, six months for punching a policeman, and another four for resisting arrest.[8] He was bad company, but that was fine with George. On Cawthray's release he rejoined Walters and George, together with another old associate, Charles Russell. Cawthray's police assault had occurred when Russell was arrested for stealing a coat.

When Detective Sergeant Franklin investigated a burglary at New Norfolk on 31 July, he found the quartet at nearby Dromedary four days later. He recognised them, having mugshots of George and Walters. The men were living in a small hut, apparently scrub-cutting, and when Franklin arrived, he found George making damper.

On 10 August, Franklin met the four again at a Hobart hotel, and this time he arrested them. Once more George and Walters were the usual suspects, for what was described as 'A Burglary Epidemic'.[9] The police lacked evidence, so remanded the men repeatedly. On their first court appearance, the charges were being idle and disorderly, frequenting a public place with intent to commit a felony, and robbing a safe at the Wheatsheaf Hotel on 10 August. On their second appearance nine days later, they were also charged with the burglary at New Norfolk: entering Julian Brown's store and stealing food and cash. On 27 August they appeared again, pleading not guilty to being idle and disorderly.

Found on Walters was a New Zealand banknote, whose serial number had been recorded by Brown's manager. That meant Walters could be charged with receiving, and at the end of September he was sentenced to seven years' gaol. No one had witnessed police find the note, suggesting it may have been planted on him.

The others appearing on 27 August fared differently, thanks to Police Court Magistrate Bernard Shaw. He ordered their discharge:

> The whole of the defendants had been found in possession of money in a hotel, but not a word of evidence was produced to suggest that they had obtained that money dishonestly. [...] Of course, it was known that the defendants were bad characters, and were suspected of all sorts of depredations, but a man could not be convicted on suspicion alone, and as far as the charge of being idle and disorderly persons was concerned the case would be dismissed against them.[10]

A judge who examined the evidence must have been a surprise to George. Otherwise the case demonstrated the problems faced by ex-convicts. The four were undoubtably trouble, but every time a crime was committed the police arrested them, with or without evidence.

With Walters back inside, George and Cawthray kept company, travelling to Zeehan on Tasmania's west coast. In October they were charged with stealing a safe from Dundas railway station. That charge withdrawn, they faced the lesser charge of being 'suspected persons', with money for which they could not account.

Certainly the accused had been penniless before the robbery, and when questioned by Sub-Inspector Anderson they were impudent. Anderson testified to George's reaction: George said Anderson had a

'— cheek', even threatening to 'put a nail in his coffin'. This time Magistrate L.E. Chambers noted their prison records. He sentenced them to six months' gaol, stating: 'It was the duty of the bench to protect the public against men of the description of [the] accused. They could obtain employment if they chose, and there was no doubt they were in the district for no good.'[11]

George returned to Hobart Gaol. For the first time his name appeared in the book of requests, asking permission to write letters. It meant one a month only, but he must have written to his mother. Ominously, his name reappeared in the medical register regularly.

At the end of the six months, in April 1904, George and Cawthray walked free. Three months later came another burglary charge, this time for jewellery and goods valued at £40 taken from the Montpelier Retreat Hotel. Licensee Thomas Enright had retired to bed on the wet and stormy night of 15 July. In the early hours he awoke to hear keys rattling and found an intruder in his room. Enright followed the man out and later claimed to have seen him clearly by streetlight, although he could not testify if the thief had a beard or not.[12] Enright also saw another, unidentifiable, man on the doorstep. Earlier that night, partygoer Elizabeth Petitt had noticed three men under the hotel bar's window. She could only describe the clothes of one.[13]

Constable Longman of the Shipwright's Arms robbery was summoned, and immediately suspected George and Cawthray. They happened to be living nearby with Cawthray's grandmother Elizabeth – being 'very close companions' who patronised the Tasmanian Coffee Palace, a temperance hotel.[14] After searching the streets, Longman staked out Mrs Cawthray's house and saw George return near dawn. Later that day Cawthray and George ordered new suits from a local tailor, paying the deposit of £1. Shortly afterwards police arrested the pair, along with Cawthray's associate Nobby Edwards, as the 'third' man seen by Petitt.

The police lacked evidence, no stolen goods having been found. They manipulated the line-up to get a positive identification from the witnesses, who were shown photographs of the accused. It was witness tampering, trying to influence their memory, but at the time the practice was police business as usual. Now it is known as the displacement effect (the second memory displaces the original) and is illegal. As Enright and Petitt had described men dressed for bad weather, George and Cawthrey were given hats and coats to wear in the line-up. Enright identified George, but Petitt could only recognise Cawthray's clothes – a damp hat and mackintosh fetched from his grandmother's. Police had pointed out George and Cawthray as 'notorious characters' to all of the other witnesses called in evidence, even prior to the crime. Christina Davies was married to a policeman and testified she told her husband every time she saw the pair.

The trial revealed that George had now adopted new aliases – John Ash and Atkinson, the name of his maternal grandmother – understandably, given the endless police scrutiny. He pleaded not guilty, which might have been true. In most of his Tasmanian trials the offence with which he was first charged would be unproven, with an eventual conviction for a lesser charge. Of the two others arrested, Edwards was never charged, and although Cawthray was charged, the case did not proceed against him.

The case drew wide coverage, even interstate. A reporter noted that George looked a 'respectable' man in his thirties, although he was actually forty-eight. His years inside had protected his skin.[15] More significantly, one report suggested the evidence was so flimsy that the defence lawyer attempted to get it thrown out of court prior to the trial. The full transcript shows that was hardly surprising. Enright's evidence was contradictory, cross-examination highlighting he could not see the intruder well. Yet he never wavered, suggesting that the police had coached him. Had Enright shown the slightest doubt, George might have walked free.

At the trial's end, George was asked if he had anything to say, as was customary. His reply was unusually angry and articulate. The

Tasmanian News reported his speech in detail, suggesting the reporter felt some sympathy.

'I am an innocent man,' George said, 'found guilty on the unsupported testimony of one man, influenced by the police. I only wish the penalty was death, so that I might be done with it all.'

George's counsel sought to interject, but George said: 'Mr Kennedy, you will oblige me by not speaking?'

He and Mr Justice McIntyre sparred:

HIS HONOUR: 'You say you stand on that dock an innocent man [...] convicted through a witness being wrongfully influenced by the police. I don't believe that for one moment, and I am sure that not one of the jury believe it. I have no doubt whatever that the jury gave your case their most careful and earnest consideration. I don't think that anyone who heard the whole of the evidence would object to that verdict. The crime of burglary, of which you have been convicted, is a most serious one, and often leads to violence on the part of the criminal in attempting to escape, and, therefore is always accompanied, when a conviction follows, by a severe sentence. This is by no means your first conviction. I have your record in my hand, and it is a very bad one.'

THE PRISONER: 'Have you any proof of these convictions?'

HIS HONOUR: 'I have your photograph.'

THE PRISONER: 'A photograph taken in 1879! – how can you tell it is mine. I say it is not, and it has not been proved to be mine.'

HIS HONOUR: 'I am going to take it as proof, and am prepared to accept the record, for there is not only the photograph, but there is your name – Thomas Harding.'

PRISONER: 'It is not evidence unless it has been proved. I am not the man.'

HIS HONOUR: 'There are several convictions against you – mostly in other states, but one in Tasmania. They are as follows – Two years, two years, twelve months, ten years, six months, three years and six months – nine convictions in all. The sentence on this occasion must be an exemplary one. It is that you be imprisoned for the period of ten years.'

PRISONER: 'It is a vindictive sentence.'

HIS HONOUR: 'It is not a vindictive sentence; but is in keeping with the crime and the records of your past life.'[16]

George would have protested more, but McIntyre ordered his removal. His mother's *Detective's Album* was based on the mug shots of criminals, and here a prison photograph of George sealed his fate, a bitter irony.

At Hobart Gaol yet again, George worked, boot-making. In the book of requests he formally asked to be recorded as a Wesleyan, suggesting he had taken the pledge and was now teetotal. He also requested writing paper again. His name appeared sometimes as George and sometimes as Thomas Harding, a continuing confusion.

His medical condition continued to deteriorate. The table below shows that at one stage he was prescribed a bed, something rarely ordered for prisoners unless they were acutely sick. Yet he was kept boot-making, with the exception of Sundays and the Christmas period. Doctors rarely found a prisoner unfit for work.

DATE	NAME	TREATMENT
18.[?].1904 On Remand	Thomas Harding	Seen
4.8.1904 On remand	Thomas Harding	Mist of Pro Gou Mist of Expect check

28.9.1904	Thomas Harding	Certified healthy
29.9.1904	Thomas Harding	Mist of Bismuth
4.11.1904	Thomas Harding	Tea instead of gruel
8.11.1904	Thomas Harding	To have a bed

George's good behaviour meant he became a wardsman again, briefly. In June 1905 he was tried, together with another prisoner. Victor Masuglia was also a former Victorian felon, having served seven years for burglary and receiving. Their charge was attempted escape, to which both pleaded not guilty.

In-gaol trials were transcribed but recorded almost exclusively the gaolers' testimonies. It seems George and Masuglia could cross-examine, but only fragments of George's words survive. Either through a gaoler's neglect, a faulty lock or George picking it, the pair got out of their cells. Warder James Wilson testified:

At about 5 minutes past 6 when I saw Masuglia and Harding the accused standing in front of Masuglia's cell – I drew my revolver and pointing it at them told them to stand or I would shoot. I then rang the electric bell – Masuglia went into H Division – I followed him – it was then I touched the electric bell – and brought him back

I and Masuglia went to the gaol front – I did not find Harding where I left him. I found him afterwards standing in front of his own cell in No. 4 Yard – Warders Purkiss and Filby came over then and the prisoners were again locked up in their own cells

Harding was strip searched but had enough time to dispose of anything like skeleton keys. While not exactly threatening the warder, he did say: 'you had better get us to go back into our cells & say nothing about it – if you don't it may be all the worse for you.' Cheeky as ever, he commented: 'if they have defective locks they must expect a man to get out.'

A Tasmanian solitary confinement cell.

For his prank George suffered a sentence harsh for a man in poor health: a further twelve months, six of them spent in irons, and a fortnight in solitary confinement. At Hobart the solitary cells were underground, with thick stone walls. They were cold year-round, but especially punitive during a Tasmanian winter. By 1900 prisoners were not supposed to endure solitary for more than three days at a time. The authorities compromised, splitting up the sentence, with one day between bouts. The diet for solitary confinement was only bread and water. Diet 2 applied during the six months of wearing irons.

Subsequently George's visits to the doctor become more frequent. On 15 December 1905 there was a request for him to be removed from work. No decision was recorded, and the workbook showed him making or cleaning shoes. Months later urine samples were sent to Hobart hospital for testing, revealing protein, a sign of renal failure. The hospital's Dr Edward Roberts examined George on 7 April 1906 and diagnosed Bright's disease.[17] From 12 May to 10 June 1906, the records note him as ill, and Roberts ordered his removal to the gaol hospital on 11 June. Finally he was exempt from prison work.

Bright's disease, now known as chronic nephritis, was recognised and treated in the nineteenth century. It had at least one famous contemporary victim, US president Chester A. Arthur, who died in 1886. The cause of Arthur's case is unknown, as is that of George's. With both men a post-streptococcal infection can be posited – and Hobart Gaol was hardly pristine. But Dr T. Grainger Stewart, a contemporary expert, also noted that '[e]xposure to cold and damp or to sudden changes of temperature [was] a fruitful cause, not only of the initiation, but of the prolongation, of kidney disease'.[18]

That suggests the crucial factor for George was the inhumane conditions in the solitary cells. Stewart again: '[all] will agree that patients suffering from Bright's disease should avoid cold, and especially variable climates.'[19] In prison George had no chance of recovery. Hobart Gaol, if it did not cause his kidney disease, profoundly exacerbated it. He could have been misdiagnosed for some time; the request to have him stop work suggested fatigue, a symptom the prison would usually dismiss as laziness. By this time he must have been really ill. Without the modern options of dialysis and kidney transplant, he faced a death sentence.

Certainly when Dr Roberts saw George he prescribed potassium soda, used to treat kidney damage, and a mustard poultice, recommended for pleurisy – a painful complication of Bright's disease.[20] Yet it took another month before George was moved to the gaol hospital. In

September he had acute pains in his abdomen, so severe a hospital doctor was summoned.

A third factor was diet, so carefully recorded by the prison. At the time it was known that Bright's disease was best treated by a diet constantly low in protein, in severe cases no more than 50 grams per day. In the nineteenth century, for those who could afford it, meat consumption was excessive. Gaol economies meant less meat for inmates, but still high protein levels. The highly variable diets, from the relative feast of Diet 1 to the famine in solitary, would have placed extra stress on the kidneys. The gaol's hospital diet comprised 1 pound of bread, 2 ounces of butter, 1 pint of milk, 5/16 ounces potatoes, 3 ounces of sugar and ½ an ounce of tea. Although lower in protein, it still exceeded the healthy limit. Elsewhere he was assigned half a pound of tripe a day, suggesting a balancing act between treating anaemia and adding extra protein.

As Harding's kidneys failed, he would have lost weight, with nausea from the toxin buildup, fluid retention and high blood pressure. He requested more writing paper, which was always granted. In March 1907 he was allowed to write two letters 'because he is so ill', at least one of them to his mother.[21]

The final deterioration of Harding's health was recorded by the gatekeeper. Late on 10 May, Dr Wetherall visited. The next day: 'Warder Carpenter with 4 prisoners to carry Thomas Harding to General Hospital.'[22] That he was carried could indicate a sign of respect by his fellow prisoners, for a man who had cocked his snook at prison. The carrying of a prisoner to hospital was unusual: they were more commonly transported by cart.

He died on 16 May at 9.30 a.m. For the last time he was newsworthy: this time, for his inquest. The verdict was death from natural causes, kidney failure from Bright's disease. Michael McSherry, the deputy gaoler, deposed that 'during [the] deceased's illness he had been exempt from work, dieted according to medical instructions, and tended by another prisoner constantly'.[23] The *Tasmanian News* added:

'Deceased told witnesses that he could not be better treated at the General Hospital.'[24]

George had gained notoriety in Tasmania as part of a two-man crime wave, with Walters and Cawthray. The police had a down on him, to use his mother's *Detective's Album* expression, and had few scruples in sending him to gaol. Old prisoners could use the vagrancy laws creatively, reoffending to gain food and shelter; but George did not return to Hobart Gaol willingly. He left it only to die, with a pauper's burial in Cornelian Bay Cemetery.

He was documented by his mother from boyhood, and his misdeeds filled newspapers and prison registers. Yet still he remains elusive. While his repeat offending indicates a hardened criminal, and he associated with brutal men, he was not violent himself. George Fortune was a complex character: a man damned by dodgy friends, a compulsive liar, an eternal boy and an optimist almost to the last.

21

———

MARY FORTUNE ALONE

IN 1885 GEORGE HAD DESCRIBED HIS mother as aged; now Mary Fortune really was elderly. While she wrote on, some of her outlets had folded, and she was getting too old for the day jobs of housekeeping or governessing. Yet she still achieved new markets and syndication, her work appearing widely in both reprints and new material. Her work for *The Advocate* was reprinted in her country of birth, appearing in journals such as the *Irish Catholic*. The woman who had frequented Melbourne's Free Presbyterian Church now wrote about the Celtic cross and novenas like a true Catholic. Was she ecumenical? No evidence suggests that she converted.[1]

Old associates began to decline and die. Percy Brett went to Albury in September 1900 to testify in a case of sheep-stealing. Although suffering from bronchitis he was in good spirits. He went to bed only to overdose on his cough mixture, which contained morphia. Being a conscientious man of law, he had previously submitted his deposition. The case proceeded the next day without hindrance. Obituaries recalled him as a genial friend, ever courteous and obliging, a contributor to the public good of his district.[2]

If Mary Fortune knew of his death, it was not directly reflected in her fiction – although an Inspector Brett appears in a 1907 story, 'The Bank Robber'. Brett family history records that when Percy's eldest son was in his dotage, he spoke of a woman who would not leave his father alone – which caused him to lose all respect for the paterfamilias. Certainly Fortune never left him alone in her fiction. If she had indulged in some quiet real-life blackmail, it ceased with his death.

From 1902 she gained a significant point of legal equality, with the right for women to vote in federal elections. Nearly fifty years before, George Wilson had enrolled to vote at Kangaroo, and Fanny Finch voted municipally in Castlemaine. For whatever reason, Mary Fortune did not appear on the 1903 roll, although she was enrolled later.

She had made a new young friend. Minaille (Minnie) Furlong, née Douglas, was born in Geelong, 1852. In 1860 her family went to farm in Queensland, and in 1873 she married widower John Mackay, a newspaper proprietor and mayor of Cleremont. Family historian Janine Myers reports the family lore that Minaille was forced into the marriage – Mackay was eleven years older. He died in 1877, leaving Minaille with two stepchildren and a daughter, also called Minaille. The young widow took the children back to Victoria.

In a photograph, Minaille is pictured with a bicycle looking very much the New Woman. She met William Romuald Furlong, a composer, music teacher and choirmaster at St Patrick's Cathedral. Furlong had grieved a series of deaths, firstly most of his children and then his wife; Minaille was hired to nurse one of his daughters, who was dying of tuberculosis. On Christmas Day 1890, Minaille and Furlong were married at the cathedral by Archbishop Carr. Minaille had been Presbyterian but now became Catholic. At the time sectarian tension between the bride's and groom's families would have been nigh inevitable. Certainly Minaille became estranged from her own daughter.

The second Mrs Furlong had one son, who died soon after birth. Bereaved and suffering postnatal depression, Minaille had a consoling vision of a white dove. Mary Fortune would write a poem about the incident, dedicating it to her friend. Minaille now became a professional artist, active in society, concerts and fancy-dress balls. She also volunteered for charity – a cause for many middle- and upper-class colonial women. The Austral colonies lacked the British Poor Laws. The ideal was self-sufficiency, with government assistance not a right, even in a land where many migrants lacked the support of family networks.

Although colonial Victoria had great wealth, unemployment benefits were a utopian dream, even during the depression of the 1890s. While prison had been a government responsibility since convict days, charity devolved upon a network of volunteer organisations, sometimes supported by government grants, sometimes by the churches. Such organisations ran the Immigrants' Home and the Home for Governesses, which had housed Fortune in the 1870s.[3]

A good example, in both senses of the word, was the Ladies' Benevolent Society (LBS). Unlike the Immigrants' Home, it provided home visits, offering what was intended as temporary relief. The organisation was district-based and decentralised, with committees of middle-class women (with a few token males on the board) whose business it was to assess and assist applicants in a state of penury. In his book *Poverty Abounding*, historian R.A. Cage praises their humanity, their dutiful care and the financial and emotional support they provided.

Similar but smaller was the Ladies' Association of Charity (LAC) of St Vincent de Paul, from 1887. The St Vincent de Paul Society's laymen volunteers could not visit single women, for reasons of propriety, and here the LAC was needed. The first Melbourne branch operated from the cathedral, with William Furlong performing in fundraisers for it. Given that association, Minaille's charity was probably the LAC. She may have met Fortune, who had recurrent problems with housing, at the LAC's shelter for women in central Melbourne. Subsequently the two women both resided in South Yarra. Although Fortune was Protestant, the Catholic agencies ministered to the poor regardless of creed or race.

Crucial to both the LBS and the LAC was the visitor. A Lady Charity visitor would enquire into the bona fides of new applicants for help, and subsequently visit the successful regularly. Fortune would have received tickets (vouchers) for the grocer, which would have provided her with food and tea but not money, lest she spend it on alcohol. The grocers returned the ticket to the charity, who paid the bill. Fortune had prized her independence, but with increasing age she lost it.

Fortune's poem 'A Sister of "The King's Guild"' was about Minaille. It depicts a relationship that began with charity but became a true friendship. Fortune even forgave a younger woman's vanity, when once she would have condemned 'the train / that sweeps the dust, & sometimes rain'. Despite dressing to the nines, Minaille did godly work without being a nun.[4]

Various Victorian royal commissions into charitable institutions commended the female-dominated charities, not least for staving off the introduction of government-funded poor laws. Yet after the depression of the 1890s, government could not shirk responsibility for this crucial area, as charities were overwhelmed by the demand. In the new century, social welfare schemes became legislative policy.

That was forward-thinking, but still the notion of the deserving poor persisted, with relief a privilege dependent upon good conduct. A major demerit was alcohol abuse. Without drink, Mrs Louise Dunne of the LBS testified to the 1890 Royal Commission on Charitable Institutions, 'there would be no poverty'. She did not mention pay inequality, far less gendered. Although Fortune might be poor, she was not respectable, given her bouts of drinking.[5]

In 1901 Victoria instituted a means-tested old-age pension. As one of Fortune's characters commented: 'What would I do only for the pension [...] the pension keeps me, poor though it is, and if I hadn't it I'd have to go to some poorhouse or other.'[6]

The process of gaining a pension began with an applicant submitting a statutory declaration. It would be followed by an investigation regarding their respectability, involving the police, and an appearance before the Pension Commissioners at the local court of petty sessions.

Mary Fortune had previously been judged for her parenting and for her drunkenness. She met some of the criteria for the new pension, being over sixty-five and a long-term resident. However, she would have failed the stricture of having for five years lived 'a sober and reputable life'.[7]

She was also still working, although with increasing difficulty: her sight was failing, affecting her handwriting. Copies of Fortune's poetry in another's handwriting have survived, as well as typescripts, suggesting an amanuensis. Fortune's publishers did not necessarily ascribe her work lasting literary value, but Minaille did. In 1899 the Australian Literature Society (ALS) was inaugurated, with Minaille as assistant secretary. Its early meetings were held in the Furlongs' Music Studio in the Royal Arcade, Melbourne. The members included professional women and some writers, such as the young and internationally successful Ethel Turner. Thomas O'Callaghan, now police commissioner, joined; he knew Fortune as a writer and more.[8]

William Furlong set Australian poetry to music, including poems by Kendall, Gordon – and Fortune. In 1903 he recited her 'Wattle Blossom' at an ALS literary evening.[9] Two of Fortune's poems, 'A White Dove' and 'King's Guild', were handsomely printed, in separate pamphlets. The ALS or the Furlongs paid for the printing and the poems were sold for one shilling each.

Minaille's copy of 'The King's Guild' was dedicated by Fortune: 'To my sister of the King's Guild'. On it Minaille wrote: 'Regret lost Mrs Fortune's kind note dedicating this song to me and requesting Mr Furlong to set it to music which he did and published.' As a consequence of Minaille's promotion via the ALS, Waif Wander's poems gained a wider audience.[10]

Above all Minaille was a friend, to whom Mary could talk about George. She still wrote stories, such as 'Every Man a Chance' (1904), in which a criminal gets just that, and reforms. In fiction at least, she could hope he might change.

What seems her only surviving letter was written to Minaille:

95 Hope St. S. Yarra
Saturday

Dear Mrs Furlong,

Your kind letter just to hand. I will try and write as plainly as I can but can only do my best. Thank you very much for information about Australasian & your appreciation of my verses. Dr Bage wrote me a most also appreciative note about them. The Ed Aust appreciated by sending 15/. I seem to be in luck at present. The Times today intimated acceptance of my last sent in story. I have, I *think*, sent in my last Detective should it be unaccepted. So many have been declined that it appears useless for me to put my poor eye to such continuous strain for nothing. I had a letter from my son yesterday. In it he explains in a measure his feelings. They are regarding religious matters what *his* grandfather's were. He says 'to say there is no hereafter is too large an order for me' & 'I have my own ideas.' He is not better and knows he will never recover. Many thanks for your most kind offer about the old night gear. I shall be thankful for them as I am quite rags in that line. I am now wearing one of Mr Furlong's old Jager [Jaeger] under flannels & it has greatly helped my back.

It is with much hesitation I enter the subject of a certain person. I am quite aware of the nature of that 'friendship'. I advertised & got 5 replies all out of the way. Having no one to help me I cannot even *see* anything in my but now I am *almost* used to *it*. I asked Father Lynch to look out for me, but you see even had I a place to go I would not meet necessary expenses. I believe & think I told you, that there is a want in that brain somewhere nothing else can possibly account for the muddle.

I am sending to *The Argus* office to try and get the Australasian for 24th ult.

With a many thanks dear friend,
Yours sincerely and gratefully
M H Fortune

[In Minaille's handwriting]

Very miserable
Poor Mrs Fortune

Minaille added that Fortune wrote to Massina for an annuity: 'which he granted with grace & I feel grateful to him & glad for her'.

This letter can be dated from the two sales mentioned: to *The Australasian* and *The Weekly Times*. On 23 March 1907 Fortune's poem 'Achernar: a Dream' appeared in the former. It refers to the ninth brightest star in the sky, a binary most visible in the Southern Hemisphere. Both Minaille and Bage (Fortune's doctor) wrote to Fortune appreciating the verse. That Bage knew her pseudonym shows trust as well as literary interest.

The wobbly handwriting shows how badly her sight was affected. Her stargazing days were long over. Yet *The Weekly Times* story was one of eleven she published there in 1907, with four poems in *The Australasian*. She kept writing, if at shorter length. Her statement that her *Detective's Album* stories were being rejected has to be treated with some caution. Certainly her handwriting was difficult, even for compositors experienced with her work. The quality of the stories was another factor – although she had always varied between pulp and inspiration.

That her detective stories were now old fashioned, in the era of the ratiocinative Holmes, was another. She had opinions about Doyle, expressed by Detective Sinclair: 'We D's get many a lift by chance that we are not wont to blow about. Even the great "Sherlock Holmes" owed a wonderful deal to the chapter of accidents.'[11]

Yet the *AJ*'s audience remained loyal. Of the twenty-nine stories that appeared under her pseudonyms in the *AJ* in 1906–7, twenty-four of them in *The Detective's Album*, the majority were consistent with her oeuvre. If the *AJ* was trialling another detective writer under the W.W. pseudonym, the results were dubious. Some stories do read like pastiches: 'Bernard's Double', with Sinclair's adventures in third person, or 'Of Unsound Mind', with its Detective Sleuth – a truly unimaginative name. However, the series continued for another two years, still displaying her writing traits. Whether Minaille took dictation for Fortune is unknown, but somebody must have helped.

Fortune also had perennial money and housing worries. The Father Lynch mentioned in the letter was Reverend Father Thomas Lynch, who was parish priest at St Mary's, East St Kilda, and also conducted services at St Patrick's. Lynch was Irish-born, ascetic but generous: 'every person in distress had in him a true friend and help'.[12]

That Fortune did not name 'a certain person' with a problematic 'friendship' suggests she may have been concerned that someone other than Minaille would read her letter. That the next sentence discusses accommodation suggests the unnamed person was her landlady at 95 Hope Street: Helen Corbett, née Mills. In 1897 she had married Frederick Corbett, an inventor and manufacturer, and the couple had several young sons.

In 1908, in the Victorian electoral roll, Fortune appears as Mary Ellen Fortune at the same address, with the Corbetts. Both women were listed as having 'home duties', but Fortune was still publishing fiction and poetry: thirteen that year in the *AJ*, and ten in *The Herald/Weekly Times*. In May her story 'The Bell of the Dead' said of a murder victim: 'She usually had in the kitchen some wreck of her own sex, who had no choice but to take any shelter offered for a mere pittance of wages, though none of them remained when they could find a home elsewhere.'[13] The 'wreck', a Mrs Jewry, is fond of beer. If Mary was not being similarly exploited, then some form of elder abuse can be suspected.

At the end of 1908, after forty years, the *AJ* ended *The Detective's Album*. The final story was 'Catermole and Terris', just under three pages long. Fortune's editors and supporters were dwindling. George Walstab died in February 1909, survived by two daughters. James Skipp Borlase, in Brighton in the UK, died later that year.

The *AJ*'s editor, William Smith Mitchell, retired in 1909 after thirty years. So did Alfred Massina, from the family print business, aged seventy-five, although he remained on the *Herald* board. Massina granted a newspaper interview for the occasion, which termed him a 'Son of Caxton'. The reporter found him hale, energetic and full of bonhomie, and noted of the *AJ*:

a glance at the first and latest numbers shows that at least one of the earliest and most versatile of its contributors – 'Waif Wander' – is still in the land of the living, an article from her pen appearing in the current number.[14]

Fortune was only just surviving. The article referred to was 'The Dead Witness', a reprint of her 1866 story. From January, starting with 'The Madman's Tale' (co-written by Fortune and Borlase), the *AJ* revived her old *Detective's Album* stories, maintaining her readership. Not all the stories were considered reprintable, and copies of the *AJ* held at the Mitchell Library show edits, cuts and alterations. They had 'the most obvious archaisms deleted or altered'.[15] What, if any, money came to her from the reprints is unknown.

In 1909 she published only eight stories in *The Weekly Times*, not enough to keep her. Her situation became desperate, with not only blindness but perhaps dementia: the 1907 letter had used an ominous phrase, 'want in that brain'. She had used the same wording in a 1902 story, 'Poor Little Miss Wenn', describing a shell-shocked child who soon after dies.

Quite when the annuity began is unclear. It is recorded that in 'her declining years' the *AJ* gave her 'financial assistance'.[16] Massina certainly recognised Fortune's long service to his magazine. He had not forgotten

Adam Lindsay Gordon, but how obligated did he feel to Fortune, an ailing and ageing writer? It might be wondered if their relationship resembled that of George Robertson (of Angus & Robertson in Sydney) with Henry Lawson, a writer similarly gifted and alcoholic and perpetually arriving on the doorstep for hand-outs.

The difference was that Fortune kept writing as long as she humanly could, and she did not feel, as Lawson did, that the world owed her a drink. She only requested the annuity in her last years. While pride could prevent a middle-class professional from applying for benefits, she was in dire need. The notion of the deserving poor was poison for a woman who liked a drink – although her longevity suggests that she was less a constant drunk than an occasional binger.

The story is not straightforward. Why, if she had the annuity, did she spend ten months in what was essentially a poorhouse? On 15 January 1910, Mary Fortune, described as a journalist, was admitted to the Benevolent Asylum in North Melbourne. The grounds for application was given as 'failing vision', and she had been recommended by the Old Age Pension Commission.[17] That indicates she had applied to them, did not fit their prescriptive criteria, but in their mercy they sent her to the Benevolent Asylum.

Her religion was recorded as Wesleyan, although previously she opined:

'She's a Methody!'
    'What's them?'
    'Oh, a sort that purtends so hard to be religious that they get to b'lieve they are after a while's practice.'[18]

George had also claimed to be Wesleyan. Her need for the pension may explain why she took the pledge.

The Benevolent Asylum in North Melbourne was a grandiose Gothic building on ten acres, including vegetable gardens and orchards.

When built in the 1850s, it was intended as a refuge for those unable to work due to age, disability, illness or other factors. It functioned as part of the colonial network of charities, with government funding for buildings and the like, but administered by volunteers.

Like many goldrush-era buildings, it was jerry-built and not fit for purpose. Over the years more wings were added, without a major problem being addressed: steep stairs, of no use to the unfit or the infirm aged. The 1890s Royal Commission on Charitable Institutions heard it was a firetrap, difficult to evacuate in an emergency.

Within the asylum, men and women were segregated in wards and in eating halls. The aim was self-sufficiency through gardening and activities such as sewing and oakum picking. By the time Mary Fortune entered, it was largely a geriatric home, with the charities for the blind directing elderly applicants there. The day began early with tea, porridge and bread. The main meal was dinner, with meat, potatoes and a little fresh fruit and vegetables. For those unable to work – the increasing majority of inmates – the monotony was total, relieved only by religious services or reading aloud from newspapers and journals. For the first time in decades Mary Fortune was unable to write. Only two of her stories appeared that year – perhaps earlier contributions finding a belated printing?

Her time at the asylum was brief. She was released on 19 October because her old-age pension was restored. In December the state pension was superseded, when women began to receive federal payments. Fortune left with Helen Corbett, returning to the South Yarra address. Now she was released, she may have written again, with a story appearing in *The Weekly Times* in April 1911. Otherwise she seems finally to have retired.

She survived another thirteen months, but not with the Corbetts. She moved to 35 The Avenue, Windsor, home of the widowed Emilie Schatz and her daughter Cora, a dressmaker and manufacturer. The family were Germans from Hamburg. Emilie is listed in street directories as a nurse, which may explain why Mary went to live with them. At the end of October 1911, Mary Fortune suffered a cerebral haemorrhage, dying a fortnight later on 9 November.

Dr Bage, who liked her poetry, signed the death certificate. The death certificate gave her age as eighty-two, but she was seventy-eight. Her name was given as Ffortune, which had only appeared once before, in 1895. Nothing about her writing appeared on the certificate, only that she was an old-age pensioner and housewife.

The following day she was interred in the Anglican section of Springvale Botanical Cemetery, established in 1901, and then semi-rural. George had a pauper's grave, but Mary's was in the Massina family plot. The *AJ* 'paid for her burial in another person's grave' – unmarked. The magazine to which she had contributed so much looked after her in death. Coincidentally, only a short distance away is now the Police Memorial, her subject matter for over forty years.[19]

Decades earlier she had written, in 'Melbourne Cemetery':

A lonely place is a primitive burial-ground 'up in the bush'. There are few engraven names there, and not many flowers, save the wild beauties that are at home under the sheltering trees; but there are rustling branches and sweet sighing evening breezes there, and instead of the loud careless laugh, there is the gargling *reveillé* of the merry magpie, although his notes will not wake the sleepers below. It little matters, I suppose, where we are laid to sleep, but could I choose my own resting place it would not be in Melbourne cemetery.[20]

She had indeed no choice, but magpies can be heard warbling near her grave in Springvale.

THE AFTERMATH

THE *AJ* PUBLISHED NEITHER DEATH NOTICE nor obituary for Mary Fortune. A month before her death, *The Detective's Album* had been handed over to a new writer, W. Gladstone Simons. He only lasted two issues: the series then reverted to Fortune reprints, with other occasional contributors. It survived the First World War, appearing alongside a new generation of writers such as Katharine Susannah Prichard. The reprints only ceased in 1919, when A. (Alex) C. Eiseman was hired to write new instalments for the series, which ended her fifty-four years of crime fiction in the magazine. The same year her last reprint in *The Advocate* appeared, 'The Widow Neil', about St Patrick's Day.

In reprinting the serial, the *AJ* had extended Fortune's readership. The magazine's wide circulation meant she potentially influenced a new generation of Australian crime writers. It is possible that Arthur Upfield (who emigrated to Australia in 1909 and became best known for his Detective Napoleon 'Bony' Bonaparte novels about an Aboriginal detective) noted her mix of Australiana and crime, not least the benefit of featuring a distinctive detective.

In late 1922 an aspiring writer, Ronald Campbell, went for an interview with Stanley Massina, grandson of Alfred, at the *AJ*'s offices. Campbell needed extra money to eke out his teaching salary. On the strength of his submitted story, he was asked to try out for *The Detective's*

Album. Eiseman had found writing 10,000 words of detection every month too much of a strain. If Campbell proved satisfactory, *The Detective's Album* was his.

Campbell had never written any crime fiction, but the chance was too good to miss. In his memoir he recalls going immediately to the nearby State Library of Victoria and reading the back issues of the *AJ. W.W.* in effect was his teacher. Next day he started writing:

> To invent a plot, and characters, write the yarn in longhand, revise it and finally type it on my old machine, all in the spare time of ten days, was quite a task for a novice, but it was worth it, for Massina declared it to be just what was wanted, and instructed me to keep going. I took him at his word, month after month for about thirty years.[1]

Campbell wrote as Rex Grayson, his association with the magazine producing 4.5 million words. He recalled the pay as 'not princely ... but well above the rate paid to casual contributors'. In 1926 he began working editorially, as the editor, William E. Adcock, was then good for little else than 'donkey work'. As with *The Detective's Album*, Campbell had no editorial experience, but he learnt quickly on the job. Four years later, Adcock retired, leaving Campbell officially the editor. While including international serials, he also sought paid work from locals, including Upfield (writing on travel), Xavier Herbert and Jon Cleary.[2]

Fortune was gradually fading from memory, although in the 1930s her poem 'Our Wattle Bloom' figured in interstate elocution competitions. Those who knew her were dying, and they left no record. O'Callaghan (d. 1931) wrote a history-memoir, 'Police and Other People', the other people not including Mary Fortune. Massina died in 1917. Only Minaille Furlong thought enough of Fortune to preserve her letter and poetry manuscripts; she died in 1941. Eight years later Campbell wrote *The First Ninety Years*, his history of the Massina firm. It mentioned Borlase, but not Waif Wander.[3]

Fortune, now forgotten, might have been irretrievable without J.K. (Jack) Moir, a bibliophile and enthusiast for Australian literature. He aimed to own every Australian book published and acquired a copy of W.W.'s *The Detective Album*. In 1950 he advertised for more information, claiming 'Mrs Fortune' had been the first female crime writer in the world. He also contacted Campbell, who relayed what the firm recalled about her. Minaille's small cache of Fortune materials was acquired by Moir and donated to the State Library of Victoria.[4]

Moir was a curious man, a cultural nationalist at a time when Australian literature was conventionally regarded as inferior and crime writers went overseas, abandoning local settings to appeal to a wider market. His business activities financed his collecting habit, and although married with a child, he lived alone in a shopfront filled with books. Outside his work, he was convivial, even bohemian, hosting the Bread and Cheese Club, devoted to 'Mateship, Art & Letters'. Despite his conservative views, he forewarned his left-wing guests that he would be reporting to the security services about them.

Campbell recalled him as rough-spoken, rather looked down upon by the literati – although Miles Franklin attended his gatherings, where she was 'like an electric spark'. Perhaps nobody else would have bothered with W.W., and while he did not solve all her mysteries, he did establish her name. Moreover, he got the information about 'Mrs Fortune' into reference books. Moir, without modern data indexing tools, could not get far with his search, although he searched the Melbourne General Cemetery records. In turn, Campbell compiled an anthology of the *AJ*, including an extract from Fortune's memoir. The anthology was never published.[5]

In 1955, Massina & Co. sold the *AJ* to Keith Murdoch's Southdown Press. The magazine continued for a few years, before declining and dying in 1961. The *AJ* had been by this time thoroughly overshadowed by *The Bulletin* in canonical memory – when it was recalled, it was chiefly in connection with Marcus Clarke and his circle. Moir died in 1958, Campbell in 1970.

It seemed Fortune had been forgotten not once but twice. Yet several factors led to her rediscovery towards the end of the twentieth century. One was the growing status of crime fiction as a subject for serious study. Al Hubin's 1979 *The Bibliography of Crime Fiction* listed W.W. Another was the worldwide feminist interest in women writers.[6]

Lucy Sussex writes:

At what point should the biographer enter the story they are telling? Maybe best at the end, which is indeed correct, chronologically. In 1987 I moved from librarianship to working as a researcher for Professor Stephen Knight at Melbourne University. He is a distinguished medievalist, but also had a grant to research the history of Australian crime fiction. So, I got the delightful job of largely reading old and vintage crime texts and reporting back whether they contained anything of interest.

Stephen asked me to look into 'Mrs Fortune'. An entry for 'Twenty-Six Years Ago' in the Mitchell catalogue meant I learnt the crucial date of her arrival in Victoria. Information could be checked, thanks to microfilming of emigration records, which verified that Mrs Fortune and her son George had indeed disembarked in Melbourne in 1855.

The first of many serendipitous moments occurred next. I went to the Baillieu Library to examine and list her writing, and began with the earliest *AJ* volume they had, for 1868–69. It contained her first journalism, including 'How I Spent Christmas'. Among the more conventional, even florid, offerings in the *AJ*, here was a uniquely vibrant and attractive voice. Whoever Mrs Fortune was, she was clearly a significant writer.

The crucial factor next was a discrepancy between 'How I Spent Christmas' and the known facts of Fortune's life. A close reading of 'How I Spent Christmas' revealed Waif Wander's young companion was her son, but if he had never seen a ship before, he was not the child who had disembarked with her in 1855. If so, could he be found in the birth records? And if the firstborn was not with his family at Christmas time, might he have died?

As the memoir ended in 1857, the search began in 1858. Here the unusual name Fortune was a boon. The death record for George Fortune, born in Canada, was found, giving his parents' names. That revealed the mystery writer was Mary Helena Fortune. However, her second son could not immediately be located. Might she have remarried? Again the 1858 registry indexes revealed her marriage to Percy Rollo Brett, mounted trooper. So that was how she knew so much about the police! The coincidence that Brett had a grandson with the exact same name led me to the Brett family, including Judith, his daughter. The Bretts knew nothing about Mary Fortune.

Having got so far already, I was not about to give up. Stephen Knight told me that Mary Fortune was no longer his research project, but mine. 'You have that gleam in your eye!' he said, something for which I am forever grateful. At issue was whether Fortune was the first woman writer of detective fiction, as claimed by Moir. She certainly predated the Americans Anna Katharine Green and Seeley Regester (aka Metta Victor), whose novel *The Dead Letter* began its serialisation in January 1866.

So began a process of presentations, advocacy, reprints, articles and anthologies of Fortune's writing. I ended up writing a PhD and then a book on the mothers of crime fiction, and a novel based on the search for Fortune, *The Scarlet Rider*. But the flow of information was intermittent, with many dead ends. Also, the sheer intensity of the personality I was studying meant I had to retreat from the search.

A biographer has to develop distance from the subject, and I lacked that experience at first. 'Do you ever dream about your subjects?', I asked biographers Deirdre Bair and Michael Holroyd. The former said firmly: No! Holroyd smiled and said that while he didn't, Maggie (his wife, the celebrated writer Margaret Drabble) did it for him. Sometimes the biographer can only wait, Nadia Wheatley says.

If the search had its novelistic moments, another came with the eventual discovery of the identity of Mary's second son. It resembled A.S. Byatt's *Possession*, in which rival scholars investigate a secret love affair between two Victorian writers. Unknown to me, another researcher had found George Fortune's extensive criminal record, which included mention of his mother as a writer. She advised theatre historian Mimi Colligan: 'Don't tell Lucy!' Another historian, informed of the discovery, started up their own investigation. Eventually, via Judith Brett, it leaked to me, together with a photocopy of George's prison record.

What ensued was a polite but most surreal phone conversation, with sound effects by the Rival Researcher's cat, mewing in the background for its dinner. R.R. told me we had coincided only that day while researching, I completely unaware, she observing me covertly. That produced paranoia: had I left my notebooks unguarded and open on a desk? We carefully and evasively compared notes on what we had and didn't have, such as a death record for Mary Fortune, still elusive at that stage. The conversation ended with R.R. informing me I wouldn't easily find the information she had.

Mimi Colligan suggested the *Police Gazette*. So, I sat on the steps of the State Library one afternoon, phoning my mother Marian and reading out Mary Fortune's 1874 police description. I also stopped the presses of a Canadian edition of Fortune's crime stories to get the new information inserted.

George's criminal career showed more research was needed. Mother and son were complementary and could not be separated. Megan Brown had completed a PhD on Mary Fortune at the University of Wollongong, and we joined forces. We read and reread Fortune's bibliography, consisting of over 500 items. Late in the process, a Trove search for the word 'fizgig' meant we discovered her nearly 100 contributions to *The Herald*. That meant we had to stop writing and read furiously.

We discussed the Fortunes constantly, a collaborative sounding board.

Megan Brown writes:

I had naively intended to write a PhD thesis on female journalists in colonial Australia. I started my research with the *Australian Journal* and soon realised that in fact the majority of contributors were women. They were loud, not silent, and like Ken Stewart, I began to feel that part of my cultural heritage had been hidden from me. While many were, as Lucy described, florid, one writer who kept reappearing page after page and year after year, and who could happily shift between writing gruesome crime, soppy romance or flâneuse-style reportage, particularly intrigued me. I decided she had to be my subject. I read Lucy's books and articles about Mary Fortune, met Lucy at conferences where I complained about the misinformation that abounded about Fortune, and completed my PhD.

Like Lucy, I discovered that just when you think you must step away from this subject, you discover yet another Mary Fortune story and find yourself back in her labyrinth of truths, half-truths and hidden cheeky self-references. It was inevitable that Lucy and I would join forces to untangle it.

One of the revelations that changed the course of my research was discovering Sylphid – the pseudonym that Fortune used to write 'The Ladies' Page' in the *Australian Journal*. It stood out as her work because of the rhythm of the writing, particular usages of the words, certain biographical references and biases. It also stood out because it was nothing like any of the other ladies' columns in the journal. With Fortune at the helm, the columns transformed from being short, choppy notes on fashion and gossip to rounded narratives in which fashion took a back seat and human observation and social and political commentary took front row. The fact that this work was commissioned gave Fortune confidence and authority. In some ways Sylphid is the most honest of Fortune's writing, and every event she talks about, from burning houses to striking cabmen and protests by cabbage sellers, can be verified as true. It was another piece of the complex puzzle.

It was also through Sylphid that I formed a theory about Fortune's strained relationship with Marcus Clarke. At a joint conference presentation with Lucy at Ballarat, I chose to discuss this relationship, pointing out that Fortune, like Clarke, modelled her writing on Dickens and Sala. Fortune also made overt references to Clarke's writing, but Sylphid trespassed further by purposefully wandering the streets making satirical observations as she went – it was a different style of satire but describing the same city. Knowing that Clarke was a prominent member of the Yorick Club she even decried the lack of an equivalent for women.

It seemed no coincidence, then, that when Clarke took over editing the *AJ* (in March 1870, according to Andrew McCann), Sylphid disappeared. Her last column was in February. 'The Ladies' Page' in March sounded like Clarke. It refers to 'women' or 'the sex', whereas Fortune had always included personal opinions and did so in first person. By June, the 'Ladies' Page' included a paragraph in the style of Clarke's shameless self-promotion. 'That amusing writer, the "Peripatetic Philosopher," has lately come out gallantly with a *tu quoque* for the indiscriminate deriders of feminine modes'.[7]

In the same month the *AJ* published Fortune's 'Under the Verandah', so clearly she was not too indisposed to write. 'Under the Verandah' was also the title of Clarke's other regular column. She is at pains to point out she is not 'trespassing on the ground of the Peripatetic', but if the echo attracts some extra readers that would be nice. She also includes a sarcastic jibe about the 'Ladies' Page', implying that it would be improved if she was still writing it. 'Talk of your "Ladies' Pages," indeed! If you had a description of *that* bonnet in it, you might get ladies to copy your patterns'.[8]

Lucy and I both felt that there were sure to be more pseudonyms, which turned out to be true. When Lucy told me about the Police Stories in *The Herald*, I started a further search and found that W.W. had written an article on the Melbourne Cemetery in 1879 in *The Herald*.

This was exactly ten years after M.H.F had written a very similar article in the *AJ*. The articles were too similar for this to be a coincidence. Fortune was now also writing for the 'Ladies' Column' in *The Herald*. There were no more articles attributed to W.W., but I read every lady columnist and found Nemia. Not only did she use Fortune's distinctive voice, she also wrote about visiting Pentridge at Christmas, and we knew George was incarcerated there at this time. I rang Lucy and danced around the room telling her what I'd found. Down another Fortune rabbit hole we went – more police stories and more ladies' columns to make sense of.

It has been quite a process: from reading, absorbing and making sense of Mary's vast output to chronicling George's colourful criminal history. I created chronologies and timelines for both Mary and George, then combined them so that we could clarify who was where when. I've created searchable databases for all the stories in the *AJ* and *The Herald* so that reoccurring themes, places and crimes can be traced. The sheer volume of writing and the quantity of criminal conviction dates made this a complex exercise.

George's criminal history was a revelation. The Simpson Road bank robbery was one of the most audacious and widely reported crimes in Melbourne in the nineteenth century. His later Victorian convictions attracted attention as well, but usually because of his involvement in the earlier bank robbery. This notoriety followed him to Tasmania, and I followed George's path to Hobart. I chased (dragging various family members with me) his exploits through newspapers, then through the archives in Hobart Library and to his grave. Many of the archives of Hobart Gaol were destroyed by fire, but what does exist is very detailed. They were zealous record keepers. The loss of archives pertaining to George's years in goal made the hunt for information a process of detection. I searched nominal rolls, ration books, medical registers, correspondence books, gang rosters, discipline hearings, gatekeepers' books, rules of the gaol and gazettes. There were many mysteries to be solved – he went in and out of Hobart Gaol regularly in the seven years he lived in Tasmania. There were two main mysteries that bothered me: how did he gain an extra conviction while in gaol, and where did he die? In both cases the gatekeeper's daybook provided the clues, and fortunately the records I needed survived. In the end I knew what George did and ate almost every day he was in gaol. There are still some details I wonder about. Why was he carried by four men to hospital? Why was he named in the daybook when it only ever referred to others as 'prisoner/s'? We get involved with our subjects – I want to like George. Was he in some way special in the gaol? Was he named because he was liked, or carried because of some sort of regard? Was this a kind of guard of honour to farewell a prisoner who had made a mark on those around him?

The August afternoon I decided to find George's grave was one of the wettest days I've ever experienced. The rain was torrential, and with long-suffering family members in tow I set forth to Cornelian Bay Cemetery. We knew George was buried in the paupers' section, we had a map, and his burial notice mentioned the section of the cemetery. His denomination was given as Church of Rome and his name as Thomas H. Fortune. Even in death his name was a hybrid and his wishes regarding religion were not honoured. Remarkably the rain cleared while we were there, and we were able to wander around the cemetery until we found the section. Although one will never find specific graves in the unmarked paupers' section, we found the area where he was buried.

There is a lovely memorial built to commemorate the paupers who rest there. The eucalypts and birds could have been from one of Mary's stories. It may not have been the bush grave she aspired to, but it was the next best thing. The sound of the sea from Cornelian Bay, the bird song and the wind through the eucalypts provide a calm and peaceful resting place – probably the only restful place George ever had in his ramshackle life. It was a pity Mary never got to see her son before he died or where he rested. I wonder just how much the prison told her about the way his life ended and the aftermath. Did she read the inquest results in the newspaper, or did they keep her updated? Eerily, as soon as we left the cemetery, the rain started bucketing again.

On another trip I visited the chapel of the old gaol. While the graveyard emanated a sense of peace, this visit was unsettling. A long-suffering daughter joined me on this mission. I pay tribute to my family for being good humoured about accompanying me on many of my research escapades. The main part of the gaol is long gone, with the chapel and a few associated buildings all that remains. The solitary cells and the chapel were cruelly integrated, with some cells located under the raked floor of the chapel. It may have brought the prisoners closer to the good word, but it made the cells even smaller than usual. In some it was impossible to stand upright.

We know George spent a significant amount of time in these cells. Being physically in this space brought home the indignity, the dank air, the lifeless surroundings and the bone-chilling cold. Similar treatment is still used for torture.

I discovered George was both villain and victim. While we'll never know whether he committed that last crime, he didn't deserve his ending.

Lucy Sussex:
One final example of how the novelistic process of research intersected with the twenty-first century. On a cold and grey Melbourne day in July 2016, I drove off to Springvale Cemetery, with a neighbor's bunch of wattle, to find Mary Fortune's unmarked grave. Then I drove to Ballarat, to give a paper with Megan Brown at the conference of the Australasian Victorian Studies Association.

As we presented, sitting in the audience at the Mechanic's Institute was graduate student Carolyn Lake, with her laptop. During the Q&A session, she entered the database Austlit and 'excitedly updated' (her words) the entry on Mary Fortune. And so the news that we had found

Mary's grave, a mystery finally solved, entered the public domain very shortly after.

No doubt more information, even more of Fortune's writing, will appear, but now what we have fills a book. If there is an image with which to end it, it is a bunch of wattle lying on the cut grass of an unmarked grave. 'The Wattle will bloom for me!' she wrote in 'Our Wattle Bloom'. On that day it did, but her work also blooms, singularly vivid, similarly recurring.

APPENDIX 1:
READING MARY FORTUNE

To read Mary Fortune now, the easiest way is via Trove for her newspaper work, and for the *AJ*, the Gale database 'Nineteenth Century UK Periodicals'. The most immediately attractive of her work to today's readers are the memoirs and journalism, a selection of which was published in 1989 as *The Fortunes of Mary Fortune*, edited by Lucy Sussex.

Most of Fortune's work was either short stories or novelettes. They vary in quality, but 'The White Maniac' has been widely reprinted and translated. A collection of the detective stories, *Nothing but Murders and Hanging and Bloodshed*, is published by Verse Chorus Press in 2025.

Fortune's serialised novels are either good but not extraordinary (*Bertha's Legacy*), interesting but flawed (*Dora Carleton, The Bushranger's Autobiography*) or enjoyable but completely wild (*Clyzia the Dwarf*). A selection of her longer crime work was published in 2019 by Corella Press at UQP as *Bridget's Locket and Other Mysteries*, the 'others' being *Dora* and *Bride of the Mountain*.

Critical reactions to Fortune's work, contemporary and modern
In the nineteenth century, the first known appreciation of Fortune's work was for 'The Deserted Hut', described as 'as usual very good'

in the *Launceston Examiner* on 31 March 1866.[1] It was the only story in Borlase and Fortune's crime series to be praised. Of her journalism, the *Bendigo Advertiser* commented that Sylphid was 'very well written, and suitable to the ladies of Australia. It cannot be expected that "Ladies Pages" written for English and French ladies are applicable to their southern sisters'.[2] *The Bushranger's Autobiography* was compared to Marcus Clarke's concurrent serial: '"His Natural Life" is advanced another stage, and as the story draws to a close the interest seems to increase. "The Autobiography of a Bush-ranger" is also increasing in interest, and most of the scenes are graphically portrayed'.[3]

The first lengthy appraisal of Fortune's writing was by Henry W. Mitchell, who termed her 'this gifted lady … beyond all doubt one of the most talented, versatile and interesting writers of fiction that we have, or have ever had, in the Australian colonies'. Across the Tasman, she attracted similar comment: 'That able writer of fiction known by the name of "Waif Wander" […] is beyond doubt one of the most pleasant and agreeable writers we have in the Colonies, and her contributions to a well-known and popular monthly serial published in Melbourne have for fifteen years been amongst the most attractive features it contains. I should be pleased to see more contributions from her pen appearing in our papers'.[4]

Even after Fortune's death in 1911, readers could recall her fondly. Writing in the *AJ* in July 1933, *A.A.C.* reflected:

> At the age of twelve years I had read a large collection of back numbers of the 'A.J.' without any ill-effect other than a taste for good, clean reading matter, and a dislike for so-called detective stories that failed to reach the high standard of excellence set by 'W.W.' […] his characters are live ones and each story creates the impression that the events related really did happen as written. To him 'I doffs me lid'.[5]

However, later critical reaction was less informed, and was influenced by a perception of the *Bulletin* as a high point for Australian literature and the *AJ* as pulp. In 1961, H.M Green in volume 1 of his *A History of Australian Literature* described the *AJ* as appealing to the 'semi-literate', or to better readers lacking anything else to read on a journey. He quoted from Waif Wander's bushranger story 'Dare Devil Bob', without naming the author, describing it as a crude 'ancestor of the modern thriller', and an example of the magazine 'at its worst'. He added that it might have been written by 'some writer capable of better things, of Clarke himself even, writing with his tongue in his cheek'.[6]

Ronald Campbell, as an *AJ* editor and crime writer, knew better: 'a very remarkable writer … undoubtedly a master of plot, although her highly melodramatic style, reminiscent of Gaboriau would scarcely pass today', is how he described Fortune in a letter to Angus & Robertson editor Beatrice Davis in 1952.

When *The Fortunes of Mary Fortune* was published, reviewers were impressed. 'Twenty-Six years Ago' was called the most 'vital account of those exciting days' by Patricia Clarke in *The Canberra Times,* and 'the first instance of Australian, as opposed to colonial prose' by Adrian Rawlins in *The Australian.*[7]

Responses this century have been overwhelmingly favourable, particularly from Fortune's fellow crime-writers. 'Mary Fortune is my favourite 19C Oz writer,' commented David Whish-Wilson. Candice Fox, in her introduction to *Bridget's Locket*, declared that Fortune should be put 'in her rightful place among Australia and the world's best crime writers!'[8]

In 2020, Mary Fortune even appeared as a cross-dressing character in Fin J. Ross's young adult novel *Billings Better Bookstore & Brasserie*:

Fidelia took an immediate liking to the feisty Irishwoman, some thirty years her senior and rough as a reused grain sack, but could not initially understand why she had chosen to write under a man's name.

'To be heard, girl, to be heard,' Mary responded, still showing traces of her Belfast accent. 'No man will read something penned by a woman unless they don't know it's a woman. So if you want to be a writer for *everyone*, it's a shame, but you must be a man.'[9]

APPENDIX 2:
ANNALS OF RECIDIVISM

Was George Fortune exceptional in his recidivism? His stints in the Industrial School, reformatory and prison devoured his life. Of his associates, some could not be traced. The fate of others is known, and some already detailed in this book. Here is what happened to the remainder. Where known, their prison number (for easier archival searching) is given.

At least three suffered mental illness. **William Fitzgerald**, the lively Bellman whom Mary Fortune met in Kangaroo Flat, appeared in goldfields courts for unpaid bills and drunkenness. In 1861 at Dunolly, he was declared a dangerous lunatic and sent to Castlemaine for treatment.

Two of the others were convicted with **George Fortune** for the 1890 safecracking. **Thomas Griffiths,** aka Henry Wilson, b. 1858, 14557, had a record for larrikin violence and theft. During this prison term he was transferred to Ararat Asylum and released at the end of his sentence in 1898. **John Watson**, aka, William Henry, b. 1863, 18251, had a similar record, with more theft but less violence. During his 1890 sentence he was sent to the Yarra Bend Asylum for nine months, but completed his sentence in prison.

Some belonged to families with criminal records. **John Spence,**

b. 1830, 14971, and his wife Rosalinda, 3550, hid their son **James Alexander Spence**, b. 1864, 21109, when he escaped from the Industrial School. John had six convictions – three for assault – and Rosalinda three. James repeatedly absconded as a juvenile, but as an adult served one month for larceny, in 1881, and a year in Pentridge, 1888, for having a picklock.

The Huxley family comprised generations of villains, first as transportees. The next generation served time for theft, forgery, assault and confidence trickery. **Harriet Huxley**, while her husband was imprisoned, successfully extracted her two sons from Industrial School, but they repeatedly offended. **John**, b. 1855, 8473 and 30097, was convicted mostly for theft, in two states, with his last conviction in 1903. **Edward**, b. 1852, 11639, was a repeat escapee, with convictions for thieving in the 1870s and short sentences for violence in the 1880s.

Some kept offending, if intermittently. **Francis Holmes**, b. 1857, 9778, was convicted of burglary with **George Fortune** in 1873. He was an Industrial Schoolboy, and like his associate **Edward Huxley**, an absconder. His crimes tended to thefts, with short sentences, the exception being two years for an 1879 spree that included assault. His eighth and last sentence was two months for larceny in 1894.

James Williams, b. Henry McNally in 1858, 14895, was convicted with **George Fortune** for his second offence at Bylands. He was a notoriously violent Richmond larrikin, with twelve convictions, mainly for assault, between 1870 and 1888. In 1899, he served twelve months for imposition.

Victor Masuglia, b. 1872, 28256, was convicted in Hobart Gaol with **George Fortune**. He returned to Victoria, with convictions for theft and receiving during the 1930s.

Some never really stopped. **William Montague Parker**, b. 1828, 21344, got off lightly after Simpson Road, with six months for dealing. He moved to Sydney and continued to put up, with occasional receiving charges. In 1903, his alibi for a burglar who murdered a policeman resulted in five years for perjury. In 1921, as a nonagenarian, he took an active part in an assault, as reported in *Truth*.

Thomas Furlong, aka Thomas Kilrain, b. 1863, 18180, was the fourth member of the 1890 safecracking gang. He was an Industrial Schoolboy and absconder. Many minor offences followed. Although he lost an eye in prison in the 1890s, upon release in 1897, he burgled post offices and received a sentence of five years. In 1902, he was sentenced to another nine years for receiving. In 1910 and 1914, he was convicted for drinking and drunken assault.

Some died in prison. **William Freeman**, b. 1865, 22392, accompanied **George Fortune** to Tasmania as Joseph Waters. He had eight convictions in Victoria, including five years for being an accomplice in an armed robbery. He apparently died of a heart attack in Hobart Gaol.

Some apparently reformed, against all expectations. **Joseph Cawthray**, from a transportee family whose men were given to drunken violence, had seventeen convictions before meeting **George Fortune**. Yet after the Montpellier robbery, he only had one further charge, for drinking on the Sabbath. It seems inheriting money upon his grandmother's death gave him his chance. Did he change his name, maybe leaving Tasmania to start a new life?

And one had a remarkable career. **Patrick Boardman** (1856–1923), 14872, testified at the 1882–23 Royal Commission to the abuses of the detectives. In 1906 he would testify at another Royal Commission into the Police, as a friend and associate of John Wren. Boardman was described as the brains behind Wren's business and appears in Frank Hardy's *Power Without Glory* as Paddy Woodman, a garish gambling identity. Certainly Boardman ran gambling clubs for Wren or on his own behalf. The *Australian Dictionary of Biography* entry on Squizzy Taylor asserts that Taylor had a business 'squaring juries' with Boardman. However, Roy Maloy, Squizzy expert, has never heard of Boardman. He comments: 'Wren may have been involved in illegal activities, but he underwent his activities like a businessman. He was systematic and risk managed on the most part. In contrast, Squizzy was a loose cannon.'

ACKNOWLEDGEMENTS

This book could not have been written without many hands who offered help, and in token of our gratitude, we list them:

The anthologists, editors and translators who have worked on getting Mary Fortune back into print, beginning with the late Spender sisters, Dale and Lynne; Susan Hawthorne; in Canada, George Vanderburgh and Georges T. Dodds; Sorcha Nì Fhlainn and Xavier Aldana Reyes of the British Library.

The Association for the Study of Australian Literature and the Australasian Victorian Studies Association – who became extended academic families. Cathy Waters, Meg Tasker, Michelle Smith, Julia Kuehn, Kirby-Jane Hallum. Mandy Treagus, Judy Johnston, Margaret Harris, Kris Moruzi, Duc Dau. In particular, the late Elizabeth Webby, the most generous of scholars.

Bibliographer of Mary Fortune Elizabeth Gibson.

The Bibliographical Society of Australia and New Zealand and its members, including Caren Florance, Paul Eggert, Brian McMullin and Shef Rogers.

The team at Black Inc., especially Sophy Williams, Chris Feik and Denise O'Dea.

Alex Adsett for contract help.

The Brett family, including Judith Brett, Percy Rollo Brett and

Margaret Dupleix. Other researchers with a family connection to the Fortunes included Anne Black and Janine Myers. In Canada, Fortune family descendants Lorraine Chevrier and Glen Porteous.

The historians generous with research and advice: literary historians Nan Bowman Albinski, Mimi Colligan and Elizabeth Morrison; Janet McCalman, Marjorie Theobald and Kacey Sinclair. Crime historians Roy Maloy and Kevin Morgan. In Bristol, Pam Lock. In Canada, Mary Lu MacDonald.

The historical societies consulted: the Royal Historical Society of Victoria; Kilmore Historical Society with Francis Payne, Rose King and Barbara Wilson; at Taradale Historical Society, Andy Indrans.

The libraries in which we spent many hours: the British Library; Libraries and Archives Canada, Ottawa; the State Library of Victoria, which gave Lucy Sussex a fellowship to research this book, and librarians Jock Murphy, Richard Overell, John Arnold and Des Cowley; the National Library and its research staff; at the State Library of New South Wales, the Mitchell library, especially Rachel Franks. And the archives: the Public Record Office Victoria (PROV); the South Carolina Department of Archives and History; Carol Morgan of the Institute of Civil Engineers, UK. Particular thanks to the Tasmanian Library and Archives' staff for their generous assistance during trying Covid times. On one visit, they, and the staff from the National Archives who share the space, all pitched in to help Megan tame a really creased prosecution file. I can't thank them enough.

On police history: Brian Hardiman, Ralph Stavely, Sandra Nicholson and Claire O'Meara (Collections Manager, Police Museum). Sisters in Crime, particularly Carmel Shute.

The universities which gave us support: Professor Stephen Knight at the University of Melbourne and the University of Wales, Cardiff; at La Trobe University, Professor Sue Martin and Juliane Römhild; at Wollongong, Sharon Crozier-De Rosa, Louise D'Arcens, Anne Collett and Dorothy Jones.

And others: Jason Steger and Carolyn Webb of *The Age*; Clarissa Tedder; in Canada, the late Douglas Barbour; in the US, Harriet McDougall and John D. Berry; in Ireland, Sharon Slater at the website Limerick's Life; Kay Craddock, Paula McGrath, Hugh McKay, Seán Ó Séaghdha, Catherine Voutier, Tom Darragh, Elizabeth Gertsakis, Brian Rieusset and Danielle Clode.

And the various people who wished to contribute anonymously.

~

Lucy Sussex: many thanks to my family and to Julian Warner for tolerating an obsession.

Megan Brown: thanks to Anne Lear, who introduced me to the voices of nineteenth-century women; Carmel Pass, who suggested the title; Leigh Dale, the voice of scholarly reason; Sarah Ferber and Sarah Ailwood. And to my family: thanks to David for his patience and advice, and to the next generation of extraordinary women, Elly, Laura, Marion and Alison, who visited so many graveyards over the years …

NOTES

INTRODUCTION: THE MYSTERIES OF MARY FORTUNE

1   *Tasmanian Times*, 1 April 1869, p. 2.

2   'A Woman's Revenge: or, Almost Lost', p. 363.

3   'How I Spent Christmas', p. 365.

CHAPTER ONE: ORIGINS OF A CRIME WRITER

1   This marriage certificate lists Mary's parents and her father's profession and states that she was born in Belfast in about 1832. Via the Ulster Historical Society Online it was possible to find the baptism record of Mary Wilson, daughter of Eleanor. It fits in all but one detail: the father was named as William. In her life, as in family history in general, names prove unreliable: mistaken, misspelled, deliberately altered or aliases.

2   'How I Spent Christmas', p. 364. In it she writes of 'good old Sir Walter Scott, whose genuine portrait we are so familiar with, and near whose home – beautiful Abbotsford – is the old home of *our* forefathers'. Near Abbotsford in Roxburghshire, in the borderlands, is the ancient town of Melrose, 31 miles from Edinburgh. George Wilson also addressed his daughter in Scots dialect, calling her 'lassie'. 'Twenty-Six Years Ago', p. 65. In the one census record that can probably be identified as George Wilson's, for Quebec in 1851, he was stated to be Canadian-born, with his birthdate given as c. 1802.

3   'Twenty-Six Years Ago', p. 52.

4   Angélique Day and Patrick McWilliams (eds), *Ordnance Survey Memoirs of Ireland*, Vol. 37: Parishes of County Antrim XIV, 1832, 1839–40: *Carrickfergus*, Belfast, Institute of Irish Studies, Queen's University.

5   'At the Shop Windows No. 1', p. 3.

6   *Dora Carleton*, p. 827.

7   'The Rustling of Wings', p. 279.

8   'Down Bourke Street', p. 335.

9   *The Secrets of Balbrooke*, p. 113.

10 'Little Peepshow', p. 3; Sylphid, 'The Ladies' Page', August 1869, p. 755; 'Flotsam', 1 December 1866, pp. 9–14.

11 *AJ*, 9 December 1865, p. 239.

12 'The Key of the Street', p. 592.

13 This computer analysis was conducted with the late Professor John Burrows, University of Newcastle. See Lucy Sussex and John Burrows, 'Whodunit?: Literary Forensics and the Crime Writing of James Skipp Borlase and Mary Fortune', *Bibliographical Society of Australia and New Zealand Bulletin*, 21(2), pp. 73–93.

14 'How I Spent Christmas', pp. 362–3.

15 Jan Noel, *Canada Dry: Temperance Crusades Before Confederation*, Toronto, University of Toronto Press, 1995; Sylphid, 'The Ladies' Page', 1 December 1869, p. 242.

16 Leaf 135, Shipton and Melbourne, Quebec Diocesan Archives, Bishop's University, Lennoxville. Information about the early history of the Fortune family can be found in the South Carolina Department of Archives and History, and Libraries and Archives Canada in Ottawa. Information has also been kindly supplied by Fortune family descendants Lorraine Chevrier and Glen Porteous.

17 See Harold Pollins, 'Railway Contractors and the Finance of Railway Development in Britain', in Mike Chrimes (ed.), *The Civil Engineering of Canals and Railways Before 1850*, Aldershot, Ashgate, 1997, pp. 321–37.

18 In Mary's story 'Delia Loney', a father advises his unhappily married daughter: 'Oh! My girl, you were always self-willed and headstrong; and now that there's nothing before you but misery, it's on my mind that you'd better leave him.' He asks her to accompany him on his emigration – 'You will get rid of that scoundrel' – but she refuses (p. 607).

19 For Canadian law on this issue see Constance Backhouse, *Petticoats and Prejudice: Women and Law in Nineteenth-Century Canada*, Toronto, Women's Press, 1991, pp. 167, 187, 203.

20   'Fourteen Days on the Roads', p. 218.

21   'Sandridge Pier', p. 3.

22   'Jack M'Crae', p. 161.

CHAPTER TWO: ARRIVAL

1   All the Fortune quotations in this chapter are from the first instalment of 'Twenty-Six Years Ago'. An extract, edited by Ron Campbell, is online at https://tomcollinsandcompany.github.io/annotate/texts/storybook.

2   Finlay is covered by the Melbourne press via Trove: *The Argus*, 1 April 1856, p. 4; *The Age*, 30 April 1856, p. 2; *The Age*, 10 December 1855, p. 6; *The Argus*, 26 December 1855, p. 6; *The Age*, 1 February 1855, p. 5.

3   *The Argus*, 15 October 1855, p. 8; Semple, b. 1820, from Stranraer in Scotland, was in 1848 ordained a minister of the United Presbyterian Church (like Finlay's Free Church of Scotland, an evangelical offshoot of the Presbyterians) in Peebles. When he resigned in 1853, 'The congregation made no effort to retain him'. Robert Small, *History of the Congregations of the United Presbyterian Church*, Edinburgh, Small, 1904, vol. 1, pp. 575–6. Semple arrived in Melbourne 1854. He worked for *The Mount Alexander Mail* for two years and died in Castlemaine of tuberculosis. His obituary appeared on 25 February 1859, p. 5, recording his lecturing on Scots poets, amateur dramatic appearances and general service to the community.

CHAPTER THREE: ON THE GOLDFIELDS

1   'Twenty-Six Years Ago', part 1, p. 37; 'The Diggings', *The Mount Alexander Mail*, 12 October 1855, p. 2.

2   All further references to 'Twenty-Six Years Ago' in this chapter are from the second installment, pp. 280–5, and the third, pp. 338–43.

3   'Twenty-Six Years Ago', p. 280.

4   'Twenty-Six Years Ago', p. 280.

5   F.B. Smith, 'Curing Alcoholism in Australia, 1880s–1920s', *Journal of Australian Colonial History* 8, 2008, pp. 137–58; 'Fourteen Days', p. 217.

6   Janet McCalman, *Vandemonians: The Repressed History of Colonial Victoria*, Melbourne, Miegunyah, 2021, p. 108.

7   'Twenty-Six Years Ago', p. 281.

8   Frederick Standish in 'The Contributor' column, 'Reminiscences and Adventures', The *Leader*, 23 April 1887, p. 16; Standish as transcribed

by Coroner Curtis Candler, 'Notes about Melbourne and diaries, 1848– [19??]', MS 9502, State Library of Victoria, [n.p.].

9   *The Mount Alexander Mail*, 30 November 1855, p. 3.

10   'Twenty-Six Years Ago', p. 284.

11   *The Mount Alexander Mail*, 14 December 1855, p. 284.

12   *The Age*, 7 February 1855, p. 5.

13   'Twenty-Six Years Ago', p. 338.

14   *Dora Carleton*, pp. 721–2.

15   Letter to Lucy Sussex from Robyn Annear, 27 May 1996; *Music of the Diggings: Songs and Tunes of the Central Victorian Goldfields*, Friends of Mount Alexander Diggings, Castlemaine, 2000.

16   'Twenty-Six Years Ago', p. 338.

17   Regarding Charles Saint, see Marjorie Theobald, *Accidental Town: Castlemaine 1851–61*, North Melbourne, Australian Scholarly Publishing, 2020, p. 51; *Kyneton Observer*, 3 December 1866, p. 3; obituary, *Gippsland Times*, 13 December 1886, p. 3; *Telegraph* and *St Kilda, Prahran* and *South Yarra Guardian*, 11 December 1886, p. 5. In retirement, he devoted himself to religious instruction of the young. He died of cancer and was attended in his last illness by Dr Bage, who would later perform that same task for Mary Fortune.

18   'Twenty-Six Years Ago', p. 338.

19   'Curlew's Gully', p. 693.

20   'The Stolen Specimens', pp. 106–7.

21   Standish, *The Leader*, 23 April 1887, p. 16.

22   'Twenty-Six Years Ago', p. 338; *The Mount Alexander Mail*, 14 March 1856, p. 3 and 18 March 1856, p. 2; *The Argus*, 18 March, p. 6. The press coverage of the case was scathing.

23   *Miners' Right*, 12 March 1856, p. 3.

24   'Twenty-Six Years Ago', p. 338; *The Bushranger's Autobiography*, p. 154.

25   *The Mount Alexander Mail*, 18 March 1856, p. 2; *The Argus*, 14 March 1856, p. 6; *The Age*, 14 March 1856, p. 3.

26   *The Mount Alexander Mail*, 7 December 1855, p. 3.

27   The plaque is on the site of Nicholson's Commercial Hotel, High Street, Taradale, her third hotel. The Taradale Hotel was her first. She operated as a hotel licensee from 1856 to 1868, 'an unusually long stint'. Marjorie Theobald, *Untold Tales of the Victorian Goldfields*, forthcoming 2024.

28   'Poor Gold', p. 625; *The Age*, 14 March 1856, p. 3; 'Twenty-Six Years Ago',
     p. 339.

29   James Flett, *Dunolly: Story of an Old Gold Diggings*, Melbourne,
     Hawthorn Press, 1974, p. 192; 'Sketches of the Diggings',
     The Australasian, 27 January 1866, p. 2.

30   'Killed in the Shaft', pp. 447–8; 'The Gutter Flag', p. 130.

31   'Traces of Crime', p. 220.

32   [Martha Clendinning], 'Recollections of Ballarat: Lady's Life at the
     Diggings Fifty Years Ago by M.J.C.', *The Leader*, 31 March 1906, p. 29.

33   See Jill Bavin-Mizzi, *Ravished: Sexual Violence in Victorian Australia*,
     Sydney, UNSW Press, 1995. For coverage of the Gray case see *The Age*,
     22 December 1856, p. 6; *The Argus,* 23 December, p. 5.

CHAPTER FOUR: A FATHERLESS CHILD

1   J.M. Barr, 'Round the Country, XVI', *Independent* (Footscray),
     10 December 1887, p. 3; *The Mount Alexander Mail*, 5 October 1855,
     p. 3; *The Argus*, 11 January 1856, p. 6.

2   'Twenty-Six Years Ago', pp. 341–2.

3   'Twenty-Six Years Ago', p. 340. The population of Buninyong was
     estimated by *The Age*, 23 February 1856, p. 3.

4   'Twenty-Six Years Ago', p. 341.

5   'In the Cellar', p. 549.

6   'Twenty-Six Years Ago', p. 343.

7   'Twenty-Six Years Ago', p. 343.

8   *The Mount Alexander Mail,* 14 December 1855, p. 5.

9   'Twenty-Six Years Ago', p. 343; *The Star* (Ballarat), 12 January 1856, p. 3.

10   'Twenty-Six Years Ago', p. 379.

11   'In the Cellar', p. 380.

12   'Twenty-Six Years Ago', pp. 445, 447.

13   'Twenty-Six Years Ago', p. 510; *Bendigo Advertiser*, 7 April 1857, p. 2.

14   *Bendigo Advertiser*, 3 March 1857, p. 2; 'Twenty-Six Years Ago', p. 445.

15   'Recollections of a Digger', p. 68.

16   Kingower is a Djadja Wurrung word, *gower* referring to a big hill.
     John Tully, *Kingower Maps*, Dunolly, Weila, 2022, p. 2; *Chronicle*
     (South Australia), 1 November 1902, p. 11.

17 'Delia Loney', p. 609.

18 'Twenty-Six Years Ago', pp. 508, 448.

CHAPTER FIVE: BIGAMY

1 'Little Georgie's Grandpa', p. 322.

2 'Her Death Warrant', p. 102.

3 *The Age*, 16 July 1857, p. 6.

4 Information about the Brett family comes from family historians Judith Brett, Percy Rollo Brett and Margaret Dupleix.

5 'The Deathstone', p. 72.

6 *The Bushranger's Autobiography*, p. 34.

7 *The Bushranger's Autobiography*, p. 94.

8 *Maryborough and Dunolly Advertiser*, 4 September 1857, p. 2; 8 September 1857, p. 2; inquest on Jane Fife, VPRS 24 PO Unit 49, item 1857/124; 'Melville's Fatal Shot', p. 309.

9 *The Age*, 3 March 1858, p. 5.

10 'Jim Dickson's Fit of the Horrors', p. 332.

11 'The Double Cross on the Rock', p. 524.

12 'The Stolen Specimens', p. 106.

13 'Grey's Gold', p. 417.

14 *Dora Carleton*, p. 739.

15 'The Stolen Specimens', p. 107.

16 'The Star-Spangled Banner', p. 44.

17 'The Star-Spangled Banner', pp. 45–6.

18 'The Double Cross on the Rock', p. 524.

19 'Yatalonga', p. 525.

20 Robert Haldane, *The People's Force: A History of the Victoria Police*. Carlton, Melbourne University Press, 1986, p. 104.

21 'Leaves from my Notebook', *Maryborough, Majorca and Carisbrook Independent*, 1 April 1870, p. 3.

22 George Buckmaster, 'Desultory Victorian Police Recollections', *The Ovens and Murray Advertiser*, 17 August 1895, p. 8.

23 'The Twenty-Ninth of November', p. 214.

24   'The Stolen Specimens', p. 107.

CHAPTER SIX: THE LADY VANISHES

1   *Clyzia the Dwarf*, p. 322.

2   'Mrs Larner's Revenge', p. 682.

3   'Mary Hester Armour', p. 579.

4   'Yatalonga', p. 526. This motif recurs in 'Mary Reardon's Christmas Eve', with a husband returning to Ireland seeking what he is owed. The setting reads like a disguised Kingower.

5   *The Age*, 20 October 1862, p. 6.

6   Henry Downing joined the Victorian police in 1852 and was described on his defaulter's sheet as aged twenty-four, a Protestant draper from Ireland, born in Belfast, the son of a clergyman. He was promoted to sub-inspector (on probation) in April 1860. In 1862, when in Geelong, he discovered the body of his superintendent, Samuel Freeman, who had cut his own throat. In 1867 Downing was transferred to Beechworth and was dismissed the following year following an inquiry into the police. Possible reasons for the dismissal include misbehaviour, such as condoning or taking bribes from sly grogging. He died in Ballarat, 1872, aged thirty-nine. Fortune fictionalised him as Sergeant Downing in an untitled *Detective's Album* story of August 1870. She gives his full name in two other tales, 'Melville's Fatal Shot', 1877 (in which he is shot by a bushranger) and 'Dead and Alive', in which she comments 'and a sad end he made of it' (p. 451).

7   'The Murderer's Claim', p. 479.

8   'Jim Dickson's Fit of the Horrors', p. 333.

9   'Dead or Alive', p. 451.

10   *The Mount Alexander Mail*, 2 December 1859, p. 4.

11   'The Dead Man in the Scrub', p. 774.

12   'Gustav Kupper, Vormals Ellinger', p. 509.

13   For Sullivan's history see the *Cornwall Chronicle*, 18 December 1874, p. 3; also *The Illustrated Australian News*, 30 December 1874, p. 218. He remains notorious in New Zealand.

14   'Our Golden Girl', p. 184.

15   Wehla or Weila is the word for brush-tail possum in Djadja Wurrung; 'Tully', p. 11; *Ballarat Courier*, 24 September 1884, p. 4.

16 'Our Colonial Christmases', p. 255.

17 'Simple Sam', p. 346.

18 Chubb MS, Box 4238, 23 August 1864, p. 47. Batchelder's images are held at the State Library of Victoria and available online. Their exhibition is described in the *Inglewood Advertiser*, 29 September 1866, p. 2.

19 Gus Peirce, *Knocking About: Being Some Adventures of Augustus Baker Peirce in Australia*, ed. Mrs Albert T. Leatherbee, Wangaratta, Shoestring, 1984, pp. 32–3.

20 'Recollections of a Digger', p. 68.

21 'A Jaunt to Jericho', qu. in Leila Gillespie, *Kingower*, L. Gillespie, 1975, pp. 81–3. Kingower is also described by 'The Sketcher' in *The Australasian*, 17 March 1866, p. 2.

22 'The Double Cross on the Rock', p. 524.

23 'The Murderer's Doom', p. 394.

24 *The Leader*, 7 July 1866, p. 21.

25 Gillespie, *Kingower*, p. 82.

CHAPTER SEVEN: FORTUNE WRITES

1 For the *AJ*'s history, see Ronald G. Campbell, *The First Ninety Years: The Printing House of Massina, Melbourne, 1859–1849*, Melbourne, A.H. Massina, 1949.

2 Campbell, The First Ninety Years, p. 41.

3 *South Australian Register*, 12 September 1865, p. 3; *South Australian Advertiser*, 14 September 1865, p. 2.

4 Walstab was born in London, the son of a former West Indian plantation owner who became successful in auctioneering and real estate after the family's emigration to Victoria in 1852. For Harrison, see Lucy Sussex, 'From Faery Sprite to Trilobite: The Writer "Robin Goodfellow"', *Notes & Furphies* 35, October 1995, pp. 6–8. Harrison was the son of a country storekeeper in Kent, and his brother Benjamin became a noted paleontologist. Both brothers wrote scientific papers, Thomas while working for the Melbourne Patent Office. A trilobite he found is named for him, *Trimerus harrisoni*. For the colonial magazines he wrote travelogue and fiction.

5 Borlase would be sacked from the *AJ* for plagiarising Sir Walter Scott. For more on his complex career, including repeated plagiarism, see

Lucy Sussex, 'Bobbing Around', *Victorian Periodicals Review* 87(4), Winter 2004, pp. 98–110, and also 'Our Whatnot', *AJ*, December 1870, p. 219.

6   'Looking for Lodgings', p. 267.

7   See G. Thomas Couser, *Vulnerable Subjects*, Ithaca, Cornell University Press, 2004.

8   Reprinted in 1993 by Mulini Press, Canberra, with a preface by Lucy Sussex. The book is also available as an electronic text from Clan Destine Press: https://www.clandestinepress.net/products/force-and-fraud.

9   Clarke's 'Wonderful' was identified by Nan Bowman Albinski, 'Marcus Clarke's First Australian Publication', *Margin* 21 (1989), pp. 1–10.

10   James Cordy Jeaffreson, review of *The Night Fossickers*, *Athenaeum*, 27 July 1867, p. 114.

11   'The Stolen Specimens', p. 106.

12   Gillespie, Kingower, p. 98.

13   'The Murderer's Doom', p. 394.

14   Henriette Nieman Inquest, VPRS 214/P0000, 1865/312.

15   The only known image of Borlase is an engraving, accompanying the article 'Some Interesting Notes About Mr James Skipp Borlase', *Derby and Chesterfield Reporter*, 11 November 1887, p. 2; Lucy Frost (ed.), *The Journal of Annie Baxter Dawbin: July 1858–May 1868*, St Lucia, UQP, 1997, p. 348. H.W. Steel and C. Nowlan Walstab died at the ages of three and seventeen months.

16   'Chay Jay', *The Bulletin*, 25 February 1855, p. 9. Ron Campbell would respond that Massina was 'pulling his leg', 25 March 1953, p. 9. Still the remark had an essential truth: Mary Fortune had married into the police and learnt from her husband and his fellow troopers.

17   *AJ*, [date], p. 156.

CHAPTER EIGHT: IMPERSONATING THE POLICE

1   Stephen Knight, *Australian Crime Fiction: A 200-Year History*, Jefferson, McFarland, 2018, p. 30.

2   The story appears with the e-reprint of *Force and Fraud* by Clan Destine Press.

3   Nemia, 'Social Sketches and Interesting Chit-Chat', *The Herald*, 29 August 1879, p. 3.

4   'Mr Furbush', *Harper's Monthly*, April 1865, pp. 623–6, 624.

5   'The Dead Witness; or, the Bush Waterhole', p. 329.

6   'The Dead Witness; or, the Bush Waterhole', p. 331.

7   'Our Whatnot', *AJ*, 1 December 1870, p. 219.

8   Christopher Philippo, Emails to Lucy Sussex, 2022.

9   Cecil Hadgraft, *The Australian Short Story Before Lawson*, Melbourne, OUP, 1986, p. 18. The story has also been reprinted elsewhere under Borlase's name, even after the misattribution was revealed.

CHAPTER NINE: THE YEAR OF NOVELS

1   James Skipp Borlase, 'Melbourne in 1869', *Temple Bar*, 30 September 1870, pp. 225–35. See 'Our Whatnot' for the *AJ*'s riposte.

2   Henry's comments were reprinted anonymously in Ruth Teale (ed.), *Colonial Eve: Sources on Women in Australia 1788–1914*, Melbourne, Oxford University Press, 1978, p. 226. The author was identified in Diane Kirkby's *Alice Henry*, Cambridge, Cambridge University Press, 1991, p. 43.

3   *AJ*, 24 March 1866, p. 479.

4   *Bertha's Legacy*, p. 482

5   *Bertha's Legacy*, p. 484.

6   *Dora Carleton*, p. 757. The case has inspired various retellings, of which the most recent are Deborah Benson's 2015 *Judicial Murder*, arguing for Young's innocence (Maldon, Deborah Benson) and Greg Pyers' 2017 novel *The Unfortunate Victim* (Melbourne, Scribe), which changes some names and makes a hero of Melbourne detective Otto Berliner, who had a real-life involvement. Pyers commented to Lucy Sussex that the Graham case was a 'good story', a sentiment with which Fortune would have agreed; interview, 20 March 2019. Benson is seeking a judicial pardon for David Young.

7   At least one of Chuck's images appeared as a newspaper engraving. The photograph of the hut is held at the State Library of New South Wales, SPF/1579. Chuck testified at the inquest that he only took one print of the victim and destroyed the negative. *The Ballarat Star*, 3 January 1865, p. 4.

8   *Dora Carleton*, p. 740.

9   *Dora Carleton*, pp. 722, 774.

10   10 November 1866, p. 169.

11   *Dora Carleton*, pp. 722, 774.

12   Dora Carleton, p. 788

13   *Clyzia the Dwarf*, p. 273.

14   22 December 1866, p. 271.

15   *AJ*, 2 December 1865, p. 223.

16   *Telegraph and St Kilda, Prahran and South Yarra Guardian*, 24 August, p. 3.

17   *AJ*, 30 March 1867, p. 495.

CHAPTER TEN: THE DETECTIVE'S ALBUM

1   'Our Colonial Christmases', p. 256.

2   See Laura Bovey (ed.), *About a Mile Away: The History of the Oxley Plains*, Preston, Bounce, 2013.

3   'The Midnight Watch', p. 500.

4   'The Midnight Watch', pp. 502–3.

5   'Circumstantial Evidence', p. 6.

6   Sorcha Ní Fhlainn and Xavier Aldana Reyes (eds), *Visions of the Vampire: Two Centuries of Immortal Tales*, London, British Library, 2020.

7   'The Family Secret', pp. 11–12.

8   'The Police Commission', *The Argus*, 15 December 1882, p. 11.

9   'Mr Medlet's Wedding', p. 73.

10   See Patricia Clarke, *Pen Portraits*, Sydney, Allen & Unwin, 1988, p. 210. The only record of Foott's work for Melbourne newspapers is a letter to her editor held in the State Library of Victoria, W.P. Hurst papers, LTU MS 6107, from 1873.

11   *The Bulletin*, 25 March 1953, p. 9.

12   Hal Walstab, 'The Bushranger', *AJ*, 29 August 1868, p. 2.

13   Quoted in Randolph Bedford, *Naught to Thirty-Three*, Melbourne, Melbourne University Press, 1976, p. 136.

14   Katherine Newey, *Women's Theatre Writing in Victorian Britain*, Basingstoke, Palgrave-Macmillan, 2005, p. 1.

15   For West's biography and opinions see 'Thirty Years Behind the Footlights', *The Leader*, 28 December 1889, p. 27.

16   See Viola Tait's *Dames, Principal Boys, and All That: A History of Pantomime in Australia*, Melbourne, Macmillan, 2001. Fortune's pantomime was discovered by Veronica Kelly.

17   *Freeman's Journal*, 26 December 1868, p. 15.

18   Catie Gilchrist, *Tales from a Colonial Coroner's Court: Murder, Misadventure and Miserable Ends*, Sydney, HarperCollins, 2019, pp. 100–7; *Empire*, 21 October 1869, p. 1.

CHAPTER ELEVEN: IN BOHEMIAN MELBOURNE

1   *AJ*, December 1869, p. 242.

2   *Bendigo Advertiser*, 15 January 1869, p. 2.

3   'Looking for Lodgings', p. 266.

4   'Looking for Lodgings', p. 266; Michael Wilding, *Wild Bleak Bohemia: Marcus Clarke, Adam Lindsay Gordon and Henry Kendall: A Documentary*, Melbourne, Australian Scholarly Publishing, 2014.

5   'How I Spent Christmas', p. 365.

6   Note, 30 January 1869, p. 365.

7   In December 1870 the *AJ*'s 'Our Whatnot' column stated: 'The present conductor of the JOURNAL has been so engaged for considerably more than four years out of the five and a half years of its existence'; p. 219.

8   Michael Cannon, Introduction, *Richard Egan-Lee's* Police News, ed. Michael Cannon, Melbourne, Today's Heritage, 1977, p. 1; Thomas Darragh, *Engravers and Lithographers in Colonial Victoria*, Ancora, Melbourne, 2023, pp. 140–1; obituary, *Australasian Typographical Journal* 9 (May 1879), p. 243. Egan-Lee was sentenced to twelve months' gaol for the type theft in February 1866 but may have paid a fine instead. He does not appear in surviving prison records.

9   'Our Whatnot' appeared from April 1869 through February 1871. It comprised snippets from overseas journals, answers to readers, and personal opinions. Egan-Lee's later sensational true-crime weekly *Police News* gave appreciative space to strong women. Historian Juliette Peers comments that he was 'fascinated by female agency'. See the introduction to *Outrage, Obscenity and* Madness, the exhibition catalogue of Elizabeth Gertsakis' exhibition of work based on *Police News* illustrations, Richmond, William Mora Galleries, 2015. The *Police News* was wildly successful, achieving a circulation of 17,000, but caused Egan-Lee grief. He was thrice taken to court on charges ranging from obscenity to libel but never found guilty. Egan-Lee had at least twelve children by four legal and common-law wives. His last wife, Elena, died, leaving him with three young sons. Aged seventy, he died in Melbourne in 1879 of gangrene of the lungs.

10 'By the way, I have often wondered why our editor bestowed such a *nom de plume* upon me as Sylphid, and, of course, I am conceited enough to fancy I could have chosen a much more appropriate one myself', December 1869, p. 241.

11 *AJ*, June 1869, p. 634.

12 *AJ*, July 1869, p. 689; *AJ*, January 1870, p. 291.

13 *AJ*, July 1869, pp. 688, 689.

14 *AJ*, June 1869, p. 634.

15 'My Advertisement', p. 565; Sylphid, January 1870, p. 292; February 1870, p. 350.

16 Jenny Coleman, *Polly Plum, a Firm and Earnest Woman's Advocate: Mary Ann Colclough, 1836–1885*, Dunedin, Otago University Press, 2017, p. 86.

17 'My Advertisement', p. 565.

18 'Under the Verandah', p. 599.

19 George Augustus, 'The Key of the Street', *Gaslight and Daylight*, London, Chapman & Hall, 1859. Available online: https://www.victorianlondon.org/publications2/gaslight-1.htm

20 'The Key of the Street', p. 593.

21 *The Australasian*, 'The Peripatetic Philosopher', 17 July 1869, p. 17.

22 Yorick Club Membership Book 1868–76, Box 4723/5, MS15347, State Library of Victoria.

23 Joseph Johnson, *Laughter and the Love of Friends*, Melbourne, Savage Club, 1994, pp. 24, 27; Hugh McCrae, *My Father, and My Father's Friends*, Sydney, Angus & Robertson, 1935, p. 35.

24 *Otago Daily Times*, 'Melbourne', 29 May 1871, p. 3.

25 *The Herald*, 9 December 1873, p. 2.

26 'A Colonial Literary Club by a Wandering Bohemian', *Australian Town and Country Journal*, 18 February 1871, p. 18.

27 Christopher Sly (Dr. Neild), 'A Peep at the Pictures', *Examiner and Melbourne Weekly News*, 12 December 1857, p. 8.

28 In Marcus Clarke, *A Colonial City: High and Low Life – Selected Journalism of Marcus Clarke*, ed. Laurie Hergenhan, St Lucia, University of Queensland Press, 1982, pp. 213, 277–8.

29 *AJ*, July 1869, p. 690.

30 Vandemonians were convicts transported to Tasmania who had been pardoned or had served their time and moved to Victoria, mostly for the goldfields, to enjoy their freedom.

31 *AJ*, August 1869, p. 755.

32 'A Night in the Lock-Up No. I. and II', *The Age*, 7 and 12 February 1870, p. 3.

33 *The Daily Telegraph*, 11 August, p. 4; *The Age*, 11 August, p. 3; *The Herald*, 10 August, p. 3.

34 In 1875 Caffrey again got six months for keeping a disorderly house.

35 Mark Finnane (ed.), '*The Difficulties of My Position*': *The Diaries of Prison Governor John Buckley Castieau, 1855–1884*, Canberra, National Library of Australia, 2004, p. 120.

36 'The Ghost in the Garden', pp. 687, 689.

37 *AJ*, September 1869, p. 62.

38 'The Convict's Revenge', p. 171.

39 'The Convict's Revenge', p. 174.

40 Barbara Minchinton, *The Women of Little Lon*, Melbourne, Black Inc., 2021, pp. 194, 195.

41 'My Lodger', p. 472.

42 'Unlucky No. 58', p. 547.

43 *AJ*, June 1870, p. 604.

44 'Down by the Yarra', p. 577.

CHAPTER TWELVE: THE WAYWARD BOY

1 'The Lost Shepherd', p. 362.

2 'The Double Cross on the Rock', p. 524.

3 'Only One Blow', p. 708; *AJ*, November 1869, p. 163.

4 'Down by the Yarra', p. 577.

5 'The Deed Done in the Scrub', p. 335

6 'What to Do With Our Boys: The Peripatetic Philosopher', *The Australasian*, 5 March 1870, p. 17.

7 'What Passed', pp. 347–7.

8 *The Age*, 25 July 1871, p. 3; 'A Night in the Lock-up', *The Age*, 7, 12 February 1870, p. 3.

9   'What Passed', p. 347.

10   *Punch*, 29 September 1870, p. 7.

11   Qu. In Dean Wilson, *The Beat: Policing the Victorian City*, Beaconsfield, circa 2006, p. 115; Melissa Bellanta, *Larrikins: A History*, St Lucia, University of Queensland Press, 2012; 'The D's: Lovie', *Punch* 15 August 1889, p. 103.

12   'Constable Dyason's Defeat', p. 2.

13   Chris McConville, 'Outcast Children in Marvellous Melbourne', in Guy Featherstone (ed.), *The Colonial Child*, Melbourne, RHSV, 1981, pp. 39–48, p. 44.

14   The Children's Registers for Colonial Victoria can be accessed via the PROV website.

15   The Governesses' Institute and Melbourne Home, *Annual Report*, 1871, pp. 2, 4, 7–8.

16   *The Argus*, 8 February, p. 6.

17   Ron Campbell, Letter to J.K. Moir, 26 May 1952, Moir Collection, State Library of Victoria, Melbourne.

18   Finnane, p. 198.

19   'A Woman's Revenge; or, Almost Lost', p. 333.

20   For information on the industrial schools and reformatories, see Joan Brogden, *Neglected – Or Criminal? The Sunbury Industrial School*, Melbourne, Joan Brogden, three volumes, 1995–2000.

21   'Jack's Villa', p. 393.

22   The Sketcher, 'Sunbury and the Industrial Schools, Victoria', *AJ*, 14 December 1867, pp. 252–4.

23   The Sketcher, p. 254.

24   The process of Mary Fortune's application for George is located at VPRS 3993/P000, unit 21, p. 511.

25   VPRS 937/P0000, unit 256/13/4085. Report dated 13 July 1870.

26   Harriet Huxley had assaulted her de facto father-in-law, *Melbourne Daily News*, 6 October 1849, p. 2; Nemia, 'Down Bourke Street', p. 3; Brogden, Neglected – Or Criminal?, v. 3, pp. 17–23.

27   'Looking for Lodgings', p. 266.

28   'The Worms Don't Care', p. 3.

29   'The Dead Man in the Scrub', p. 774.

CHAPTER THIRTEEN: A VERY RARE AND VALUABLE BOOK

1   John Holroyd, *George Robertson of Melbourne 1825–1898*, Melbourne, Robertson and Mullens, 1968, p. 56.

2   'Arch Leslie's First Yarn', p. 516.

3   'Our Whatnot', *AJ*, 1 December 1870, p. 219.

4   W. Park Low, typescript, PRG 53/11, State Library of South Australia.

5   Message to Lucy Sussex from Caren Florence, 24 October 2020.

6   Catherine Martin, *The Silent Sea*, ed. Rosemary Foxton, Colonial Text Series 4, Sydney, UNSW, 1995.

7   'Australian Literature in Its First Century. Poetry – III', *The Argus*, 10 July 1886, p. 3. *The Warden* contains an interesting poem on William Buckley.

8   *The Mount Alexander Mail*, 18 January 1873, p. 2.

9   See Sussex, 'Bobbing Around'.

10 Campbell, *The First Ninety Years*, pp. 74–5. This information was first brought to our attention by Sarah Ailwood, a legal academic and literary scholar at the University of Wollongong. We then checked the copyright registers in the national archive to confirm this and to see if Mary Fortune held any copyrights. None could be found.

11 Campbell, *The First Ninety Years*, p. 84. For Egan-Lee, see Cannon and Darragh. In 1873, Egan-Lee dealt even more drastically with missing copy. The *AJ* was pirating a serialised American novel, which arrived in Melbourne by instalments. When copies of the conclusion failed to arrive, Egan-Lee wrote it himself.

12 *The Bushranger's Autobiography*, pp. 396–7.

13 The Bushranger's Autobiography, p. 584.

14 In Marcus Clarke, *His Natural Life*, ed. Lurline Stuart, St Lucia, University of Queensland Press, 2001, p. xliv.

CHAPTER FOURTEEN: THE MISFORTUNES OF GEORGE FORTUNE

1   'Our Colonial Christmases', p. 256.

2   'Mag Braban's Share', p. 606.

3   *Police Gazette*, 23 January 1872, p. 27.

4   *The Argus*, 27 February 1872, p. 4.

5   VPRS 3991, Unit 1048, 78/14342.

6   'The Waif of the Slums', p. 70.

7   *The Herald*, 8 June 1871, p. 2.

8   *The Argus*, 27 March 1872, p. 4.

9   Brogden, Neglected – Or Criminal?, vol. 3, p. 57.

10 'The Stolen Deed', p. 677.

11 The hulk concerned was the *Deborah*: 'Juvenile Reformatory and Training Ship', *The Argus*, 22 July 1864, p. 7; George Duncan's testimony to the Royal Commission on Penal and Prison Discipline; Industrial and Reformatory Schools, *Report (No. 3)*, J. Ferres, government printer, 1872, p. 10, q. 263–4.

12 Royal Commission on Penal and Prison Discipline, *Report*, p. 9, q. 255.

13 'Lost in Town', p. 124.

14 Campbell, *The First Ninety Years*, p. 115

15 Brogden, Neglected – Or Criminal?, vol. 3, pp. 79–80.

16 *The Herald*, 17 February 1873, p. 2; *The Leader*, 1 March 1873, p. 13.

17 Duncan told the royal commission that reformatory children were harder to place; p. 10, q. 270.

18 'Yatalonga', p. 523.

19 'Yatalonga', p. 523.

20 'Queen of Diamonds', p. 132.

21 'The Convict Son', p. 67.

22 The Victorian *Police Gazette* is digitised and available via Ancestry.com. 21 October 1873, p. 263.

23 'Jack's Villa', p. 389.

24 *Police Gazette,* 10 February 1874, p. 30.

25 'Yatalonga', p. 523.

26 'Yatalonga', pp. 523, 526.

27 *Police Gazette,* 30 June 1874, p. 141.

28 Campbell, *The First Ninety Years*, p. 100

29 'Pentridge', reprinted in *The Ovens and Murray Advertiser*, 18 December 1875, p. 1.

30 'Death of Mr David Brown', *Kilmore Free Press*, 25 August 1892, p. 2.

31 For Bylands information: Jim Quillinan, *The Story of Bylands* [Warragul, Quillinan] 2022, pp. 71–3, 128; Our Travelling Reporter, 'Farming in

the Kilmore District', *The Australasian*, 5 August 1878, p. 23. The other Fortune story is 'The Lady in No. 4, De Lunatico Inquirendo', p. 5.

32   'The Waif of the Slums', p. 69.

CHAPTER FIFTEEN: FIZGIGS

1   'The Terrace Walk', p. 560.

2   'The Shadow on the Blind', p. 4.

3   *Household Supplement*, 10 December 1881, p. 1.

4   Brian Hardiman, interview with Lucy Sussex, 20 June 2020.

5   Donald Thomas, *The Victorian Underworld*, London, John Murray, 2003, p. 6.

6   'The Stolen Deed', p. 674.

7   Victorian Royal Commission on Police, *Special Report on the Detective Branch*, 1883, p. xiii.

8   *Telegraph and St Kilda, Prahran and South Yarra Guardian*, 24 December 1881, p. 7.

9   Royal Commission on the Police Force of Victoria, *The Proceedings of the Commission, Minutes of Evidence, Appendices, etc.* Melbourne, Government Printer, 1883, p. 534, Q 14732.

10   Sandra Nicholson, interview with Lucy Sussex, 2021.

11   'The Wages of Sin', p. 49.

12   Interview with Brian Hardiman, 2021.

13   'The Stolen Deed', p. 675.

14   'My Friends and Acquaintances', p. 197.

15   'John Fowler's Sin', p. 627.

16   See Elizabeth Morrison, *A Man of No Mean Talent: Donald Cameron and Australian Colonial Newspaper Fiction*, Queanbeyan, Restitution, 2023, p. 90.

CHAPTER SIXTEEN: THE STONE JUG

1   *The Kilmore Advertiser*, 6 February 1979, p. 2.

2   *The Kilmore Advertiser*, 14 April 1879, p. 2

3   *North Eastern Ensign*, 1 April 1890, p. 2.

4   All prison records cited are available online from the PROV.

5   'Pentridge', p. 1.

6   Samuel Gill, 'The Kelly Gang at Jerilderie', *Euroa Advertiser*, 4 March 1910, p. 6.

7   Douglas Stewart, *Ned Kelly*, Sydney, Shepherd Press, 1946.

8   *The Herald*, 22 September 1879, p. 3.

9   *The Herald*, 20 August 1879, p. 3.

10   Both Chads and Dumas were well connected. Chads was the daughter of an admiral, but an improvident husband brought her to journalism, notably art criticism, but also didactic novels. See Pieter Koster , 'A Forgotten Art Critic: Ellen Augusta Chads and the Melbourne Art Scene 1884–86', *The La Trobe Journal* 93–94 (September 2014), pp. 102–13 Dumas, who more frequently wrote as T.L. Grace Dumas, was daughter of Alex Dumas (1812–1878), clerk of the Legislative Council in Victoria. She wrote primarily fiction for newspapers and the *AJ* but died the year after her marriage, from childbirth. *The Ballarat Star* termed her 'one of the most graceful and most apt of our feminine lady writers', 9 July 1888, p. 3.

11   *The Herald*, 22 September 1879, p. 2.

12   *The Herald*, 15 September 1879, p. 3.

13   Campbell, *The First Ninety Years*, p. 110.

14   Nemia, 'Going Shopping', p. 3.

15   Nemia, 'Social Sketches and Interesting Chit-Chat', p. 3.

16   Nemia, 'A Visit to Pentridge', *The Herald*, p. 3.

17   Geoffrey Serle, 'Winter, Samuel Vincent (1843–1904)', *Australian Dictionary of Biography*, Volume 6, Parkville, Melbourne University Press, 1976.

CHAPTER SEVENTEEN: MARVELLOUS MELBOURNE

1   Campbell, *The First Ninety Years*, pp. 114–6

2   'A Colonial Literary Club by a Wandering Bohemian', *Australian Town and Country Journal*, 18 February 1871, p. 18.

3   Henry W. Mitchell, 'A Well-Known Contributor: Waif Wander', *AJ* May 1880, pp. 487–8; 'Mr. Henry Mitchell', *Table Talk*, 26 December 1901, p. 19.

4   'Twenty-Six Years Ago', February 1883, p. 338.

5   'Mag's Braban's Share', p. 606.

6   'Mag Braban's Share', p. 335; 'The Deed Done in the Scrub', p, 334.

7   *The Kilmore Advertiser*, 14 April 1881, p. 2

8   'The Forger Foiled', p. 36.

9   'Metropolitan Echoes', *The Ballarat Star*, 8 July 1881, p. 3.

10   'Metropolitan Echoes', *The Ballarat Star*, 1 August 1881, p. 3.

11   Henry Kendall, 'Marcus Clarke', *Sydney Mail and New South Wales Advertiser*, 13 August 1881, p.277.

12   *Bertha's Legacy*, p. 533.

13   Royal Commission on Police, *Special Report on the Detective Branch*, 1883, p. iii.

14   *Special Report on the Detective Branch*, p. iv; Royal Commission on the Police Force of Victoria. *Proceedings*, p. 372, Q 9450.

15   *Special Report on the Detective Branch*, p. ix.

16   For Boardman's history, see the Royal Commission, *Proceedings*, p. 312, Q 7664; *Proceedings*, p. 326, Q 8007; *The Australasian*, 23 December 1871, p. 822.

17   Forster, *Proceedings*, p. 102, Q 2552.

18   Alfred Edward Whitney, *Proceedings*, p. 316, Q774; Boardman, *Proceedings*, p. 312, Q 7664.

19   Brian Hardiman, email to Lucy Sussex, 29 October 2020. See also his 2019 statement for the Royal Commission into the Management of Police Informants: https://www.rcmpi.vic.gov.au, Exhibit RC0274.

20   *The Age* 31 December, p. 7; *The Herald*, 30 December, p. 12.

21   'Ned Pelbit's Escape', p. 358.

22   'Reforming Criminals', *The Herald*, 25 May 1878, p. 2.

23   Royal Commission, Proceedings, p. 312.

24   'Our Penal System', *The Herald*, 27 May 1878, p. 3.

25   'Reforming Criminals' *The Herald*, 25 May 1878, p. 2.

26   'Little Peepshow', p. 3.

27   'Twenty-Six Years Ago', p. 36.

28   *The Mount Alexander Mail*, 3 April 1884, p. 2.

29   *Northern Ensign Supplement*, 23 January 1885, p. 1.

CHAPTER EIGHTEEN: THE BANK ROBBERY

1   Information regarding this case comes from its trial brief, with
     depositions: VPRS 30/P0029/8, Central Criminal Court, July 1885; and
     from *The Weekly Times*, 13 June 1885, p. 2.

2   *Nabbing Ned Kelly* sets out in detail Michael Ward's hard, dedicated
     work in the Kelly case, as does an article reprinted in *The Ovens and
     Murray Advertiser*. The latter also notes that Ward was O'Callaghan's
     brother-in-law, 29 June 1889, p. 5.

3   *Truth*, 29 May 1904, p.6. Devine's exchange was with Thomas Millidge.

4   *The Mount Alexander Mail*, 26 September 1905, p. 4.

5   *The Crookwell Gazette* also named this man as Millidge, p. 4;
     Melbourne Punch, 29 August 1889, p. 135. Detective Lovie's deposition
     states that he acted on 'information received' but declines to say from
     whom. The press may have confusesd Lovie with Lomaine. Detective
     Considine deposed that vagrancy warrants were issued for the four
     named robbers on the night of 5 June.

6   *Truth*, 29 May 1904, p.6.

7   *Glenn Innes Examiner*, 16 June 1885, p.3.

8   *The Mount Alexander Mail*, June 9 1885, p. 2.

9   Richard McMahon figures in Marjorie Theobald's *Untold Tales of the
     Victorian Goldfields*, forthcoming 2024; *Riverine Herald*, 2 May 1876, p. 2.

10   See Anne Black, *Pendragon: The Life of George Isaacs, Colonial
     Wordsmith*, Adelaide, Wakefield, 2020. Isaacs was also responsible for
     the pantomime *The Burlesque of Frankenstein*, regarded as the first
     Australian science fiction. The *AJ*'s firm published it in 1865.

11   *The Age*, 8 May 1874, p. 2.

12   VPRS 515/P0000, Central Register for Male Prisoners 14257–14721
     (1876–1877), Thomas Millidge, volume 25, p. 160, prisoner number
     14413.

13   *The Weekly Times*, 27 June 1885, p. 11.

14   Raingill, born c. 1848, was described as a clerk, and ostler. UK
     Calendar of Prisons 1869–1929, via Ancestry.com, *Liverpool Mercury*,
     16 March 1870 and *Manchester Times*, 12 March 1870.

15   *The Weekly Times*, 27 June 1885, p. 11.

16   *The Weekly Times*, 13 June, p. 6.

17   *The Weekly Times*, 20 June, p. 11.

18 *The Herald*, 29 June 1885, p. 3.

19 *The Herald*, 26 June 1885, p. 2. Fraser would later write the eccentric utopia *Melbourne and Mars: My Mysterious Life on Two Planets* (1889).

20 *The Herald*, 20 July 1885, p. 3.

21 *The Weekly Times*, 27 June 1885, p. 11.

22 *Police Gazette*, 25 March 1885, p. 88.

23 *The Argus*, 24 June 1885, p. 10.

24 *The Herald*, 25 June 1885, p. 4.

25 *Table Talk*, 31 July 1885, p. 6.

26 *The Mount Alexander Mail*, 22 July 1865, p. 2; 'Recovery of Part of the Treasure', *The Herald* 9 June 1885, p. 3.

27 J. Schnittker, S.H. Larimore and H. Lee, 'Neither Mad Nor Bad? The Classification of Antisocial Personality Disorder among Formerly Incarcerated Adults', *Social Science & Medicine* 264 (November 2020):113288.

28 Schnittker et al., 'Neither Mad Nor Bad?', p. 5; 'Antisocial Personality Disorder', Health Direct (website), February 2024, https://www. healthdirect.gov.au/antisocial-personality-disorder.

29 Schnittker et al., 'Neither Mad Nor Bad?', p. 12.

30 *Clarence River Advocate*, 8 December 1903, p. 1.

31 *The Leader*, death notice, 25 August 1894, p. 42.

32 *Albury Banner*, 19 November, 10 December and 24 December 1886, pp. 19, 20 and 25. McMahon apparently did not reoffend.

33 *Clipper*, 9 June 1894, p. 1.

34 See Rachel Franks, *An Uncommon Hangman: The Life and Deaths of Robert 'Nosey Bob' Howard*, Sydney, NewSouth, 2022, pp. 216–20.

35 *The Argus*, 20 October 1902, p. 5.

36 *Bendigo Advertiser*, 15 October 1902, p. 3.

37 *The Weekly Times*, 25 October 1902, p. 14.

38 *The Argus*, 20 October 1902, p. 5.

39 *The Argus*, 27 October 1902, p. 9.

40 See Mary's story 'Trapped', p. 33.

41 *The Herald*, 21 July 1885, p. 3.

CHAPTER NINETEEN: SAFECRACKING

1   'Bridget's Locket', p. 1177.

2   'Bridget's Locket', p. 1333.

3   *Sydney Mail*, 29 March 1890, p. 721

4   *The Age*, 22 March 1890, p.10.

5   *Albury Banner and Wodonga Express*, 28 March 1990, p. 25

6   *The Age*, 24 March 1890, p. 5.

7   *The Age*, p. 5.

8   *North Eastern Ensign*, 4 April 1890, p. 2.

9   *North Eastern Ensign*, p. 2.

10 *The Argus*, 28 March 1890, p. 6.

11 *North Eastern Ensign*, p. 2.

12 *Seymour Express*, 28 March 1890, p. 2.

13 *The Leader*, 24 May 1890, p. 16.

14 *North Eastern Ensign*, 20 May 1890, p. 2.

15 *North Eastern Ensign*, p. 2.

16 *North Eastern Ensign*, p. 2.

17 'Market Street Mystery', p. 687.

18 'Regan's Doom', p. 742.

19 'Digging His Own Grave', p. 796.

20 'Regan's Doom', p. 742.

21 'Mag Braban's Share', September 1898, p. 605.

22 *Table Talk*, 25 March 1898, p. 3.

CHAPTER TWENTY: THE RECIDIVIST

1   *The Daily Telegraph* (Launceston), 3 May 1899, p. 3.

2   Commission on the State of Penal Discipline in Tasmania, *Report of the Commissioners, with the Evidence Taken, and Other Documents*, Hobart, House of Assembly, Government Printer, 24 July 1883, p. 3.

3   Commission on the State of Penal Discipline in Tasmania, *Report of the Commissioners*, p. 3.

4   Tasmanian Archives GD4/1/2, p. 165

5   *Mercury*, 8 February 1900, p. 4.

6   *Tasmanian News*, 11 May 1901, p. 2.

7   *Tasmanian News*, 21 May 1901, p. 4.

8   *Mercury*, 15 May 1903, p. 4.

9   *The Daily Telegraph*, 11 August 1903, p. 3.

10   *Tasmanian News*, 2 September 1903, p. 4.

11   *Zeehan and Dundas Herald*, 20 October 1903, p. 2.

12   'City Police Court', *Mercury*, 30 July 1904, p. 2.

13   'City Police Court', *Mercury*, 30 July 1904, p. 2.

14   *Tasmanian News*, 3 August 1904, p. 4.

15   Tamanian Archives. SGD13/1/108 Criminal Prosecution file, 11 August 1904–10 December 1904.

16   *Tasmanian News*, 28 September 1904, p. 2.

17   *Tasmanian News*, 17 May 1907, p. 6.

18   T. Grainger Stewart, 'On the Treatment of Chronic Bright's Disease', *British Medical Journal*, 16 August 1890, p. 389.

19   Stewart, p. 389.

20   Tasmanian Archives GD96/1/7, Medical Treatment of Ill Prisoners, January 1888–31 December 1938.

21   Tasmanian Archives GD116/1/2, Request Book, March 1907.

22   Tasmanian Archives GD29/1/5, Gate keeper Book, 1 February 1907–3 March 1908.

23   *Mercury*, 18 May 1907, p. 2.

24   *Tasmanian News*, 17 May 1907, p. 6.

CHAPTER TWENTY-ONE: MARY FORTUNE WRITES

1   An anti-Romish sermon in Chalmer's church drew censure from *The Age*, 12 October 1855, p. 4; at least two of her *Advocate* works had Irish reprints: 'The Celtic Cross' in the *Irish Catholic*, 1907, and 'A Bunch of Shamrocks' as 'The Punishment of Frank Audsley' in the *Irish Emerald*, 1905. We are indebted to Maitrayee Roychoudhury for the latter discovery.

2   *Albury Banner*, 28 September 1900, p. 23.

3   R.A. Cage, *Poverty Abounding, Charity Aplenty: The Charity Network in Colonial Victoria*, Sydney, Hale & Ironmonger, 1992, p. 25

4   Fortune file, Moir collection, State Library of Victoria.

5   *Charitable Institutions: First Progress Report of the Royal Commission on Charitable Institutions*, Melbourne, Government Printer, 1890, p. 577.

6   'Digging His Own Grave', p. 792.

7   Dean Wilson, *The Beat*, p. 135; William Pember Reeves, *State Experiments in Australia and New Zealand*, vol. 2, London, G. Richards, 1902, pp. 296–300.

8   For the ALS, see Susan Radvansky and Patricia Alsop (eds), '*Twixt Heather and Wattle: The First Minute Book of the Australian Literature Society, 1899–1903*, Melbourne, Monash University Library, 1990.

9   *The Argus*, 22 September 1903, p. 7.

10   Fortune file, Moir collection, State Library of Victoria.

11   'No. 95 Prosser Street', p. 178.

12   *The Advocate*, 1 January 1942, p. 11.

13   'The Bell of the Dead', p. 305.

14   *Richmond Guardian*, 13 March 1902, p. 2.

15   Ronald Campbell, 'An Editor Regrets', p. 6. Unless otherwise stated, all quotations from Ronald Campbell in this chapter are from his memoir; Roger Osborne writes on Campbell's tenure: 'An Editor Regrets': R.G. Campbell's *Australian Journal*, 19261955', *Script and Print* 41(4), 2017, pp. 226–242.

16   J.K. Moir, letter to Miss [Beatrice] Davis, 20 July 1954, Moir collection, State Library of Victoria.

17   Records of the Melbourne Benevolent Asylum, General Register, Female FBox 926/6 v.V, p. 99, FBox 626/7, p. 164, MS8366 Box 624/13, For information on the institution, see Mary Kehoe, *The Melbourne Benevolent Asylum: Hotham's Premier Building*, North Melbourne: Hotham History Project, 1998.

18   'Mona Caerwyn', p. 228.

19   Moir, letter to Miss [Beatrice] Davis .

20   'Melbourne Cemetery', p. 181.

EPILOGUE: THE AFTERMATH

1   Campbell, 'An Editor Regrets', p. 6.

2   Campbell, 'An Editor Regrets', pp. 6, 7. *The Detective's Album* continued until 1933.

3   The poem was recited at a 1932 Eisteddfod in Toowoomba (*Toowoomba Chronicle*, 11 April, p. 9) and as an elocution test piece in Perth in 1934 (*West Australian*, 30 April, p. 16); the manuscript of O'Callaghan's 'Police and Other People' is held at the State Library of Victoria.

4   For further information on Moir, see Campbell, 'An Editor Regrets', and Lucy Sussex, 'Collecting Books and Intelligence: The Curious Case of Jack Moir', *Overland* 155, 1999, pp. 16–18. Moir's granddaughter is the true-crime writer Robin Bowles. Moir advertised in *The Argus*, 4 August 1950, p. 6.

5   Campbell, 'An Editor Regrets', pp. 28, 31, 34; Campbell's 'The *Australian Journal* Story Book' is held at the University of Queensland Fryer Library UQFL120. It is available online at: https://tomcollinsandcompany.github.io/annotate/texts/storybook.

6   Allen J. Hubin, *Crime Fiction 1749–1980: A Comprehensive Bibliography*, second edition, New York, Garland, 1984.

7   'Ladies' Page, AJ, June 1870.

8   'Under the Verandah', p. 599.

APPENDIX 1: READING MARY FORTUNE

1   *Launceston Examiner*, 31 March 1866, p. 5.

2   *Bendigo Advertiser*, 6 July 1869, p. 3.

3   *Gippsland Times*, 6 January 1871, p. 2.

4   'Our Melbourne Letter', *Lake County Press*, 6 May 1880, p. 3.

5   AJ, July 1933, p. 84.

6   H.M. Green, *A History of Australian Literature, Vol. 1*, Sydney, Angus & Robertson, pp. 292–3.

7   Patricia Clarke, review of *The Fortunes of Mary Fortune*, The *Canberra Times*, 20 January 1990, p. 84; and Adrian Rawlins, *The Australian*, 28–29 October 1989, p. 8.

8   Candice Fox, introduction to *Bridget's Locket and Other Mysteries by Waif Wander / Mary Helena Fortune*, p. vii.

9   Fin J. Ross, *Billings Better Bookstore and Brasserie*, Bittern, Clan Destine Press, pp. 201–4.

LIST OF IMAGES

LIST OF MARY FORTUNE'S WORKS CITED

The great majority of Mary Fortune's works were published in the *Australian Journal* (*AJ*). The *AJ* up to 1900 can be accessed online via Gale's *Nineteenth Century UK Periodicals*, which also includes the colonies. Other publications to which Fortune contributed are for the most part available via Trove.

'Achernar: A Dream', *The Australasian*, 23 March 1907, p. 714.

'Arch Leslie's First Yarn', *AJ*, June 1878, pp. 516–23.

'At the Shop Windows No I', *The Herald*, 1 October 1879, p. 3.

'The Bank Robber', *AJ*, September 1907, pp. 561–4.

'The Bell of the Dead', *AJ*, May 1908, pp. 305–9.

'Bertha's Legacy', *AJ*, 31 March–26 May 1866, pp. 481–6, 500–3, 515–9, 533–6, 580–4, 594–7, 613–5.

'Bridget's Locket', *Australian Town and Country Journal*, 27 November–25 December 1886, pp. 1125, 1177, 1228–9, 1332–3.

'The Bushranger's Autobiography', *AJ*, September 1871–June 1872, pp. 34–40, 94–99, 154–60, 214–20, 274–81, 334–41, 394–7, 581–4.

'The Camperton Necklace', *AJ*, November 1888, pp. 164–170.

'Canada', *AJ*, 11 August 1866, p. 798.

'Caught in his Own Trap', *The Herald*, 1–2 March 1876, p. 4.

'Charley Evan's Story', *AJ*, August 1873, pp. 653–660.

'Circumstantial Evidence', *AJ*, 31 August 1867, pp. 5–8.

'Climb Up the Hill', *The Mount Alexander Mail*, 28 December 1855, p. 2; reprinted as 'Excelsior', *AJ*, November 1880, p. 133.

'Clyzia the Dwarf: A Romance', *AJ*, 29 December 1866–30 March 1867, pp. 273–6, 289–93, 321–3, 337–41, 353–7, 371–5, 385–9, 401–4, 417–21, 433–6, 449–52, 465–9, 481–3.

'Coals of Fire', *The Herald*, 4 August 1883, p. 3.

'Constable Dyason's Defeat', *The Herald*, 1 January 1879, p. 2.

'The Convict Son', *AJ*, October 1873, pp. 66–73.

'The Convict's Revenge', *AJ*, November 1869, pp. 170–4.

'Curlew's Gully', *AJ*, August 1893, pp. 686–93.

'Dan Lyons' Doom', *The Gippsland Mercury*, Supplements 400–9, 27 November 1884, 6 December 1884, 13 December, 10 January, 17 January, 24 January, 31 January, 7 February 1885, [n.p].

'A Dark Night', *The Herald*, 4 April 1882, p. 3.

'Dead or Alive', *AJ*, April 1895, pp. 451–7.

'The Dead Man in the Scrub', *AJ*, 3 August 1867, pp. 744–6.

'The Dead Witness; or, the Bush Waterhole', *AJ*, 20 January 1866, pp. 329–331.

'The Deathstone', *AJ*, October 1884, pp. 72–81.

'The Deed Done in the Scrub', *AJ*, February 1889, pp. 334–9.

'Delia Loney', *AJ*, October 1904, pp. 606–12.

'De Lunatico Inquirendo', *Weekly Times*, 25 January 1908, pp. 5–6.

'The Deserted Hut', *AJ*, 24 March 1866, pp. 473–6.

'The Diamond Ring', *AJ*, 17 March 1866, pp. 454–5.

'Digging His Own Grave', *AJ*, December 1898, pp. 791–796.

'The Dog Detective', *AJ*, May 1873, pp. 473–9.

'Dora Carleton: A Tale of Australia', *AJ*, 14 July–25 August 1866, pp. 721–4, 739–43, 756–9 772–5, 788–92, 803–7, 826–9.

'The Double Cross on the Rock', *AJ*, May 1870, pp. 524–6

'Down Bourke Street', *AJ*, 16 January 1869, pp. 330–5.

'Down Bourke Street', [Nemia] *Herald*, 13 November 1879, pp. 3–4.

'Down by the Yarra', *AJ*, June 1870, pp. 576–9.

'The Family Secret: A True Tale of the Colonies', *AJ*, 29 August 1868, pp. 9–12.

'Flotsam', *AJ*, 8 December 1866, pp. 217–22.

'Fourteen Days on the Road', *AJ*, 28 November 1868, pp. 217–21.

'The Ghost in the Garden', *AJ*, August 1872, pp. 684–9.

'Going Shopping', *The Herald*, 7 October 1879, p. 3.

'Grey's Gold', *AJ*, June 1898, pp. 417–22.

'Gustav Kupper, Vormals Ellinger', *AJ*, May 1893, pp. 509–15.

'The Gutter Flag: A Tale of the "Green Hills' Diggings"', *AJ*, November 1880, pp. 125–31.

'The Hart Murder', *AJ*, October 1870, pp. 106–11.

'Hatty Lyle', *Herald*, 11 October 1879, p. 3.

'Her Death Warrant', *AJ*, February 1904, pp. 102–4.

'How I Spent Christmas', *AJ*, 30 January 1869, pp. 362–5.

'In the Cellar', *AJ*, 27 April 1867, pp. 549–52.

'Jack McCrea', *AJ*, March 1907, pp. 161–6.

'Jack's Villa', *AJ*, March 1891, pp. 389–94.

'Jim Dickson's Fit of the Horrors', *AJ*, 20 January 1866, pp. 332–3.

'John Fowler's Sin', *AJ*, August 1877, pp. 626–34.

'The Key of the Street', *AJ*, 1 June 1869, pp. 592–4.

'Killed in the Shaft', *AJ*, April 1871, pp. 446–49.

Ladies' Column, 'The Melbourne Hospital', [Nemia] *Herald*, 28–9 November, p. 3.

'The Ladies' Page', by Sylphid, *AJ*, June 1869, pp. 634–5; July 1869, pp. 688– 90; August 1869, p. 755; November 1869, pp. 163–4; December 1869, pp. 241–3; January 1870, pp. 290–2.

'The Lady in No. 4', *AJ*, February 1867, pp. 317–24.

'The Lady's Hair-Net', *AJ*, 5 October 1867, pp. 89–92.

'The Last Scene', *AJ*, November 1870, pp. 54–9.

'Little Peepshow', *The Herald*, 2 December 1882, pp. 3–5.

'Little Georgie's Grandpa', *AJ*, June 1903, pp. 322–6.

'The Little Widow', *AJ*, November 1901, pp. 665–72.

'Looking for Lodgings', *AJ*, 19 December 1868, pp. 266–9.

'Lost in Town', *AJ*, November 1872, pp. 123–6.

'The Lost Shepherd', *AJ*, 2 February 1867, pp. 361–4.

'Mag Braban's Share', *AJ*, September 1898, pp. 605–612.

'The Market Street Mystery', *AJ*, August 1894, pp. 683–687.

'Mary Hester Armour', *AJ*, July 1878, pp. 572–80.

'Mary Reardon's Christmas Eve', *The Advocate*, 21 December 1872, p. 4.

'Miss Mathew's Proposal', *The Herald*, 11 & 13 March 1876, p. 4.

'The Masked Lady', *AJ*, April–May 1871, pp. 428–34, 524–7.

'The Medal Case', *AJ*, 1 June 1867, pp. 628–31.

'Melbourne Cemetery', *AJ*, November 1869, pp. 180–1.

'The Midnight Burial', *AJ*, September 1872, pp. 834–9.

'The Midnight Watch', *AJ*, 6 April 1867, pp. 500–3.

'The Misfortunes of "O'Shicer of Ours"', *AJ*, May 1879, pp. 456–63.

'Mr Boyce's Daughter', *AJ*, May 1904, pp. 297–301.

'Mr Medlet's Wedding', *AJ*, 26 September 1868, pp. 73–8.

'Mrs Larner's Revenge', *AJ*, August 1890, pp. 682–90.

'The Murderer's Doom', *AJ*, March 1894 pp. 393–8.

'The Murderer's Claim', *AJ*, May 1874, pp. 477–82.

'My Advertisement', *AJ*, May 1869, pp. 563–5.

'My Lady Jane', *AJ*, 21 October 1865, pp. 115–9.

'My Lodger', *AJ*, April 1870, pp. 471–5.

'My Friends and Acquaintances', *AJ*, December 1876, pp. 197–9.

"Mystery and Murder', *AJ*, 10 February 1866, pp. 376–8.

'Ned Pelbit's Escape', *AJ*, June 1902, pp. 358–64.

'No. 95 Prosser Street', *AJ*, March 1906, pp. 177–81.

'Only One Blow', *AJ*, October 1897, pp. 705–11.

'Our Colonial Christmases', *AJ*, January 1872, pp. 255–6.

'"Our Golden Girl": A Christmas Story', *AJ*, December 1892, pp. 182–6.

'Outside the Hall', [Nemia] *Herald*, 20 October 1879, pp. 3–4.

'The Phantom Hearse', *AJ*, September 1889 pp. 45–52.

'Poor Gold', *AJ*, July 1885, pp. 624–8.

'The Queen of Diamonds', *AJ*, November 1873, pp. 127–32.

'Recollections of a Digger', *AJ*, 30 September 1865 pp. 68–9.

'The Red Room', *AJ*, 7 November 1868, pp. 169–75.

'Recipe for Buckwheat Cakes', *AJ*, 9 December 1865, p. 239.

'Regan's Doom', *AJ*, October 1896, pp. 742–748.

'The Rustling of Wings', *AJ*, January 1886, pp. 279–80.

'Sandridge Pier', *The Herald*, 23–24 September 1879, pp. 3–4.

'The Second Wedding', *AJ*, December 1873, pp. 183–9.

'The Secrets of Balbrooke', *AJ*, 1 September–29 December 1866, pp.1–5, 17–21, 33–7, 49–53, 65–8, 81–5, 97–101, 113–16, 129–32, 145–8, 161–4, 177–81, 193–6, 209–13, 225–8, 241–4, 257–8, 276–8.

'The Shadow on the Blind', *The Herald*, 31 August 1875, p. 4, 1 September 1875, p. 4.

'Simple Sam', *AJ*, 23 January 1869, pp. 346–9.

'A Sister of "The King's Guild"', n.d., n.p.

'A Social Reunion', *The Herald*, 15 October 1879, p. 3.

'Social Sketches and Interesting Chit-Chat', Mignon, *The Herald*, 20 August 1879, p. 3; [Nemia] *Herald*, 25 August 1879, p. 3; [Nemia] *Herald*, 29 August 1879, p. 3

'Song of the Gold Diggers', *The Mount Alexander Mail*, 14 December 1855, p. 6.

'The Spider and the Fly', *AJ*, November 1870, pp. 145–7.

'The Squatter's Daughter', *AJ*, June 1897, pp. 458–63.

'The Star-Spangled Banner', *AJ*, September 1893, pp. 44–50.

'The Stolen Brooch', *The Herald*, 24 January 1876, p. 4.

'The Stolen Deed', *AJ*, August 1875, pp. 671–8.

'The Stolen Specimens', *AJ*, 14 October 1865, pp. 106–8.

'The Terrace Walk', *AJ*, June 1875, pp. 560–6.

'Tom Doyle's Dream', *AJ*, July 1880, pp. 585–91.

'To My Little Son on his Birthday', *AJ*, 9 September 1866, p. 30.

'Traces of Crime', *AJ*, 2 December 1865, pp. 220–2.

'The Twenty-Ninth of November', *AJ*, December 1870, pp. 214–17.

'To xxxx', *The Mount Alexander Mail*, 21 December 1855, p. 5.

'A Trooper's Tale of the Fifties: Robbing the Dead', *The Weekly Times*, 20 May 1899, pp. 6–7.

'Twenty-Six Years Ago: Or, the Diggings from '55', *AJ*, September 1882–May 1883, pp. 33–7, 280–5, 338–43, 379–84, 445–8, 508–10.

'Under the Lamp', *The Herald*, 9 March 1876, p. 4.

'Under the Verandah', *AJ*, June 1870, pp. 599–602.

'Unlucky no. 58', *AJ*, August 1898, pp. 545–51.

[Untitled], *The Herald*, 10 December 1881, Supplement, p. 1.

'A Visit to Pentridge', *The Herald*, 30 December 1879, p. 3.

'The Wages of Sin', *AJ*, January 1907, pp. 49–53.

'The Waif of the Slums: A Tale of One New Year', *AJ*, January 1898, pp. 68–71.

'The Wattle Farm Tragedy', *AJ*, July 1870, pp. 644–8.

'What Passed', *AJ*, February 1871, pp. 346–7.

'The White Maniac: A Doctor's Tale', *AJ*, 13 July 1867, pp. 725–8.

'A Woman's Revenge; or, Almost Lost', *AJ*, February 1871, pp. 333–8.

'Woman's Perseverance', *The Herald*, 7 January 1882, Supplement, pp. 1–2.

'Wongawarra: A Story of Australia', *W.H. Williams's Illustrated Australian Annual for Christmas and New Year's Day*. W.H. Williams, Melbourne, 1868, pp. 24–40.

'Work with a Will', *AJ*, October 1875, p. 76.

'The Worms Don't Care', *The Herald*, 11 February 1882, Supplement, p. 1.

'Yatalonga', *AJ*, June 1873, pp. 523–8.

ABOUT THE AUTHORS

Megan Brown completed her PhD at the University of Wollongong, examining the work of Mary Fortune. She has contributed chapters to *The Routledge Companion to Australian Literature* and *The Unsocial Sociability of Women's Life Writing*.

Lucy Sussex's books include *Blockbuster! Fergus Hume and The Mystery of a Hansom Cab*, which won the 2015 Victorian Community History Award, *Women Writers and Detectives in the Nineteenth Century* and *Saltwater in the Ink: Voices from the Australian Seas*. She has a PhD from the University of Wales and is an honorary fellow at La Trobe University.

Together they edited *Nothing but Murders and Bloodshed and Hanging*, a collection of Mary Fortune's crime writing.